RONALD REAGAN *in Private*

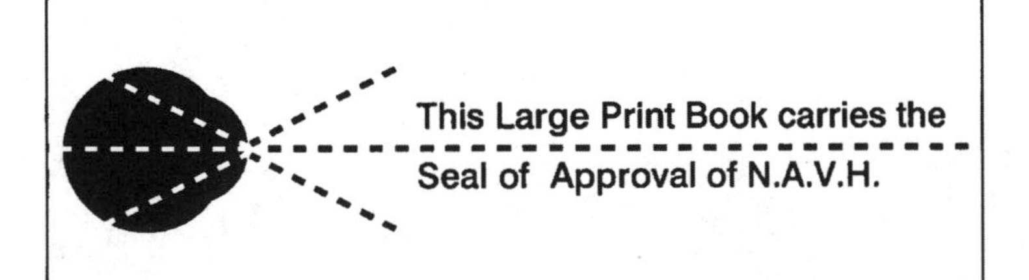
This Large Print Book carries the
Seal of Approval of N.A.V.H.

RONALD REAGAN *in Private*

A MEMOIR OF MY YEARS IN THE WHITE HOUSE

Jim Kuhn

Thorndike Press • Waterville, Maine

Published in 2004 by arrangement with
Sentinel, a division of Penguin Group (USA) Inc.

Thorndike Press® Large Print Biography.

The text of this Large Print edition is unabridged.
Other aspects of the book may vary from the original edition.

Set in 16 pt. Plantin by Minnie B. Raven.

Printed in the United States on permanent paper.

Library of Congress Cataloging-in-Publication Data

Kuhn, Jim, 1952–
Ronald Reagan in private : a memoir of my years in the White House / Jim Kuhn.
p. cm.
Originally published: New York : Sentinel, 2004.
ISBN 0-7862-7053-5 (lg. print : hc : alk. paper)
1. Reagan, Ronald — Friends and associates. 2. Presidents — United States — Biography. 3. Kuhn, Jim, 1952– 4. Presidents — United States — Staff — Biography. 5. Large type books. I. Title.
E877.2.K84 2004b
973.927′092—dc22
[B] 2004056738

To Lyn Nofziger, Ed Meese,
Senator Paul Laxalt and Mike Deaver.
Without your contribution,
Ronald Reagan might never have been
known and acknowledged by the world.

As the Founder/CEO of NAVH, the only national health agency solely devoted to those who, although not totally blind, have an eye disease which could lead to serious visual impairment, I am pleased to recognize Thorndike Press* as one of the leading publishers in the large print field.

Founded in 1954 in San Francisco to prepare large print textbooks for partially seeing children, NAVH became the pioneer and standard setting agency in the preparation of large type.

Today, those publishers who meet our standards carry the prestigious "Seal of Approval" indicating high quality large print. We are delighted that Thorndike Press is one of the publishers whose titles meet these standards. We are also pleased to recognize the significant contribution Thorndike Press is making in this important and growing field.

Lorraine H. Marchi, L.H.D.
Founder/CEO
NAVH

* Thorndike Press encompasses the following imprints: Thorndike, Wheeler, Walker and Large Pr int Press.

CONTENTS

Acknowledgments
Preface 11
1 And So I Became a Republican . . 15
2 Running Against the President. . . 33
3 The Mashed Potato Circuit. 53
4 Turmoil and Trouble 82
5 Triumph in Detroit 93
6 Victory 120
7 From California to the White House. 138
8 "We Have Every Right to Dream Heroic Dreams" 157
9 Jelly Beans and Former Presidents. 177
10 Tough Times in the Presidency . 189
11 Triumph and Tragedy. 206
12 Heading for a Second Term. . . . 243
13 Executive Assistant to the President. 280
14 Geneva and the Battle of the Coats 314
15 Falling Back to Earth 337
16 The Iran-Contra Affair 373
17 The First Lady and Her "Roommate" 399
18 Getting Personal and Getting "Borked" 422

19 The Streets of Washington
and Moscow 444
20 The Final Stretch 463
21 An Official Farewell,
but Not Good-bye 490

ACKNOWLEDGMENTS

This book would not have become a reality without Jacqueline S. Salmon, correspondent with the *Washington Post.* My highest regards to Jacqui for her writing expertise and for keeping us on deadline.

To Marlin Fitzwater for recommending me to editor Bernadette Malone as the author for this rewarding endeavor.

My sincere thanks to Michael Putzel for all of his advice, guidance and counsel on this worthy project.

To Ellen McCathran, presidential diarist, for all of her input in terms of historic accuracy.

My deep appreciation to my predecessor as executive assistant to President Reagan, David C. Fischer, for helping me assume his role in the second term of Ronald Reagan's presidency.

To Bernadette Malone, editor, for her leadership in the execution of this publication on Ronald Reagan. And to Megan Casey, assistant editor.

And most thoughtfully, to President Reagan and Mrs. Reagan for all of their kindnesses offered to my wife, Carole, and children — Caitlin, Greg and Alyssa.

PREFACE

This final tribute to Ronald Reagan was a long time coming.

But before this work could be published, I always knew I'd need to meet with Nancy Reagan face-to-face to explain my interest in writing a book about her "roommate," as she lovingly referred to the man she was so passionate about and protected so well. Theirs was indeed a special — even fairy tale — relationship that endured for decades, and any book I was to write would reflect that, in addition to recalling all the unique traits I saw in Ronald Reagan when no one else was watching him.

For these reasons, I knew it would be best to have Mrs. Reagan on board with the project. So one day in March 2004, I boarded a plane and made the long-familiar trip to the Reagans' house in Bel Air, California. President Reagan was ailing at this time, and he was in his private room in the house. I did not see him on this trip, but I felt his strong presence, and it touched me deeply.

I felt good about visiting Mrs. Reagan, and even better to be talking with her about this worthy project. But I have to admit, I was more than a little nervous about her reaction. How would she feel about my writing a book about her husband? That nervousness reminded me of old, very happy times at the president's side.

Once, early in the second term, Rita Hayworth's daughter, Princess Yasmin Aga Khan, came into the Oval Office for a presentation to the Reagans from the National Alzheimer's Association. Mrs. Reagan was supposed to attend, but wasn't able to. She called me to request that I ask the president to explain her absence and to extend her apologies for missing the event. I was also supposed to instruct the president to express that Nancy Reagan sent her love. Then I got a call from Mrs. Reagan's personal assistant at the time, Elaine Crispen, to ensure that the president was fully briefed on explaining Mrs. Reagan's absence.

Well, I forgot to tell the president, remembering only after the event was over. I was terrified. I hadn't been on the job as executive assistant very long, and I was very nervous about screwing up. I figured I could get fired over this. So as the president and I walked along the Colonnade to the White House residence that afternoon,

I explained that I'd neglected to relay to him Mrs. Reagan's request and that it was my fault.

"As soon as we get off the elevator, Mrs. Reagan is going to ask you if you explained why she wasn't there," I told the president. "She's going to be very angry with me, and rightfully so. You're going to have to tell her, but it's one hundred percent my fault."

Reagan knew that I was quite scared about my mistake. We got off the elevator, and the president walked into the bedroom and, sure enough, Mrs. Reagan asked him about it. "Honey, did you tell Rita Hayworth's daughter why I couldn't be there and that I sent my love?" she asked him.

"I certainly did," the president answered. "Everything was just fine, and they missed you and also send their love."

He looked out at me from the bedroom and winked.

Here I was in the same position some twenty years later, worried about Mrs. Reagan's reaction. I told Mrs. Reagan about the book, explaining to her that it would be comprised of my recollections — loyal, honest and to the best of my intentions and memory. I did not intend to interview other people, conduct a survey or do more reporting. She looked at me and simply said: "Jim, you don't need to do that, because you already know everything." That felt great to hear.

"I am very pleased that you are writing this book," she told me.

That made me miss working for her husband more than I already did.

So it is my goal to display Ronald Reagan just as he was: a dedicated hard worker who always maintained a big-picture policy perspective over his entire eight years in office. *Ronald Reagan in Private* endeavors to distinguish President Reagan from his predecessors and successors by honoring his unparalleled leadership and perseverance. And most important, I hope to show just how strongly President Reagan believed in the American people. In his own words, as he said over and over again to his cabinet and senior staff: "Listen to the people, as they know what is best."

1

AND SO I BECAME A REPUBLICAN

It was a sunny, uncharacteristically warm November day in Cleveland when I first met Ronald Reagan in 1975. He was scheduled to speak to a group of businessmen there. Speculation was swirling that he would declare his candidacy for president of the United States, but he hadn't yet made any announcement.

I was 23 years old at the time, and my boss, Ohio businessman Peter Voss, had arranged the speaking engagement and asked me to greet Reagan when he arrived. I looked forward to meeting the man I had seen for years on TV shows like *General Electric Theater* and *Death Valley Days* and, of course, in his national exposure as governor of California.

I stood at the entrance to the dining room of the Union Club in downtown Cleveland, waiting for Reagan to appear. What would he be like? Would he turn out to be the warm, approachable man whom I'd watched on Sunday nights in my family room? Or would I find a cold politician who had great charm only when the TV cameras appeared?

Then there he was, rounding the corner of the corridor at the Union Club and striding down the hall toward me, accompanied by one of his longtime aides, Dennis LeBlanc.

Reagan wore a light-colored suit, and he had a deep tan. He was in his mid-sixties by that point but to me he appeared much the same as when I'd seen him on television many times. He looked trim, fit and in command — very much the recent governor of a major state — and he had the aura of a successful man.

He was also right on time. I was to learn that punctuality was something of a religion with Reagan. He hated to make people wait for him — whether it was one person, 10 people or 50,000.

I was to learn much more about Ronald Reagan over the ensuing years — his hidden shyness, his stubbornness, his sense of humor, his warmth, his big dreams for America and his clear-eyed determination to make them come true. Often underestimated, sometimes ridiculed, he was also one of the few people I have ever met who was totally comfortable with himself.

Whether it was standing shirtless and unseen, watching with interest thousands of furious anti-Reagan protesters on the street below him, grieving for the deaths of hundreds of young marines or outmaneuvering charismatic Soviet leader Mikhail Gorbachev, he never lost that sense of wonder at the extraordinary role that he had been handed and he never lost the capacity to laugh at his own foibles.

Yet while he was open and totally trusting of his inner circle, he always kept a part of himself walled off. And even though he was totally confident of himself as president, he could be unexpectedly protective about his past.

I knew none of that, of course, in 1975 in Cleveland, nor could I foresee that my life's trajectory would suddenly connect with his when I stuck out my hand to one of my childhood TV idols as he approached me.

"Hello, Governor, I'm Jim Kuhn," I said. "How was your trip?"

I grew up in the 1950s and '60s on a farm in northwestern Ohio — Seneca County, Ohio, with a population of just under 30,000 people — as part of a large Catholic family that took pride in its Democratic roots. As in many farming families at the time, Franklin D. Roosevelt and his New Deal were important to our family, and when John F. Kennedy was elected the first Catholic president of the United States, it was a significant day in my parents' lives.

My dad and mother never knew a day without hard work. My father's parents both died when he was young, and he was forced to quit school in the seventh grade to go to work. We had two farms, totaling 250 acres, where we raised cattle, hogs and chickens and grew corn, wheat and soybeans. To help pay the bills, my dad also worked as a barber in the closest town, Tiffin, about seven miles from our home. Some of my earliest memories are of helping my dad and mom with chores — and there were a lot of them. Out of six kids in the Kuhn family, I was the only son, and my mom and dad and I did most of the farm work ourselves — feeding the livestock every morning and night, milking cows, hauling in the crops, tending to sick animals. Of course, farm families didn't take vacations, so my childhood horizons didn't stretch much past downtown Tiffin.

But while it wasn't much fun crawling out of bed on those frozen Ohio winter mornings to head for the barn, it was a good life. My parents always made sure I had money in my pocket and, as soon as I turned 16, I had saved enough to buy a car so I didn't have to ride the school bus anymore. I also learned the value of hard work — a lesson that would help me immeasurably when I grew up and ventured into politics.

However, those were scary times for our country. The cold war was at its peak, and I remember lots of worried conversations in our house — like in a lot of American homes — about the possibility of nuclear war. I would overhear my parents talking about their fears, and I'd lie in bed — like lots of American kids at the time — wondering if I would wake up in the morning or whether a nuclear bomb would destroy my family. I remember hearing about Soviet leader Nikita Khrushchev's famous warning to capitalist nations that "we will bury you!" in a speech to western ambassadors in Moscow.

From the standpoint of the United States and the Soviet Union, long-range nuclear weapons could have a devastating impact on the world as we knew it. I remember my parents speaking admiringly of the firmness with which John F. Kennedy had faced down Khrushchev during the Cuban missile crisis. At the same time, there was talk of building bomb shelters.

In those frightening days, I found comfort in a weekly television drama hosted by an actor — Ronald Reagan. I first encountered him on Sunday nights in the glow of the black-and-white console television in our family room. A radio announcer and movie actor, Reagan had largely turned to TV by the time I found him — first hosting the weekly drama series *General Electric Theater* and then *Death Valley Days.*

I was enthralled. There was something about him that just drew me to him. Maybe it was the warm smile or the jaunty tilt of the head. Maybe it was the easy confidence with which he faced the camera. Whatever it was, I would settle in front of the television every Sunday just to watch Reagan. I never paid much attention to the actual show, unless he was acting in it, which he did occasionally. I just loved watching Reagan.

I remember the opening: a trumpet fanfare, and then a narrator said: "For *General Electric Theater*, here is Ronald Reagan." And Reagan would appear, sometimes in suit and tie with a crisp handkerchief poking out of his breast pocket or sometimes in a costume that reflected that week's show.

"Good evening," he said with a nod. And he introduced the show. "Tonight, Thomas Mitchell and Vincent Price star in the *General Electric Theater*," for example. Sometimes, he'd riffle a pack of cards or take a swing at a punching bag in his introduction.

Before one episode, a western, he pulled a gun out of a holster hanging on the wall and turned to squint at the camera. "A man's talents may be used for good or evil," he said in that sonorous voice that stayed with him over the years. "Exceptional talents only widen the possibilities for both."

After *General Electric Theater*, he served as the host and occasional actor in *Death Valley Days*, which I also avidly followed. In one episode, "No Gun Behind His Badge," he played a soft-spoken town marshal, Bear River Smith, who stood up to the murderous town bully.

Of course, in the '60s, although I wasn't aware of it at the time, Reagan was becoming much more than just an actor; he was transforming himself into one of the leading conservative leaders in the country. Like my family, he had grown up in a family of Roosevelt Democrats. In fact, he'd cast his first vote for FDR in the depths of the Depression in 1932. But over the years, he had become disillusioned with the Democrats, believing that their party didn't do enough to curb high income taxes and the encroachment of the federal government into Americans' lives. His role as a union leader in Hollywood left him disenchanted with the power of the labor movement and concerned about the infiltration of the Communist party into American society.

Ultimately, his increasing activism cost him his GE job, which included hosting the TV series and serving as GE's national spokesman at its plants and workshops nationwide. But that activism also opened the door to the world that would embrace Ronald Reagan — the world of politics.

In 1964, he burst onto the American political scene with his now-legendary televised address, "A Time for Choosing," in support of conservative Republican presidential candidate Barry Goldwater. In it, Reagan sketched out the problems he saw facing America: an overwhelming tax burden, a wasteful government and the evils of the Soviet Union, one of the most dangerous enemies that humanity had ever faced. And he laid out the vision that would drive him for the next 30 years; America, Reagan declared, was humanity's final hope.

"You and I have a rendezvous with destiny," he told Americans. "We will preserve for our children this, the last best hope of man on earth, or we will sentence them to take the first step into a thousand years of darkness."

The speech triggered a cascade of donations to Goldwater's campaign. It didn't save Goldwater from defeat, but it launched Ronald Reagan's political career and moved the lifeblood of the country's burgeoning conservative movement onto center stage.

But none of that, at the time, meant anything to an Ohio farm boy who was enraptured by the warm appeal of Ronald Reagan the actor. As Reagan moved into his political life — running for and, ultimately, serving as California governor from 1967 to January 1975 — I moved on with mine, although I never forgot the man I met on the television screen.

In the winter of 1970, I was accepted at Kent State University. But on May 4, two weeks before I graduated from Mohawk High School, National Guard troops shot and killed four Kent State students and injured several more as the students participated in a three-day Vietnam War protest on campus. The campus shut down for the year shortly after that.

After the shootings, my parents and I debated whether I should go to Kent State at all. It was an era of widespread campus protests. I told them I wasn't any more safe or less safe at Kent State than on the campuses of many other colleges in the country at the time. What happened at Kent State, I argued, could have happened on 40 other campuses around the country. My parents ultimately decided to let me enroll the following fall. Not all parents of Kent State students were so reassured, apparently — one third of the students in my freshmen class didn't show up in the autumn of 1970.

Ironically, while Ronald Reagan was facing down campus rioters as California governor, where he'd campaigned on the slogan "Obey the rules or get out," I was throwing myself into one of the epicenters of student activism at Kent State. I grew my hair down my back, tied it into a ponytail and demonstrated against the Vietnam War, Richard Nixon and whatever else there was to protest at the time. It was an emotional time at Kent State, understandably, and the campus protests were big and loud. Kent State had many factions: radicals, gays, heavy thinkers and Jesus freaks. During the 1972 presidential campaign between President Nixon and Senator George McGovern, some friends and I collected as many NIXON NOW bumper stickers as we could, cut the "w" off the word "Now" and posted them around campus. When the voting age was lowered from age 21 to age 18, I voted for McGovern in 1972 in my first presidential election vote.

Years later, when I worked for President Reagan, I saw lots of anti-Reagan protests in my travels with him and sometimes my '70s protest experience would pop out without my realizing it. "Wow," I'd say admiringly after watching thousands of chanting students pour through the streets to protest Reagan's defense buildup or, overseas, to demonstrate against the placement of short-range nuclear missiles in Europe. "That was *great*." I remember Mike Deaver staring at me in astonishment one time. I quickly corrected myself. "I mean," I added, "that was a *big* protest."

But like millions of other campus protesters, I eventually grew up. By my senior year, I'd become close with a friend since my freshman year, David Seffens, who was three years ahead of me in school. He was very active in Republican politics and from time to time tried to convince me to change parties, but I always refused. In January 1974, as the Vietnam War deescalated, I got a congressional internship through Kent State's Department of Political Science, cut my hair and spent three months in Washington, D.C., working for Congressman Glenn Anderson, a Democrat from Los Angeles.

I loved the work. It was fast paced, it was interesting and it was important. I liked the work and the people so much that I didn't want to go back to school for my final quarter — only 11 more weeks to graduate.

Seffens persisted in his efforts to get me involved in Republican party politics. He was working on the political campaign of a businessman from Canton, who was running in the Republican Senate primary in 1974 against then-Cleveland Mayor Ralph Perk. The businessman's name was Peter Voss, and Seffens introduced me to him. I liked Voss instantly. He was smart, strong-minded, successful and not afraid of a challenge. He owned three small companies that generated most of their business as manufacturers' representatives for heavy industrial equipment for the steel and auto industries and public utilities.

Seffens, however, pointed out that I couldn't work closely with Voss and remain a Democrat. "If you want to work for him," he said, "you're going to have to switch parties." And so I became a Republican. It was surprisingly easy for me, as it turned out. As I was with Reagan, I found that I was attracted more to a particular candidate than to a particular ideology. I had always been a moderate Democrat, and now I found myself moving to a moderate Republican. But most important, for me, the man came before his politics. With Voss and, later, with Reagan, I liked and respected the individual first and then focused on the issues.

Maybe that was because of my farm upbringing, where the individual was always more important than a particular matter, issue or cause. Or maybe, also because of my farm background, the father was very important to you. It wasn't that I was looking for a father figure, but it was always important to me to be associated with the right guy. Ideology simply came in second.

In the meantime, however, across the country, Ronald Reagan faced some changes as well. After two successful terms as California governor, he had returned to private life in early 1975. He launched a successful career making weekly radio addresses that were aired on more than 200 stations, writing a syndicated newspaper column and traveling the country giving speeches that reflected his conservative philosophy. He was particularly troubled by the increasing federal spending that swelled even more immensely while Reagan was governor during Lyndon Johnson's Great Society initiative. But he was also concerned more broadly about the direction in which the country appeared to be drifting.

At the same time, some in the Republican party were urging him to take on President Gerald Ford and fight it out for the Republican presidential nomination for the upcoming campaign. The Watergate scandal was a significant blow to the Republican party and left Ford in a weakened position. In the aftermath of Nixon's departure — the same year that my candidate Ralph Perk got destroyed in the Ohio Senate race — Republicans lost 43 seats in the House, four in the Senate and four governors' seats, including California's.

Reagan was reluctant to split the party by challenging a sitting president, but he was unhappy with Ford and his policies. Reagan didn't think Ford was doing enough to counter the buildup of military power in the Soviet Union, and he opposed Henry Kissinger's pursuit of détente with the Soviets.

A shrewd former Nixon aide, John Sears, joined forces with some longtime Reagan supporters and persuaded Reagan to form an exploratory committee chaired by Reagan's friend Paul Laxalt to look into a possible run for the presidency.

And in November 1975, Ronald Reagan paid that visit to Cleveland's Union Club — a trip that would change my life.

After greeting Reagan in the Union Club that November day, I expected a perfunctory nod in return. But, instead, Reagan stopped, looked me in the eye and gave me a firm handshake. His hand was warm to the touch. He asked me my name and what I did. He listened intently, his eyes on me, as I explained that I worked for Peter Voss. For a minute or two, we chatted, and he talked with me as if I were the person he had traveled from California to see. He had the same warm appeal that had drawn me to him on television.

I learned over the ensuing years that Reagan treated everyone that way — whether it was a foreign leader, a member of Congress, a Girl Scout or a busboy. Everyone was the same in Ronald Reagan's eyes, and everyone was important. He didn't adjust his manner based on the relative importance of whomever he was dealing with — he was genuinely interested in hearing about you. It was an approach that made you feel like you mattered, and it was part of the personal magnetism of Ronald Reagan that was to capture millions of Americans.

At the Union Club, after a minute or two of chatting with me, I pointed out to Reagan that the business leaders awaited him inside the room, and Reagan went in, had lunch and gave his speech. I don't remember the details, but I recall that it reflected his concern about America — the growth in federal spending, the growing tax burden on ordinary Americans and the antibusiness environment created by excessive regulations. His audience listened raptly; he had an unusual ability to draw people in, to project his warm personal appeal to any crowd, large or small. I saw him do this an immense number of times from 1975 to 1989. People had the genuine sense that he was speaking directly to them.

Reagan stayed after the lunch, talking to people the way he had chatted with me. And after the speech, Voss asked if we could accompany Reagan and his aide to the airport, and we did so, following them in our car onto the tarmac next to the waiting plane. It was very low key. There were no press people there. Just me, Seffens, Voss, Dennis LeBlanc and Reagan. Someone produced a camera, and we each posed for pictures outside the jet with a smiling Reagan. We said our good-byes and watched the plane take off.

After Reagan departed, we could barely drive back to Canton, about 65 miles south of Cleveland, we were so excited that we'd met someone who could become the next president of the United States — and someone whom we felt we could fully support. None of us was particularly enamored with President Ford and his chief backer in Ohio, Governor Jim Rhodes. Next to Reagan, Ford seemed sluggish and colorless. And I particularly resented Rhodes for his role in the Kent State killings — as governor, he had been the one to send in the National Guard.

On the road back to Canton, we plotted how we could get involved with the Reagan campaign if he decided to run for president. All we could do at that point, however, was hope that he would take his chances against Gerald Ford. But we would help him in any way that we could.

2
RUNNING AGAINST THE PRESIDENT

On November 20, 1975, shortly after Reagan's Cleveland visit, we got our wish when Reagan announced his candidacy at the National Press Club in Washington, sounding themes that he had been pounding away at in countless speeches and newspaper columns. He wanted to "relcasc the energy that is the American spirit," he said in his speech that day.

Government, he said, "has become more intrusive, more coercive, more meddlesome and less effective," and Washington "has become the seat of a buddy system that functions for its own benefit, increasingly insensitive to the needs of the American worker who supports it with his taxes.

"A nation that is growing and thriving is one that will solve its problems," he said. "We must [seek] progress instead of stagnation; the truth, instead of promises; hope and faith instead of defeatism and despair."

It was an inspiring start to a campaign

that experienced plenty of bumps on the way to the Kansas City Republican Convention in August 1976. The Ohio primary wasn't until shortly before the convention, so Reagan had a long way to go before he got to our state. In late February 1976, he lost the New Hampshire primary narrowly to Ford, despite predictions that he would win easily, then lost in Florida and even in Illinois, where he had grown up. He hadn't waged campaigns in Vermont and Massachusetts, and so lost those uncontested states. The press started to write his political obituary, and fellow Republicans urged Reagan to quit for the sake of party unity.

In the meantime, Peter Voss decided not to challenge Bob Taft for the Ohio Republican Senate seat and launched a vigorous effort with Reagan's top campaign people — John Sears, Lyn Nofziger and Charlie Black — to be named chairman of the Reagan campaign in Ohio. Others in Ohio also wanted to run the Reagan campaign there but, in the end, Voss prevailed. Seffens and I were thrilled. We wanted to work for Reagan and help him get to the White House by making inroads in Ohio.

For a while, we weren't even sure that Reagan would visit our state. Early on,

Ohio Governor Rhodes got the entire Ohio Republican state committee to lock up behind President Ford, and the Reagan people had to decide whether to challenge Rhodes on his home turf and whether it would be worth the money they would have to spend to do it. Their alternative was to concede the state to Ford and focus on other battlegrounds.

For weeks, Voss worked to persuade Sears, Nofziger and Black that it was worth the effort to come to Ohio, assuring them that we could put an organization together and win some delegates for Reagan. Voss conceded that the number would be small, but it would have a positive impact nationally, as opposed to just writing off a critical state like Ohio. After all, no Republican president had ever ascended to the White House without winning Ohio.

It was on again, off again — hurry up and wait. We were on an emotional rollercoaster for several weeks as the Reagan campaign debated internally about what to do about Ohio. First Reagan was coming, and then he wasn't coming. Finally, in early March, we got the decision. It was a go. But another hurdle appeared. The filing deadline for delegates for the June 8 primary was just days away, and we had to find delegates for Reagan in all of Ohio's 23 congressional districts and the at-large slate, get petitions, get signatures and get them filed with the Ohio secretary of state — all the while fighting the Rhodes people.

As soon as we got the official word about Reagan formally organizing in Ohio, Seffens and I headed in opposite directions around the state in the hunt for delegates and petition signatories. We had to work outside the Republican state machinery, which made the going difficult but, fortunately, Voss had Ohio well organized for Reagan. Seffens flew around the state, while I drove practically 24 hours a day. I was falling asleep behind the wheel, so I would pull off the road, catch a short nap, then hit the road again, stopping along the way to make calls from pay phones to the Reagan people I had found in the counties that lay ahead.

In a story at the time, the *Washington Post*'s David Broder noted that Voss was "running largely a living room campaign from the homes of conservative sympathizers." It was not an inaccurate description!

Fortunately, we were able to file petitions in 15 of Ohio's 23 congressional districts, which included the statewide slate. Then we hit the road again, spreading information on the issues, working on turning out Reagan voters for the primary — anything we could do to sell Reagan from an issues standpoint and as a viable candidate.

In the meantime, Reagan had vowed to forge ahead despite the setbacks to his national campaign, and the Reagan campaign began to turn around. Reagan could be ferocious when the odds were against him — I was to see that trait emerge time and time again in the years ahead — and he was no less so on the campaign trail in 1976 when many thought his mission was impossible.

"Win, lose or draw, I am continuing this campaign," he defiantly told a press conference when he arrived in North Carolina to campaign for its March 23 primary.

Against everyone's expectations, including some of his own campaign staff, Reagan won the North Carolina primary, which fueled us immensely.

As we prepared for his campaign swing through Ohio in early June, Reagan continued to pick up steam. He won all 100 delegates in the Texas primary and then took Georgia, Alabama, Indiana and Nebraska. Ford won Michigan, Kentucky and Tennessee. The battle seesawed back and forth. With all this front loading of primaries today, you don't see classic battles like Reagan-Ford anymore.

The Reagan strategists decided that Reagan would do a five-city swing through Ohio on the weekend before the Ohio primary. It wasn't a long appearance — after all, Rhodes and Taft practically had the state in their pockets — but we figured he could pick up enough delegates to maybe make a difference when he got to the Kansas City Republican Convention in August. A strong percentage of the popular vote would also provide Reagan with significant momentum going into the convention.

At the same time, the Republican party leadership went all out to stop Reagan. At a California press conference a few days before the Ohio and California primaries, Senator Howard Baker — who later went to work as chief of staff to President Reagan — opined that Reagan was "a good governor of California [but] not careful enough to be president of the United States." Ford warned that Reagan would lead Republicans into a repeat of the 1964 Barry Goldwater debacle and ardently wooed individual states, including promising Ohio a billion-dollar expansion of a nuclear fuel plant in the southwestern part of the state. But Reagan stuck to his message — restoring America to its greatness, reducing government spending and strengthening defense.

"Under Ford and Kissinger, this country has become number two in military power in a world where it's dangerous, if not fatal, to be second best," he told cheering crowds.

One of Reagan's major campaign lines that always drew a roar from crowds involved the Ford administration's negotiations to return the Panama Canal to the government of Panama: "We bought it, we paid for it, it's ours and we're going to keep it!" Reagan would tell them.

Before the Ohio primary, Voss and I had a long strategy session with Charlie Black, who came to Canton for the meeting. Although only in his late twenties at the time, Black — a Jesse Helms guy — was a big name in national political circles and had really made a difference for Reagan in North Carolina. Black told us that the Reagan campaign strategy in Ohio consisted of solidifying Reagan's conservative base while reaching out to the undecideds.

Then a week before Reagan's visit to Ohio, his advance team showed up to prepare for his campaign appearances there. They took over, getting phones installed, reserving blocks of rooms in hotels, renting sound equipment and working on building crowds at rally event sites for Reagan.

These guys were like gods to me. It was the biggest thing in the world — that these individuals were traveling the country and working for Ronald Reagan while having weekly contact with him. They had been all over the nation, and now they were in Ohio. Voss told me to drive to Cleveland to see how I could help them out. The campaign had wired money from Los Angeles into Voss's Ohio Reagan account to cover the costs of the campaign stops, so I also took a big check to them. They were setting up a major rally in Cleveland's Lakewood Park, in a western suburb on the shores of Lake Erie, and they needed cash for advertising, the sound system and staging and logistics in general.

I learned later when I worked as an advance man that the scariest part of the job was crowd building for campaign events. Some events — like a dinner for which you're selling tickets — are difficult, but crowd events like political rallies are especially hard. No matter how popular a candidate is, it's not easy to turn people out. They figure parking will be scarce or that they won't be able to see the candidate. Security can also be a problem, and an advance man has to overcome all those obstacles.

I gave the check to Walt McCay, Reagan's lead advance guy for Cleveland, and worked for him as he put together the Lakewood rally, the centerpiece of Reagan's visit to the state. McCay was a warm, friendly Arizonian who really had a way with people. Later in the White House, I would work with him again.

In Cleveland, I met Nancy Reagan for the first time, as well as some of Reagan's California crowd. Mrs. Reagan was warm, friendly and very personable. She smiled right at you and, like Reagan, had a way of making you feel welcome. Several campaign staff came into Cleveland on the Reagans' United charter, including Michael Deaver, a young Californian who had worked for Reagan when he was governor. I also saw Dennis LeBlanc again.

The battle between Ford and Reagan got ugly and, in Columbus during the weekend he spent in Ohio, Reagan had to defend himself against a nasty Ford campaign ad airing in California that claimed Reagan would take the country to war. "When you vote Tuesday," the ad warned, "remember that Governor Reagan couldn't start a war. President Reagan could."

Reagan, who never resorted to personal attacks on Ford, said he was disappointed in the ad. "I wish they had campaigned on a higher plane," he told the press.

At the Lakewood Park rally, I watched as McCay's site advance guy — the person in charge of that particular event — greeted VIPs, got them settled on the stage and got the program going. The master of ceremonies was former Cleveland Browns All Pro lineman Dick Schafrath, whom I'd grown up watching block for Jim Brown. The site advance guy told me to introduce Schafrath to the crowd. I protested that I couldn't — thousands of people were there by this point, and I'd never spoken in front of a crowd this big.

"You have to," he said. "That's your job. You're here to help us."

So I swallowed hard and made Schafrath's introduction. I could hear my voice shaking at the outset as it echoed from the speakers across the crowd. It went without saying that my role in politics was not going to be behind the microphone or in front of the television cameras!

Lakewood Park was a beautiful setting in the near west Cleveland suburb of Lakewood, and the Saturday-evening rally came off beautifully. The weather was perfect, and the crowd was large and receptive.

At the rally, Reagan drew a cheer from the crowd by calling for strengthening the military, reducing the size of the federal government and returning money to taxpayers.

"Sometimes government does its best when it does nothing!" he told the crowd.

After the rally, we got in the motorcade — another first for me that I repeated literally thousands of times in the years ahead — and headed back to the airport hotel. I met some of the big network television reporters and celebrities who traveled with the candidate. There was Ken Curtis, who'd just finished a stint playing Deputy Sheriff Festus Haggen on the TV show *Gunsmoke*. On later campaign trips in 1976, I met Jimmy Stewart and Efrem Zimbalist Jr. The Reagans had made a lot of close friends in California, and they never forgot them.

Back at the hotel in Cleveland, the Reagans retired for the night, and we stayed up in the hotel bar with the rowdy national media and campaign staff. It was a big change from quiet Canton, and I fell in love with the whole scene.

On primary election day in Ohio, Reagan won 45 percent of the popular vote, to Ford's 55 percent, and squeezed out six delegates. We were pleased. The Ford campaign had expected to sweep all 97 Ohio delegates. Reagan's campaign staff had predicted that he might win up to two dozen delegates in the state, but Reagan himself had said he would be happy with 10. So we weren't far off, and we had been up against such an unbelievable force from Rhodes, his organization and the president of the United States. The close popular vote showed voters in states with upcoming primaries that Reagan had solid support.

On the same day as the Ohio primary, Ford also won New Jersey, but Reagan took California by a 2 to 1 margin. Reagan won a lot of kudos for hanging in there at the beginning of the race when it seemed that he would go down to defeat, and we were proud of him.

Voss and I went to the Republican convention in Kansas City that year. It promised to be historic. Most Republicans old enough to have attended a number of conventions will no doubt tell you it was one of the most exciting, colorful conventions they could remember.

Two weeks before the convention opened in August, I drove one of Voss's cars from Canton — 600-plus miles in one day — to Kansas City. It was an exhausting trip, but not nearly as tiring as the next three weeks would be. We were immediately thrown into action. I worked with Reagan's advance guys, setting up different events — rallies at which Reagan would speak, caucus meetings and receptions. We also worked on planning a major convention-floor rally for Reagan on national television, where the pro-Reagan delegates had to be loud and colorful. Walt McCay was there, as was Dave Fischer — who eight years later would lead the way for me to get my job as Reagan's executive assistant in his second term — and a guy by the name of Chuck Tyson, who ran Reagan's entire advance operation.

Reagan hadn't arrived at the convention with quite enough delegates to snatch the nomination away from Ford — most estimates put the number of Ford delegates at about 1,090 delegates and Reagan delegates at about 1,030. But a Ford triumph wasn't guaranteed. Anything could happen. The vote could go to a second ballot, for example, and since delegates were legally committed only on the first ballot, we might succeed in swinging over enough delegates from the Ford side to boost Reagan over the top. With that strategy in mind, we spent a lot of time setting up Reagan visits to state delegations in various meeting rooms and ballrooms around Kansas City. Reagan worked diligently to win over the Ford delegates.

Sears worked hard to give Reagan more of an advantage. In a bid to attract some of Pennsylvania's uncommitted delegates, he had helped persuade Reagan before the convention to announce that he was going to choose Pennsylvania Senator Richard S. Schweiker as his running mate if he won the nomination. Schweiker was liberal compared with Reagan and, though the choice helped Reagan, it angered some supporters, and there was pressure on Reagan to drop Schweiker as they came into the convention. But Reagan displayed the steadfast loyalty — to friends, to supporters, to causes that he believed in — that I was to see much of later on. We came to Kansas City together, he told

Schweiker, and we're going to leave together.

No doubt the Reagan team could have done more to push Reagan closer to the nomination, but that could have torn the party apart, and Reagan had no desire to participate in the destruction of the struggling post-Watergate Republican party.

So that's the way Reagan's bid ended in Kansas City. The final tally: Ford: 1,187 delegates. Reagan: 1,070.

For me, even though I was already a veteran of bitter electoral defeat — having watched Peter Voss lose to Mayor Ralph Perk and then see Perk get destroyed in the Senate battle with John Glenn — it was still very hard to see Reagan go down after that valiant effort.

Ford, in his acceptance speech on the final night of the convention, was gracious: "After the scrimmage of the past few months, it feels really good to have Ron Reagan on the same side of the line," Ford said to the cheering delegates from the podium, his smiling family at his side.

But after Ford's address, the cheering of the crowd only grew louder, and finally Ford looked up at the box where the Reagans were sitting. "Will you come on down," he shouted up at Reagan, "and bring Nancy," gesturing with both hands. The Reagans made their way down to the stage, where the roaring got louder as Reagan stepped to the mike at the invitation of Ford.

There, Reagan spoke of his great vision — ridding the world of the scourge of nuclear weapons — a cause that would carry him through two presidencies and would, ultimately, change the world.

"We live in a world in which the great powers have poised and aimed at each other horrible missiles of destruction — nuclear weapons — that can in a matter of minutes arrive in each other's country and destroy virtually the civilized world we live in," he said.

He told the delegates, some weeping, that he had been asked to write a letter for a time capsule in Los Angeles, to be opened in 100 years.

"It dawned on me that those who would read the letter one hundred years from now will know whether those missiles were fired," Reagan said. "They will know whether we met our challenge. Whether they will have the freedom that we have known up till now will depend on what we do here."

He may have been talking to the Republican convention, but he was also talking about, and to, America.

"And if we fail," Reagan told the virtually silent hall, "they probably won't get to read the letter at all because it spoke of individual freedom and they won't be allowed to talk of that or read of it. Better than we've done before, we've got to quit talking about each other, start talking to each other and go out and communicate to the world that we [Republicans] may be fewer in number than we've ever been, but we carry the message they've been waiting for. We must go forth from here united, determined. . . . There is no substitute for victory."

After Reagan's address, a delegate waved a hand-lettered sign: GOV. REAGAN, it said. WE ALMOST MADE THAT HARD CLIMB, DIDN'T WE?

Reagan was no less eloquent when he spoke to his volunteers later. We were exhausted and depressed, but Reagan was steady and upbeat.

"Sure, there is disappointment in what happened, but the cause goes on," he told us in a meeting room of the Alameda Plaza Hotel. "Don't get cynical. Look at yourselves and what you were willing to do, and recognize that there are millions and millions of Americans out there that want what you want."

He quoted from a Scottish ballad that he'd memorized as a child. "I may be wounded but I am not slain. I'll lay me down and rest for a while and then I'll fight again."

The drive back to the rolling plains of Canton, after experiencing all the color, life and excitement of the Kansas City convention, was one of the longest of my young life. We had gone into the convention with so much hope, and now it was over. After such a valiant fight on the part of Reagan, the Republican nominee would be Gerald Ford.

I was crushed. More than anything else in the world, I had wanted to work for Reagan. Politics, and a fierce desire to help Reagan, had gotten into my blood. Even though I might have disagreed with him on some issues, I respected and admired his fearless and unapologetic articulation of his principles. And, most important, I respected his enormous personal appeal. I didn't think I could ever get that excited about a candidate again.

Some believed that Reagan could never get elected president. He was too conservative for the county, was the thinking; he was a warmonger and his pro-life stance on abortion alienated many women. The postmortems on Reagan were withering. *Newsweek* magazine headlined a story "Into the Sunset" and drew on the last line of Reagan's convention speech — "There is no substitute for victory." The line, said *Newsweek*, "could also turn out to be an epitaph for his own political career."

Yet I was still convinced that Ronald Reagan could make a great president. He was a national figure. His strong belief system, his articulation of the issues that were important to him — getting government off the backs of the people, battling the evils of communism, fostering democracy around the world — what a great leader he could be for the most important nation in the world! Would he ever have an opportunity like this again?

As I drove, I listened to commentator Paul Harvey on the radio. In his trademark staccato style, Harvey was hitting the same themes. "Is this the end of Ronald Reagan?" Harvey asked as he announced the Reagans' departure from Kansas City that morning.

That's when it hit me. I pulled the car over to the side of the street in Kansas

City, upset by my realization. It *was* the end of Ronald Reagan. I did the calculations in my head. Reagan was 65 years old. If Ford won, he would probably become a two-term president. That would put Reagan well into his seventies before he got another shot at running for president.

It was too late for Reagan. It was over. Really over. Reagan could never come back. I saw an opportunity, for myself and for our country, evaporating in the hot midwestern air. He was too old. Too damned old. And that was too damned bad.

3

THE MASHED POTATO CIRCUIT

I was in a noisy café in Canton, lunching with a client, when Jimmy Carter was sworn in as the thirty-ninth president of the United States in January 1977. After the Reagan disappointment, I had gone back to work for Peter Voss, as a sales representative for IPS Industries. It was a hard switch after the excitement of the political campaign, but I had to look out for my future. As far as I was concerned, I was done with politics.

In the end, Ford had lost — done in by a stumbling campaign and weakened by the aftershocks of the Nixon scandal and, more specifically, the Nixon pardon. On the restaurant television, I caught a glimpse of Jimmy Carter taking the oath of office, his wife, Rosalyn, holding the bible as Supreme Court Justice Warren Burger administered the oath, although the din of the restaurant made their words unintelligible.

I watched the television with only faint interest. I had decided that, if asked, I would have worked for Ford in Ohio, but neither I, Voss nor Seffens ever got that request. I had a feeling the Ohio Ford people just didn't want us around. We didn't do anything to hurt Ford in Ohio, but we didn't do anything to help him, either. In fact, Ford lost Ohio by a slim margin, as he did New York State. If he had won either state, he would have still been president in 1977.

Reagan was criticized for not doing enough to help Ford get elected. And there were many in Ford's camp who believed that Reagan's vigorous campaign for the nomination had mortally weakened Ford, although Reagan campaigned in 20 states in the general election for Ford. But that was all history on that frigid day when Jimmy Carter raised his right hand and swore to uphold the Constitution of the United States.

The months after Carter's inauguration were hard ones for me. It was back to the day-to-day reality of earning a paycheck, and I missed the glamour and excitement of politics Ronald Reagan-style. I tried to make myself believe that politics was behind me now, and I focused on working for Voss, visiting the purchasing departments of steelmakers, bidding for purchase orders to supply power-transmission and material-handling equipment. But my future seemed pretty gray.

Then, suddenly, all that changed with a newsletter from the Ohio State Republican party in early spring 1977. The newsletter talked about a big fund-raiser coming up in Napoleon, a small town in the northwest part of the state, in July. The keynote speaker was none other than Ronald Reagan.

He was coming back.

After the '76 election, Reagan had resumed writing his syndicated newspaper column and giving his regular radio addresses, which he had suspended during the presidential campaign. He also used leftover campaign funds to form a political action committee, Citizens for the Republic, headed by Lyn Nofziger, to engage in key issues and to help Republican candidates who shared his vision.

Week after week, in his speeches, columns and radio addresses, Reagan articulated his vision for the country, defended the principles that had made the United States great and expressed his concern that it was headed in the wrong direction at a crucial time in history.

Conservatives, he contended, were the new majority in the United States. But, he said in a 1977 speech to the American Conservative Union, "the American new conservative majority we represent is *not* based on abstract theorizing of the kind that turns off the American people, but on common sense, intelligence, reason, hard work, faith in God, and the guts to say, yes, there *are* things we do strongly believe in, that we are willing to live for and, yes, if necessary, to die for. This is not 'ideological purity.' It is simply what built this country and kept it great."

As well, he continued to warn against the dangers of détente with a power-hungry Soviet Union, which he said was bent on the gradual encirclement of the West and in reducing the United States' political and economic influence on the West. He argued that the United States should continue to discuss arms agreements with the Soviets, but only with its eyes open.

Reagan also kept his name in circulation with speeches to various organizations, such as business groups, educational institutions and political gatherings. By now he was a well-known conservative icon and very much in demand as a speaker.

"There is magic in this marketplace economy of ours that we often forget as we worry about inflation, the dollar's decline and an unfavorable trade balance," he said in one radio address in 1979. "The magic is to be found in the way that someone with an idea sees a problem and comes up with a solution. The motive is, of course, profit, yet we all benefit."

I asked Voss whether Reagan had a chance of making a realistic run for president again. The assumption at that point was that Carter would win a second term.

But Voss was optimistic about Reagan's prospects.

"We don't know what's going to happen with Carter," he told me. "And if Carter is a one-term president, I don't think Ford will come back and run again."

Voss felt sure that Ford didn't have the stomach for another go-around in the brutal business of presidential campaigning. Also, as David Seffens saw it, other than campaigning nationwide in '76, Ford had never even run statewide in Michigan. He had been minority leader in the House of Representatives when Nixon plucked him from Congress to replace the disgraced Spiro Agnew.

"And," said Voss, "Ronald Reagan has the will to do it again."

"Isn't he going to be too old?" I asked.

"Maybe not," said Voss. "You saw the man. He's sixty-five going on forty-five. He's in great shape. Mind like a steel trap. Watch him. He's going to be very visible in the next four years."

And that is exactly what unfolded. Reagan took to what he called the mashed potato circuit, earning an income from speeches, writing his newspaper column and giving his radio addresses. He also never took an honorarium from any educational institution. He stayed visible and articulated the issues important to him.

My big break came just a few weeks before the Napoleon event when I got an unexpected call from Ronald Reagan's office. It was Helene Van Damme, who had been Reagan's executive secretary in Sacramento on the traveling staff of the '76 campaign and who now worked as office director for the agency representing Reagan, which was run by former Reagan aides Mike Deaver and Pete Hannaford.

The Reagan organization had kept a detailed list of all its former advance men. Helene asked me if I could advance the Napoleon trip for Reagan. "We need someone to go in a couple of days ahead of time," she said, "and hook up with the Napoleon Republican organization and get things set up for him and the group."

I was ecstatic — first that they had called and, second, that I was going to get a chance to work with Reagan again. Then I started worrying. It would be the first time I had advanced a Reagan stop by myself. I'd always had one of Reagan's top guys with me before. Now I felt the pressure. Would I do too much? Would I not do enough?

Fortunately, Voss was an old hand at this, since he'd done some advance work for Nixon, and he coached me through it. There were some challenges. The Napoleon Republican party had made a big mistake when planning the event; its event chairman had predicted that 20,000 people would attend the rally at the local fairgrounds. As I learned later in my years as an advance man, that's a huge number of people — even for a president — to draw, let alone to bring to tiny Napoleon. In the end, we drew about 7,000 people, which was a very respectable number for a small rural area. Clearly, a lot of people out there were hungry for Reagan's message.

After meeting Reagan at the Toledo airport on the day of the event, we drove him to the fairgrounds. As always, he was friendly and easygoing. When we got to the event site, I escorted Reagan to a borrowed Winnebago I had set up just outside the grandstand. People milled around as I led him into the holding room. Voss had suggested this arrangement to give Reagan time to gather his thoughts and read over the notes for his speech before I took him to the dais.

So I left Reagan alone for a few minutes, then returned to check in. Something was wrong. He looked distressed.

"I can't stand this," he said to me.

I was bewildered. What had I done?

"I feel like I'm in a fishbowl," he said. "Where are the people I'm supposed to be on the stage with?"

I felt terrible. I'd messed up. I apologized profusely and mentally kissed my bright future with the next Reagan presidential campaign good-bye.

But Reagan was kind.

"I understand why you put me in here," he said. "But put me with people. I don't like to be alone like this."

"Yes, sir," I said, and immediately took him to where the rest of the speakers, and others who would be on the dais with him, were located. I learned a valuable lesson about Governor Reagan. He was a private person, but he loved listening to what was on other people's minds and bouncing some ideas off them. Reagan never aspired to be Boss Tweed in situations like this. He always deferred to others as he was a great listener with groups of any size.

Ohio Governor Jim Rhodes had been invited to the event, but it wasn't clear whether he would attend. He hadn't been happy that Reagan had run in the Ohio primary, especially since Rhodes and Senator Taft had thrown their full support behind Ford, and he blamed Reagan for Ford's defeat.

But halfway through Reagan's speech, Rhodes appeared. He came in behind the grandstand and then popped out on the racetrack, where chairs were set up for the VIPs. Everyone recognized him, and he got a standing ovation, and it was clear that he was trying to take the spotlight away from Reagan.

My blood was boiling. How dare he try to upstage Reagan like that? But Reagan, the old pro, didn't let it faze him. He paused in his speech, graciously applauded Rhodes and then continued as if nothing had happened.

It took a lot more than the Jim Rhodeses of the world to throw Reagan off his stride.

After the event, Helene called to tell me everything had been fine and to ask if they could assign me to other Reagan events. I didn't even have to think about that. I said yes immediately.

So for the next two and a half years, I got a call about every two months to advance another Reagan visit, mostly in the Midwest and on the East Coast. We met in various states — Iowa, Illinois, Missouri, New Jersey, Pennsylvania, Ohio — as he spoke to gatherings. Sometimes he and I were alone, sometimes Mike Deaver or Pete Hannaford came along.

It was clear that Reagan was striking a chord with his audiences. They were eager to hear him, cheered him lustily and always stayed afterward for a chance to meet him. Reagan liked to remain, too. He always said he figured that if someone paid good money for a ticket to hear him speak, the least he owed them was a personal hello and a handshake.

I watched him greet people in the airports and on our plane rides. People almost always recognized him. They looked at him for a few seconds and smiled. Some called out "Governor Reagan, how are you?" while others stopped him and wanted to talk. He always took the time to do so.

Reagan and I talked a lot on those trips — in car rides, in airplanes and before and after receptions, rallies, dinners and other events — about myriad issues. He asked me about my life and told me about his.

It didn't take me long to realize how completely genuine Ronald Reagan was. On a plane, in a hotel room, at a big reception, in front of the press, he treated everyone the same with his unassuming, self-effacing style. You could tell it was real, that he had probably been that way his entire life, and if he ever became president, he would still be that way. That made a huge impact on me.

On those trips in the late '70s with Reagan, I also learned that he was proud of his past. He'd grown up as "Dutch" Reagan during hard economic times in the small town of Dixon in northwestern Illinois. He loved his parents — Jack and Nelle — and his older brother, Neil. His father was an alcoholic, but Reagan's mother helped the boys understand his sickness, as she called it.

Later, to small groups in the Oval Office, Reagan enjoyed talking about his mother and the impact she had had on the family and the community. One favorite story Reagan told was when his Eureka College football team was on the road, and a motel refused to allow the team's only black player to stay there. Reagan called his mother, and Nelle Reagan brought Reagan and the player to her house, where they spent the night.

In 1977, I met Reagan at Upper Iowa University in Fayette, in northeast Iowa, for a speech. Reagan had roots in Iowa, having worked as a radio announcer in Davenport and Des Moines shortly after graduating from college in the depths of the Depression in the 1930s. He remembered it fondly. In fact, in his second term when we flew back to Washington on Air Force One after political trips to Michigan and Nebraska, I went into the stateroom to talk to the president. He was gazing out the window at the patchwork of gold and green below, and he called me over.

"Look down there," he said.

I squinted. "I see a little town," I said.

"Look again," said Reagan, pointing at something on the ground.

I located an open structure in the landscape. "I see a round thing," I said.

"Do you know what that is?" he asked me. I said I didn't know.

"That is the University of Iowa's Kinnick Stadium," he said. "I used to announce Big Ten football games there." It was his first job out of college — Dutch Reagan's first big break.

Somehow, on that flight more than 40 years later, he'd been able to find it in the vast landscape of the country as we streaked our way to Washington. In fact, one of the games he had announced back then was a contest between the University of Iowa and the University of Michigan that had featured a Michigan center — Gerald Ford.

Walking across the Upper Iowa University campus, Reagan asked me about the school. He had attended Eureka College, about 100 miles from Dixon, which had fewer than 250 students.

"This place is *small*," I said, thinking of the thousands of students at my alma mater, Kent State. "Very small." I must have smirked a bit, because he stopped walking and turned to me with a slight smile.

"Let me tell you what small is," he said. "Small is where I went to school — Eureka College. When I was there, Eureka was so small that if every man didn't go out for football, then we couldn't field a team. I'm sure this school is much larger than Eureka."

I said that, yes, most definitely it was. Reagan smiled again and resumed walking.

I think Reagan was trying to tell me something about his origins, but he also wanted to set me straight. Don't underestimate what's in front of you, he seemed to be saying. There's nothing wrong with being small.

He was immensely proud of the small town where he grew up and the small college that he had attended. He always said that growing up in a small town was a good foundation for politics because you got to know people as individuals, rather than as blocs or special interests. And, he liked to say, if he'd gone to a larger school, he might have become just part of the crowd and never discovered things about himself that he had found at Eureka.

He had loved playing football in high school and at Eureka and had a real affinity for athletes because of that experience. Later, in the White House, he enjoyed it when athletes came to visit and he could show off his athletic prowess. When the Washington Redskins came to meet Reagan at the White House after winning the Super Bowl in January 1988, we decided to take the team to the South Lawn, where Reagan would make a short speech. We also determined that after the speech he would throw a pass from the outdoor stage to one of the Redskins offstage.

Reagan liked this idea, but he wanted to practice first.

"Don't we have a couple of footballs in the closet in your office?" he asked that day in the Oval Office. "If I'm going to throw this pass, I'm going to have to loosen up."

I took a commemorative Super Bowl ball into the Oval Office, but I said I didn't know where we could practice, pointing out that we couldn't go out to the Colonnade or the Rose Garden because we could be seen by the press and others.

"We're going to throw the ball here," Reagan said.

"Here?" I said. "In the Oval Office? We can't do that!"

"Why not?" asked Reagan.

"What if we hit something?" I said, turning to look at the gleaming room, with its precisely placed furniture, western sculptures, porcelain eagle figurines and breakable lamps.

"We won't," Reagan said confidently.

"You'll just have to catch it."

Fortunately, I had been a receiver on my high school football team, so that assignment wasn't too difficult. We tossed the football back and forth; the president still had a perfect spiral on the ball. Eventually, the president's secretary, Kathy Osborne, heard the snap of the pigskin against our hands and looked through the peephole to investigate. She called in the White House photographer, who took some shots of us throwing the ball back and forth.

Later, the president gave his speech on the South Lawn to the Redskins and guests, which culminated with a picture-perfect pass to wide receiver Ricky Sanders, who ran out in front of the press and the audience. The president had a huge smile on his face.

Reagan also took great pride in staying in shape and worked out almost every day when he was in the White House. Those workouts, combined with the hard physical labor he put in at his California ranch, had left him in better shape than most men 20 years younger.

At Upper Iowa University, we met a prominent alumnus of the school, former Oakland Raider punter Mike Eischeid. Reagan and Mike really hit it off, and they traded stories about Mike's playing football at Upper Iowa and Reagan at Eureka.

Another time on the mashed potato circuit, we met at Chicago's O'Hare International Airport and flew together to Youngstown, Ohio, for a speech at Youngstown State University. We sat in the front row seats and had a chance to talk on the plane. Reagan told me he'd seen a woman drink four Bloody Marys on the flight from Los Angeles to Chicago.

"You know, people wouldn't do that at home," he commented. "So why, when they get on the plane, do they act differently?"

"Maybe some people are afraid to fly," I said, "and that's how they make themselves comfortable."

He thought about it for a moment. "You're probably right," he said. "That hadn't occurred to me. I fly so much, it's a routine. I just take it for granted. But some people who don't fly very much may have a real dread of it."

For a long time, Reagan hadn't really liked to fly, I was to learn later. He'd gotten over it before running for governor, although he and Nancy had rarely flown together when he was governor because they were concerned that their children would be left without both parents if their plane went down.

But it never would have occurred to him to resort to an escape like alcohol to deal with his fears. He was, in many ways, a fearless man. He had enough inner confidence and natural optimism to prevail in even the toughest times, and one of his favorite sayings was "Never say never." That inborn buoyancy served him well when he took over the White House during difficult times in our country.

Also on our trips in the 1970s, we talked about his ranch, Rancho del Cielo — "Ranch in the Sky" — high up in the Santa Ynez Mountains northwest of Santa Barbara that he and Nancy had purchased shortly before he left the California governor's office. Reagan just lit up when we got on the subject of the ranch. I visited it frequently while working in the White House, and it really was a special place. Reagan and his close friends — Barney Barnett and Dennis LeBlanc, who were former California highway patrolmen who protected Reagan as governor — had put in a lot of work to fix it up, particularly after Reagan left the governorship.

On this trip to Youngstown in 1977,

Reagan told me about the fences they were building. He and LeBlanc had devised a system of using old telephone poles to construct fences around the property to make sure the horses didn't get out and onto the property's road. The poles last forever, he told me, and made great fence material. He, Barnett and LeBlanc used some as posts and then cut and notched others for the fencing.

During Reagan's presidency, the Reagans tried to visit the ranch in August for two or three weeks — sandwiching in a trip to Los Angeles to see friends — and again for Thanksgiving. We also squeezed ranch trips into the president's schedule other times during the year. When necessary, the president would forgo trips to the ranch; during the hostage crisis in 1985, for example, when passengers from a TWA flight departing Athens were hijacked and taken hostage, he canceled his ranch trip to stay in Washington to monitor the situation.

Ranch trips energized him. He and Mrs. Reagan rode in the mornings, had lunch, then he did paperwork until it was time to go out and get some ranch work done, such as cutting down trees, clearing brush and chopping wood. There wasn't as much up there for Mrs. Reagan, but she stayed busy with her projects as first lady and stayed in touch with friends via the telephone. She knew how good it was for Reagan, mentally and physically, to be there.

It was on that Youngstown trip that I noticed Reagan, despite his background of acting and politics, was really a rather quiet man, reserved and shy. As I got to know him, I learned that although he had an unparalleled ability to come across as larger than life in public, he was, in many ways, very private. He was neither a back slapper nor verbose. Like many actors, he was more at ease in front of large groups than in smaller groups.

When I was working as his executive assistant in the second term, I found that he liked his time alone; he preferred reading, answering letters, writing speeches and formulating policy decisions to empty chatter. In fact, small talk was not his forte. Sometimes it took him a little while to get warmed up in small settings, and I learned to recommend a few topics to small groups or some people who hadn't met Reagan and were about to visit with him in the Oval Office, in case he had a lot on his mind or if his natural shyness took hold and he wasn't talkative. I generally suggested that they ask him about the ranch and the horses; he loved talking about them. Hollywood was also always a big hit.

But I was always surprised when people described Reagan as "distant" and incapable of relating to people very well. In fact, some people complained in the media or in books that Reagan couldn't even remember people, citing as evidence his tendency not to call people by their names. In the White House, for example, there was only a small group of people — his chief of staff, his national security adviser, his executive assistant, his secretary, old Hollywood friends — that he addressed by name. I was amused to find out when actor Jimmy Stewart visited the Oval Office during the second term that the president called him Jim. Reagan knew Stewart very well from their Hollywood days.

I realized after I'd worked closely with President Reagan throughout '85 and into '86 that he really did know many more names than he ever got credit for. When we were in private conversations, he quite easily used the names of many people he knew. But he had a deep concern about offending anyone if he got their name wrong and, if anything, he was too careful and too kind in avoiding the use of their names for fear of mistakenly insulting anyone.

In our conversations and in all his speeches on the mashed potato circuit, Reagan talked about the issues that would always remain important to him — downsizing the federal government and reducing government waste, fostering democracy around the world, lowering taxes and rebuilding our military. He used to talk about planes that couldn't fly and ships that couldn't sail — how our armed forces didn't have enough money to purchase spare parts or have the mechanics who knew how to fix them, and he warned that the United States was falling behind the Soviet Union in military might.

The issue of government waste and lowering taxes resonated with me, having seen my parents, who owned two small farms, work so hard to pay their taxes along with their other bills. I realized that Reagan cared about the little guy. If there was a way to make the government more efficient, by helping it get more value out of the dollars it brought in, then Reagan was on the right track.

It took me a few years longer, however, to come around to his message about the need to build up America's military might again. I was in some ways still a child of the '60s, still antimilitary from my years at Kent State during the Vietnam War, and my natural reaction wasn't sympathetic support for buying more guns, tanks and fighter jets. America already had enough of those, I thought.

But later, in 1981, I finally saw what Reagan was talking about. I was at Langley Air Force Base near Hampton, Virginia, preparing for a Reagan appearance in Williamsburg for the bicentennial of the Revolutionary War Battle of Yorktown. The Reagans were likely to helicopter to Williamsburg on Marine One (the helicopter that transports the president, first lady and senior staff), but might fly on Air Force One into Langley. I met with the base commander to work out the logistics, and we drove around the base, where I spied rows and rows of F-15 fighter jets — 97 in all — lined up on the tarmac.

I complimented the base commander on a magnificent sight. But he told me that the last time crews had tried to undertake a full-fledged drill with the jets, they could get only 37 of them to start! That's when I realized that those Reagan stories about malfunctioning military equipment that he had related in radio addresses, columns and speeches were actually true. I was seeing it firsthand.

Also on the Youngstown trip, Reagan did a question-and-answer session with the students and faculty attending his speech. He loved doing Q-and-As. He would start out by saying, "When I was in your place, I always felt that if I could ask someone a question about what they've been saying, that this would be a good opportunity to really find out what they're made of. So I want you to fire way. Here's your opportunity. Ask me anything — anything that I just said that you think might be factually incorrect or that you disagree with me on."

He always got an abundance of questions until someone in charge stepped in and cut it off. He would have stayed all night answering questions. He loved to do it.

When he ran for president and was in the White House, this tendency sometimes got him into trouble. He always said what he believed, but that sometimes could create a story that we didn't want. For example, he once got a question about why he didn't propose more money for the homeless in his budget. The accusation was that the president wasn't doing enough for them and that bothered him. Reagan responded by saying that the United States spent sizable amounts on the homeless and that many programs were in place to help them. He said that he was hard-pressed to believe that there weren't already enough programs, and it appeared to him that there were those people on the streets who were there because they wanted to be.

Of course, those remarks became a running controversy for several days — that Reagan didn't care about people living in poverty. But that's not what Reagan believed.

So when he was in the White House or on the road and got the urge to do a question-and-answer session, we often tried to talk him out of it. For the most part, he accepted our guidance, but he knew what we were doing. One morning, he told me he planned to do a question-and-answer with a group of students he was scheduled to speak to in the White House Old Executive Office Building. I spoke up quickly and told him he didn't have time because some items had to be added to his schedule.

Well, he knew what I was up to!

"You guys always think I'm going to

drop a bomb every time I take questions, don't you?" he said, eyeing me sternly.

I looked at him and started laughing and said, "Well . . ."

And he said, "Well, I'm taking questions, and I don't care."

"You're the president," I said. "You're in charge and you can do whatever you want to do."

In the '70s, Reagan always started his speeches with a prepared text, usually written on half sheets of paper, handwritten in block letters in his special shorthand. But he almost always digressed from the text. He was a voracious reader and was always clipping out anecdotes, stories and statistics that he would cite in the speeches. As president, he would come down to the Oval Office in the morning with a stack of clippings, and he would point out to us what he'd read. *We ought to look into this. Can we get more information on that? This is wrong, what can we do about it?*

He kept the clippings, along with notes to himself and other such paraphernalia, in a thick folder in the lower right-hand drawer of his Oval Office desk, and we never went into that drawer. Occasionally, he pulled an article out of the drawer to make a point and, when he went over drafts of speeches, he got that old folder out and inserted facts, statistics and stories collected through the years.

It drove the speechwriters crazy. They would come to me, asking to pull the president's insertions out. I always argued with them, maintaining that it was the president's speech and if he wanted to insert this fact or that fact from his folder, then that was his call. He was the boss. Then the staff secretary, through whom every bit of paper that went to the president flowed, would weigh in with me, saying that the new facts couldn't be confirmed or fact checked. The staff secretary would ask me to talk to the president and ask him about the background of the specific information.

Invariably, I refused to bring it up with the president, insisting that we would leave the information in unless someone found something dangerously wrong with it. Otherwise, we could upset the president and if we did that, I would point out, he would just put his foot down anyway. Despite the concerns of speechwriters and the staff secretary that the president's insertions would cause trouble, they never really did.

Going from city to city with Reagan in the 1970s, I could see that he was in excellent condition for a man in his late sixties. He was in great physical shape, and his mind was keen. I could also tell that he wanted to challenge Carter because he was increasingly troubled by the direction in which Carter was taking the country. Reagan didn't like the Carter administration's approach to arms control, and he believed the United States was sacrificing its military might and not asking for enough concessions from the Soviets.

He talked about the Carter administration and its war on poverty. "Unfortunately," he liked to say in speeches, "poverty won." The crowd always responded to criticism of Carter with cheers and roars of approval for Reagan.

I became convinced that Reagan had the ability to get elected and to govern effectively. Sometimes that's hard to find in one politician. Reagan, however, had both qualities — a warmth and personal appeal that attracted voters and a clear agenda for the country — and would be a great president. In my mind, he was in an absolute position of strength from which to run the country.

Plus, he was very competitive. In the White House, he used to tell the story of a rainy, muddy football game he played in while at Eureka. He was being beaten the entire game by the defensive lineman across from him who constantly got into the Eureka backfield, stopping the running backs and sacking the quarterback. Reagan was frustrated.

Well, there was this big puddle of water in between Reagan and his opponent. So the next time the ball was snapped, Reagan scooped up as much water as he could and threw the ice cold water in the defensive lineman's face. The guy staggered back and Reagan stormed over him.

As I continued to learn over the years, it was very easy for people to underestimate Ronald Reagan. But his amiable personality included a fierce determination that was too often overlooked. And if Reagan was beaten, he didn't stay beaten for long.

4

TURMOIL AND TROUBLE

Nineteen seventy-nine was not the best year for many Americans. Chronic gas shortages meant long lines at the pumps in some parts of the country, inflation and unemployment raged at double-digit rates and the prime rate hovered around 21 percent. In November, Iranian extremists seized 52 Americans at the American embassy in Tehran, holding them hostage amid the chaos of revolutionary Iran, where America was being slammed as the "Great Satan."

Also in November 1979, Reagan formally declared his candidacy for the Republican presidential nomination — the tenth candidate to do so. He was going up against former CIA director George H. W. Bush, former Texas Governor John Connally and Senator Bob Dole of Kansas, among others. Ronald Reagan was officially back in the political saddle.

Although Reagan was crowned the front-runner as soon as he entered the race, he was to lose that title not long after.

I still lived in Canton, but climbed aboard Reagan's presidential bid when the

Reagan campaign gathered about 50 potential advance men, some of whom had worked on Reagan's '76 campaign, for a two-day conference in mid-October in Chicago. There was a new director of scheduling and advance, Nick Ruwe, a former Nixon aide, and I was fortunate enough to be chosen by Ruwe as one of five from the Chicago conference to be hired for the national campaign. Many others would come aboard when Reagan won enough primaries in the Republican nomination race or later in the general campaign.

By the fall of '79, much the same team as had run Reagan's '76 campaign was back again. Paul Laxalt was national chairman, John Sears directed the campaign, Mike Deaver was political strategist, Ed Meese served as a senior adviser and Lyn Nofziger was also a senior strategist and press secretary.

Because of Reagan's nearly successful capture of the Republican nomination in 1976 and the years he had spent building his political base, everyone was confident he would capture the nomination this time. In early November, I went to New York City to help plan Reagan's official announcement at a big dinner on November 13 and to assist with the national campaign launch.

Sears had decided that it was best to bring Reagan right into the lion's den — New York — which Reagan hadn't even entered in the '76 campaign. New York was critical to the election, but voters there did not have a strong understanding of Ronald Reagan. The idea was to present New York voters, and the nation, with a man with strong conservative principles who could indeed represent the entire nation.

The announcement dinner was co-chaired by Charlie Wick, a longtime Reagan friend from California, and held at the New York Hilton. Afterward, I would assist with the final stop of Reagan's 10-city announcement tour in Orlando.

At the time, we knew virtually nothing about Wick except that he was very close to Reagan — he later chaired the '81 inauguration. But we learned that he was very challenging to work with. He had definite ideas of how the announcement was to be made — how to get everyone in the ballroom, who else would speak, how to present Reagan — that contradicted everything we'd learned about putting Reagan in the best perspective and getting him the best press coverage. He was temperamental and, at times, given to long rants about how wrong we were for the Reagan campaign. After many such tirades, Wick was forgiving, but it was rough going.

Wick had this unorthodox idea of how to formally present Reagan at the announcement dinner. Normally, it would be handled in a very dignified manner. Reagan would be announced into the room, "Ladies and gentleman, Governor Ronald Reagan" or "The next president of the United States," and he would come in stage left or right and take his seat to fanfare.

Wick decided to first show the crowd a short biographical film on Reagan's life, then the lights would dim, the curtain on the stage would open and the lights would come up on Ronald Reagan himself. We hated the idea; we thought it was not at all presidential. But the Reagans went along with Wick's idea, and Charlie got his way.

Well, as we had feared, it fell flat. There was an awkward pause after the film, and when Reagan appeared, it surprised the crowd. But after dinner, Reagan gave a great speech in which he talked about his father and laid out his optimistic vision of America. He talked about the Christmas

Eve when his father got a layoff notice during the Great Depression. He repeated the phrase from his 1964 Goldwater speech that Americans had a "rendezvous with destiny." He was interrupted several times by enthusiastic applause from the diners in the packed ballroom.

"I don't agree that our nation must resign itself to inevitable decline, yielding its proud position to other hands," he said. "I am totally unwilling to see this country fail in its obligation to itself and to the other free people of the world."

After the speech, we headed for the airport for our next campaign stop in Washington, but we had a few mishaps along the way. First, our motorcade to LaGuardia Airport got split up. Somehow, the New York City police escorting us made a wrong turn and went down one of those narrow, car-clogged byways that pass for side streets in New York City. Then we all had to turn around. The main part of the motorcade containing the Reagans and the Secret Service vehicles (major presidential primary candidates had Secret Service coverage back then) managed to make the turnaround and continue to the airport. But the buses with members of the media planning to travel on the campaign plane with the Reagans couldn't make the U-turn. So there we were — I and others — trying to stop traffic in the middle of Manhattan so the buses could back out! It was a mess but, finally, the buses made it and we were again on our way to LaGuardia and the waiting charter.

Worse than that, we discovered after the Reagan charter departed that one of Mrs. Reagan's bags had somehow gotten separated from the rest of the luggage sent to LaGuardia earlier that evening. It was a small bag, usually used to carry makeup, but Mrs. Reagan was very protective of it. I never knew for sure what it carried, but we knew it was very important.

Whatever was in it, there was much consternation when it was discovered that the bag was left behind in New York. A campaign worker ended up driving it down to Washington that night. Years later, Mrs. Reagan always made sure the bag stayed within her immediate reach. I or another senior White House staffer would carry it when we were traveling, instead of entrusting it to others. I even saw Don Regan, the White House chief of staff, carry it a couple of times during Reagan's second term.

★ ★ ★

In December '79, I went to Shelby County, Iowa, in the far western corner of the state, only weeks before the crucial Iowa caucuses on January 21 to put together a rally for Reagan in a high school gymnasium in the little town of Harlan. This was our last campaign stop of '79. Because of his radio broadcast experience in Iowa, Reagan was practically a native son, and his opinion polls in the state were high. Campaign higher-ups were confident he would do well. A poll by the *Des Moines Register* and *Tribune* in late November appeared to confirm that belief, showing Reagan at 50 percent of the vote and his closest rival, Bush, at 14 percent. Internal campaign polls had Reagan even higher. In fact, so certain were campaign strategists that Reagan had the state wrapped up that they focused on the Northeast — where Gerald Ford had swamped Reagan in 1976 — instead of Iowa.

However, I got a rude shock when I got to Harlan. Instead of finding enthusiastic volunteers and Republican party officials ready to throw themselves into the campaign stop for Reagan, I found a bunch of furious people. The message from these Reagan loyalists was a resounding: "Where the hell have you been?" Bush had been virtually living in the state for months, patiently building a county-by-county organization, and Reagan had made only periodic drop-in appearances.

In the minds of the Iowans I was talking to, Reagan had taken the state for granted — a major mistake when it came to stubborn Iowans. I had trouble finding volunteers willing to pitch in with the Reagan effort; Republican party officials who were leaning toward Reagan were hostile, and rank-and-file Republicans told me they were either going to boycott the caucuses or vote for Bush.

Reagan had worked so hard those years on the mashed potato circuit to build his political base. Now it appeared to be coming apart in one of the crucial opening events of the campaign. I couldn't help but wonder — was it just Harlan?

I made a frantic call to my boss, Nick Ruwe, in Los Angeles, giving him the scoop. "It's really bad here," I told him. "People are saying they're not going to support Reagan. We're losing people to Bush."

But I got nowhere. Ruwe just kept reciting the campaign's weekly tracking poll numbers to me. "You don't know what you're talking about," he'd tell me. "We're at sixty-five percent in the Iowa polls. People are just upset because Bush has been there so much." Just do your job, he told me, and don't worry about it.

Nonetheless, I kept calling for three days, trying to warn Ruwe of trouble. Finally, he threatened to pull me out of the state and send someone else in. So I swallowed hard and told Ruwe that I would put together a great event and stop overreacting. I tried to tell myself that I was still young and not as experienced at this as Ruwe and others in the Reagan camp. Maybe I was wrong in having misgivings about Reagan's prospects in the state.

We managed to fill the high school gym with an overflow crowd that cheered enthusiastically when Reagan came in for his campaign appearance. Reagan ended up making more appearances in the state in January of '80 as the caucuses drew closer.

But his rivals were pummeling him. Connally and Bush repeatedly hit Reagan, then 68, with the "he's too old" accusation. With the cameras rolling, Bush, 55, took an aerobics class, and his state campaign manager assured reporters tongue in cheek, "We're not doing this to emphasize Reagan's age. We're just letting the world see what great shape George Bush is in." Connally even suggested that Reagan might not have either the mental or the physical capacity to be president.

When the final results came in, they were as ugly as I had feared. Bush clobbered us in the caucuses something like 33 percent to 27 percent and, jubilantly informing the country he was no longer an "asterisk," headed for New Hampshire with momentum. "Big Mo'," he called it. The Reagan campaign could only lick its wounds. NBC national correspondent Tom Pettit declared that "Ronald Reagan is politically dead," and commentators opined that Reagan prospects for the presidential nomination were over.

I learned something valuable that night. Whatever happens, don't believe the polls. When you're ahead, don't believe them because you could lose that lead. When you're behind, don't believe them because you just have to keep plugging away to the end.

After Iowa, most of us in the Reagan campaign were scared and in various states of depression and shock, but we all had to go forward and do our jobs and see if we could turn things around for this guy.

* * *

The day after the caucuses, I headed to my next stop in Huntsville, Alabama, to start building Reagan campaign events for Alabama's upcoming primary.

I arrived in Huntsville in the middle of a freezing rain and checked into my hotel, where I discovered that the heat in my room was off, the room was ice cold and water leaked through the ceiling. I turned on the television, and there were shots of George Bush running around in the blowing snow on an airport tarmac in New Hampshire, smiling, grabbing hands and talking about Big Mo again.

What the hell is Big Mo? I wondered.

I crashed down on the bed and stared up at the dripping ceiling. Everyone thinks it's over.

We've got to pick ourselves up, I told myself. But can we?

5

TRIUMPH IN DETROIT

After the Iowa debacle, I was buoyed by a warm reception in Alabama. The Reagan people weren't bitching about being snubbed by him. Instead, they told me not to worry about Iowa and assured me that Alabama was solidly behind Ronald Reagan. The next primary, New Hampshire, wasn't until February 26, so there was still plenty of time for Reagan to regain his momentum.

Reagan came in from campaigning in New Hampshire for an appearance in Huntsville, and it was tremendous. We felt like we had our footing again. We decided to forget about Iowa and think about New Hampshire, then Massachusetts, and then South Carolina, followed by Florida, Alabama and Georgia. We were going to turn this thing around.

Unfortunately, we were missing some important Reagan loyalists. Reagan had brought Sears in to help him broaden his support beyond his loyal base of conservative supporters, and Sears was working on bringing in the swing voters — moderate Democrats and independents. Sears was a brilliant strategist, but there had been a lot of friction between him and Reagan's longtime staffers. After repeated clashes with Sears, some of Reagan's California team, including Deaver and Nofziger, had left. But most of us on the campaign figured they would be back at some point as Reagan wound his way through the primaries and, we hoped, got the Republican nomination. Reagan couldn't really go on without them — they were too much a part of him.

Just before the New Hampshire vote, something unusual happened. My boss suddenly sent me to Worcester, Massachusetts. An advance team was already in there, but Ruwe told me he wanted me to go in and help since Reagan would be coming down for a series of campaign appearances.

But I realized that Ruwe had sent me for another reason. He told me to keep my eyes and ears open for a meeting the Reagans might have with a man by the name of Bill Casey.

"Let me know the minute it happens — if it does," he told me. I had no idea who Bill Casey was, but I dutifully promised to stay alert for him.

Sure enough, what seemed like mere

moments after the Reagans arrived in their hotel suite in Worcester, I spied a man who I confirmed was Casey. He went to the Reagans' suite, and I called Ruwe right away.

"Good job, Kuhn," he said cryptically. "Thanks."

He then ordered me to Florida to put together campaign events throughout that state. I was still mystified, but obeyed orders and headed south.

On the Saturday night before the New Hampshire primary, I was driving through Daytona with a Floridian, surveying the area for an upcoming campaign blitz to be held before the Florida primary. We listened to news reports about the debate between Republican primary candidates being held that night in Nashua, New Hampshire.

A New Hampshire newspaper, the *Nashua Telegraph*, had offered to sponsor a debate between Bush and Reagan only. But after the Reagan campaign had ended up paying the costs of the event, Reagan had invited other candidates to join it. However, Bush campaign manager Jim Baker objected when Phil Crane, Howard Baker, Bob Dole and John Anderson showed up at the Nashua High School gymnasium for the event. Baker insisted that Bush had agreed to debate only Reagan, and the *Nashua Telegraph* editor refused to change the ground rules to include the others.

Over the radio, we could hear the crowd of 2,500 people in the gym jeering and shouting as confusion reigned. Over the noise, Reagan started to explain the situation to the crowd. But the *Nashua Telegraph* editor ordered that Reagan's microphone be turned off.

Then we heard Reagan's voice boom out of the radio: "I *paid* for this microphone, Mr. Green."

He sounded as commanding and presidential as I had ever heard him.

The crowd went wild.

I turned to my friend in the car. "Ronald Reagan just won New Hampshire."

Three days later, New Hampshire voters went to the polls. Would they come to the same conclusion as I had?

Reagan, in the meantime, didn't wait for the results to make changes to his campaign. On the day of the primary, February 26, he asked John Sears, Jim Lake and Charlie Black to resign. They did. Then Bill Casey, whom Reagan had already quietly hired as Sears's replacement, stepped in.

There was a lot of shock and bewilderment among the staff about Casey. He was an unusual choice for such a significant political position. Heavy-set, stooped and perennially rumpled, a lawyer and former head of the Securities and Exchange Commission during the Nixon administration, Casey had never run a campaign, although he had been active in Republican politics for 30 years. He didn't connect with people very well. He mumbled so much that later, when Reagan became president and named Casey as director of the Central Intelligence Agency, we used to joke that Casey never had to use a secure phone because you couldn't understand him to begin with.

But Casey was a staunch conservative and reassured Reagan supporters who had never trusted Sears. He picked up the pieces and did a competent job of getting us through the primaries.

Ronald Reagan got a badly needed win when he took New Hampshire with 51 percent of the vote. Reagan commented that he was surprised by his margin of victory. Bush received 23 percent, and Howard Baker got 13 percent. That night, Reagan told cheering supporters that he planned to continue campaigning as he had in New Hampshire, "meeting the people of the country as I was able to meet you." He said he wanted to give people "an opportunity to question us and talk." This was forever a strong part of Reagan's central belief system — that in being an effective leader, you always had to "listen to the people — let them question you," as I heard him say often in the White House.

After Sears's departure, Deaver returned and, later on, so did Nofziger. Unfortunately for staffers like me, the campaign lost Nick Ruwe, who left out of loyalty to Sears. I was sorry to see Ruwe go. He'd given me my big chance when he'd hired me out of a crowd of 50 advance staffers back in October at our seminar in Chicago, and he had tremendous wisdom and great institutional knowledge about campaigning nationally. With Nick, we had reported in every day, and he talked to us, guided us and asked the right questions. We always knew when we were on the right track.

I remember when I was planning a campaign bus tour for Reagan through Massachusetts. One of the scheduled stops was Plymouth, home of the famous Plymouth Rock where, legend has it, the Pilgrims landed in 1620 (actually, they'd landed in Cape Cod, but the myth persisted). I figured Reagan could stop by the rock.

I called Nick, excited by my idea. Nick was horrified.

"You can't do that," he said.

"Why not?" I was baffled.

"Age, Kuhn," he said. *"Age."*

I still wasn't getting it.

"Think about it," Ruwe said. "Reagan's *age*. The *age* of the Plymouth Rock. The press will be all over it. Forget it."

The Reagan campaign was already sensitive about the age issue. Reagan had turned 69 just 20 days before the New Hampshire primary. Now, he didn't much care. In fact, he made it a running joke of it throughout his presidency. On his seventy-third birthday, he told a Eureka College convocation that he had what every man with that many candles on his birthday cake needs: "A large group of friends and a working sprinkler system." He joked to a group of senior citizens during the 1984 presidential campaign that he "planned to campaign in all thirteen states." Later, in his second term as president, when he was introduced to an older-looking person who turned out to be years younger than he, he would smile and remark, "Just a kid."

Reagan loved jokes, and he was great at

telling them. He had the cadence and the timing down so that, even if it was a joke he'd told time and time again, it was still funny to those of us who were constantly with him. When he was in the White House, he usually tried to begin or end meetings with a joke. He knew we had tough jobs, and he understood the importance of keeping everyone loose. I used to wonder where he got his jokes from. I knew there was a system and, throughout the second term, I accused the president's secretary, Kathy Osborne, of guarding this process. At the end of Reagan's presidency, Osborne told me that a retired marine general by the name of Charles Krulak had been feeding jokes through her to Reagan since his days as California governor.

In the end, Nick Ruwe was overruled on the visit to Plymouth Rock, and a trip to the Rock was added to Reagan's schedule at the last minute. While there, though, we narrowly averted a disaster, but not because of the age issue. When Reagan arrived at the Rock, he leaned over to take a look at the seven-ton landmark on the shore of Plymouth, Massachusetts. It is set down in the ground under a columned portico and is a little difficult to see unless you stoop over to look. Once you do, however, the famous Rock turns out to be thoroughly uninteresting but covered with spray-painted graffiti. So when Reagan leaned over to take a look, he was confronted with scrawled obscenities. True to his actor's training, Reagan didn't react, and no one else really noticed. Thank goodness nobody got any photos of it. I was relieved when the day-long bus tour was over, and it was back to Alabama.

On a high note, the Massachusetts tour was memorable for another reason — in a hotel ballroom in North Falmouth, Reagan was presented with a live 17-pound lobster. The thing was bigger than a suburban mailbox, and it had an American flag clenched in its claw. Reagan and his senior staff dined on it that evening. They said it was kind of tough.

After Nick Ruwe left the campaign, we got only brief instructions from campaign headquarters in Los Angeles, telling us which state and which cities to go to. From there, we had to decide the campaign events with our Reagan regional political directors, come up with the venues, decide on the schedule — all the big and small details that make an event tremendously successful for a candidate or a disastrous waste of time and money.

After Bill Casey arrived, money also got tighter because Reagan's campaign expenses were hovering close to the federal limit on primary spending for candidates' accepting federal matching funds — and we were also running out of cash. The farther we went, the more we cut costs. We switched from a United charter to a Braniff charter and, by the time we got to Ohio in May, we were squeezed into an Evergreen Airlines prop plane.

In South Carolina, we toured many small towns by bus. It was a heavy-duty trip put together by a brilliant fellow we heard from a lot more in the 1980s — Lee Atwater.

We also had a barracuda of a chief financial officer for the campaign, Angela "Bay" Buchanan, Pat Buchanan's sister. She was a tyrant. She was convinced that the advance teams were misspending campaign money, so she set impossibly tight budgets for each stop and then fought us tooth and nail if we ran even slightly over budget. We were questioned on every expense. She especially hated any expenditure for rope. Well, rope is essential at campaign stops. We used hundreds of feet of it at rallies and other big campaign events to designate various areas — the press area, for example, and the VIP section. Plus, we put up a rope line, along which people could line up to shake hands with Reagan.

Sometimes we could borrow the rope from the local police or fire departments. But other times we just had to go to the nearest hardware store and buy it. But Bay couldn't understand repeated rope purchases. At one point, she actually asked, "Why can't you just take it with you?" It was no use explaining to her that we couldn't just wind up hundreds of feet of rope around a giant spool and lug it on a commercial flight to our next stop!

Along with the cash crunch, another big problem loomed shortly after New Hampshire.

Gerald Ford.

Reports that he would run for president again had begun appearing and, after New Hampshire, they escalated. By early March, the press was full of speculation. In a *New York Times* interview, Ford pointedly said that Reagan could not win a presidential election even if Reagan became the nominee, and he invited Republican leaders to publicly urge him to enter the campaign.

I was exasperated at the timing. Why

now? I had thought this roller coaster of a campaign was beginning to even out. We lose in Iowa, pick up the pieces and win big in New Hampshire. Then our campaign leadership is turned upside down. And just as we begin to regain our momentum and win another primary — Massachusetts — we start hearing that Ford would insert himself in the race.

The Ford people had always believed that Reagan had prevented Ford from getting elected, and I guess getting Gerald Ford to run again would be their revenge. But despite his rhetoric, I didn't think that Ford would decide to go again. As David Seffens had once pointed out, Ford had never even run statewide in Michigan prior to running for president. I believed '76 had been enough for him.

But along with Reagan's campaign staff, one other person was extremely concerned that Ford would jump in — Nancy Reagan.

I was in Florida with the Reagan campaign in early March, the day of the South Carolina primary. Mrs. Reagan's aide, Carol McCain, asked me to drive Mrs. Reagan to visit a friend in Miami that Saturday afternoon.

I hadn't spent a lot of one-on-one time

with Mrs. Reagan, and I was nervous — particularly since I didn't know Miami very well. Very quickly, I managed to get lost. But Mrs. Reagan seemed preoccupied. As we drove, she suddenly spoke up.

"Jim, what are we going to do?" she asked me.

I thought she was worried about my driving, and I tried to reassure her.

"We're going to get there, Mrs. Reagan. It's not that far. We'll be there soon."

Mrs. Reagan spoke again: "No, Jim. What are we going to do?"

I thought, Oh, God, she's talking about something big here. Think, Jim, think. What's she talking about? Don't be stupid. Then it hit me. She's talking about Ford.

I said, "Mrs. Reagan, he's not going to do it."

"What do you mean, he's not going to do it?" she asked me. Neither of us needed to mention Ford's name.

"He's not going to run for president," I assured her.

She wasn't convinced. "Jim, haven't you seen the news? It's all over the place."

"I know," I said. "His people want him to do it. The media wants him to do it because it would add drama to the campaign for them. But I just cannot comprehend

Gerald Ford making the decision to go back in. Mrs. Reagan, it's not going to happen."

I made the why-Gerald-Ford-won't-run-for-president argument. "He never had the desire to run for statewide office in Michigan. He never had any intention of running for president and was thrust into it. He doesn't have it in his heart to run again. He'll make the decision not to go."

I didn't convince Mrs. Reagan.

"Jim," she insisted, "it's going to happen."

I was equally as adamant. "I just don't believe so."

I was confident that the days of Ronald Reagan versus Gerald Ford were over. Ford hadn't really wanted to be president in the first place, and he would not come back after losing the way he did to Carter.

Fortunately, I was proven correct later when we were in Chicago during a campaign blitz through Illinois. On the Saturday before the Illinois primary, Ford held a press conference outside his home in Rancho Mirage, California, and announced that he would not run for president again.

"I have determined that I can best help the cause by not being a candidate for president, which might further divide the party," he said in reading his statement. "I am not a candidate. I will not become a candidate. I will support the nominee of my party with all the energy I have."

But that wasn't the last we heard from Gerald Ford.

Even before Ford's announcement, the momentum was building for Reagan. The crowds were getting larger and even more enthusiastic. I remember the especially rapturous welcome we got in Miami before the Florida primary. Reagan visited Little Havana, where many Cuban immigrants live. Many had lost their businesses, their homes and their possessions when Fidel Castro took over the island and they were forced to flee. Because of Reagan's emphatic anti-Communist stance, they loved him.

On that steamy day, Reagan plunged into the huge crowd in Little Havana at a Cuban street festival. People crowded around him, shouting and calling to him: "Governor Reagan!" "Mr. Reagan!" They wanted to touch him, to talk to him. The pocket of his shirt was torn away in the melee. But Reagan was in his element.

Texas was the next big primary, and I surveyed the entire state for a Reagan campaign onslaught. I took charge of a big rally in Amarillo. We called it the Texas Panhandle rally and set it up at a big hangar at the local airport. Ronald Reagan was also very popular in Texas, where he had taken 100 delegates in the state's winner-take-all primary in 1976 against Ford, and it had helped him immensely at the '76 convention.

We had a huge, enthusiastic crowd that day. The hangar was long and narrow, so I had positioned the stage for Reagan along one long side so the crowd could be close to him. But as Reagan left the hangar, an immense number of people lined up along the rope line to greet him and shake his hand. Reagan was supposed to take only two or three minutes along the rope line before getting in the motorcade to return to the campaign charter to fly to our next stop in Nebraska. But I should have remembered that Reagan could not walk by anyone without shaking hands and spending time with them, and the rope line was so long that it took Reagan 45 minutes to get out of that hangar because so many people wanted to meet him. Reagan could have just grabbed a few hands and raced out the exit but instead he shook hands all along the rope line — a real handshake for each person — signed autographs and talked to people.

Dave Fischer, his personal assistant at the time, didn't even try to hurry him along. Fischer knew that once Reagan was planted like that, he was going to greet everyone, even if it put him way behind schedule. Later in Reagan's presidency, at a hotel ballroom in Miami, I made the mistake of trying to coax Reagan away from a long rope line in order to keep us on schedule. But Reagan would have no part of my urgings. Soon after we left the ballroom, he came down on me. "You can't pull me away like that," he said. "It's rude and it's wrong. I will never turn my back on people like that. Please don't do it again." I got the message.

In the '80 campaign, I knew I was in trouble for putting Reagan so far behind with such a long rope line in Amarillo. In a tightly scheduled presidential campaign, every minute is crucial and 45 minutes is an eternity, so when we finally got on the plane and headed for Grand Island, Nebraska, I felt better. However, shortly after we arrived at the hotel there, I got a call from campaign headquarters. Chuck Tyson, who was running scheduling and advance for the campaign at that point, ripped into me.

"You had a great event," he said. "But you had a *two-hundred-foot rope line*. You can't put Reagan in a situation like that. If he's going to work a rope line, make sure it's only fifteen or twenty feet. He'll take all day with those people. He just can't walk away from them. You really wrecked our day. You cost us forty-five minutes."

After winning the Texas primary, we had lost all our other rivals except Bush. John Connally had dropped out after losing big in South Carolina while spending $12 million to win exactly one delegate — forever known as the $12 million delegate. In late May, Bush quit the race, too.

After Texas, I had a few days off, and I went back to my small Canton house after 63 straight days on the road. I scraped the dust off my furniture, collected my mail and then headed back out again. But after the excitement of the campaign trail Canton didn't seem like home anymore.

After Bush quit, the road to the 1980 Republican National Convention was suddenly clear. The only question — and it was a big one — was who Reagan would pick as a running mate.

Suddenly, we started hearing about Gerald Ford again.

To get ready for the convention, we arrived in Detroit about two weeks early. We were headquartered at the Renaissance Hotel on the riverfront in downtown Detroit — three glass-sheathed towers connected at the base by a massive rotunda. It had the most confusing layout I have ever seen, and many Republican delegates probably spent most of their time riding up and down the wrong elevators and getting lost in the warren of lobbies. But it was only a few blocks from Joe Louis Arena, the convention site.

Even before the Reagan entourage got to Detroit, there was talk of bringing Ford on as Reagan's vice president — a sort of "dream ticket." Some in the Reagan camp talked to Ford and his people about the idea. But most of us thought that bringing Ford on as Reagan's running mate was a terrible idea. There was a great deal of mistrust between the two men and their staffs because of the contentious '76 race, and each camp would have continually tried to undermine the other. It would have been an unwise, unproductive and dangerous way to run the country.

Nevertheless, by the time the convention got under way in mid-July, everyone was buzzing about the prospect. Other names were being tossed around, too — George

Bush, former Senator Paul Laxalt, Congressman Jack Kemp of New York, former Defense Secretary Donald Rumsfeld and former Treasury Secretary William Simon. Supporters lobbied for their candidates vigorously. Kemp's supporters even distributed hats advertising a Reagan-Kemp ticket.

Chuck Tyson saddled me with one of the worst jobs of a political convention: I was placed in charge of all Reagan campaign motorcade movements. That meant managing a fleet of about 30 cars, several buses and dozens of volunteer drivers to transport Reagan, his family, his staff, his vice-presidential choice (whoever that would be) and entourages to and from the Joe Louis Arena and wherever else in the Detroit area they needed to go. It also required much complicated coordination with the Secret Service.

It was, to put it bluntly, an awful assignment. In the days leading up to the convention, I had to beg, borrow, rent and lease a massive motor pool from as far as 100 miles away and then line up the volunteers to drive all those vehicles over the four-day convention. As a result, I spent a lot of the convention in the basement parking garage of the Renaissance Hotel.

On the first night of the convention, however, I did escape the garage to accompany Mrs. Reagan and all four of the Reagan children — Michael, Maureen, Patti and Ron — to the arena, where they watched the proceedings. As is customary, the presidential nominee — Reagan — does not go over to the arena until after he is officially nominated.

Instead of the usual box for the nominee's family, we had reserved a special section of Joe Louis Arena for the Reagan family. I remember the Reagan family was announced in through a special door and, as they entered, Patti froze. It seemed to suddenly occur to Patti that she didn't want to be there. I finally had to give her a shove to get her through the door. And when Mrs. Reagan walked through the surrounding seats to get to their assigned seats, she tripped and fell, disappearing completely in that section of Joe Louis Arena. Everyone in the arena gasped, but she popped right back up, fortunately, and everyone applauded.

It's no secret that the Reagans weren't a close family, and I don't recall seeing Patti at the White House during Reagan's second term, although Ron — a ballet dancer at the time — visited every now and then. Later, TV correspondent Sam Donaldson took Ron under his wing when Ron expressed an interest in television journalism. I saw Ron in Geneva in '85 when he covered the president's meetings with Soviet leader Mikhail Gorbachev as a correspondent for *Playboy*.

However, Maureen and Michael — Ronald Reagan's oldest offspring by his first wife, actress Jane Wyman — worked diligently for months to get their dad elected. Sometimes they filled in for Reagan at various campaign stops, and Maureen, in particular, was a very effective campaigner — she knew the issues, she connected well with voters and she was so positive. She was a smart, very determined woman, although if she was in a bad mood, she could take your neck off!

Early in the primary campaign, she traveled to Iowa to fill in for her dad on a stop I had been assigned to. I remember Nick Ruwe telling me, "She's a workhorse. She's very good, but you're gonna have your hands full. Take care of her."

We also had Senator Orrin Hatch of Utah with us on that trip and campaigning together, Maureen and Senator Hatch were a powerful force for Ronald Reagan. They believed in the man and spoke so strongly on his behalf. Later, Maureen lived for a while at the White House and served with distinction as cochair of the Republican National Committee.

At the 1980 convention, the speculation on Reagan's running mate reached a fever pitch. The assumption was that Reagan would announce his choice on the last day of the convention — Thursday night — and that the two would then travel to Joe Louis Arena, where Reagan would present him to the convention delegates.

By late Wednesday, the public speculation had settled on Bush or Ford. Ford conducted a not-so-subtle campaign for the job, making it clear that if he got the vice-presidential slot, he wouldn't settle for being a mere number two. He told CBS anchor Walter Cronkite that if he were Reagan's vice-presidential choice, he wanted a "meaningful role across the board in the basic, crucial and important decisions that have to be made in a four-year period."

Cronkite said that sounded like a "copresidency," and Ford agreed. "That's something that Governor Reagan really ought to consider," he told Cronkite.

Earlier Wednesday night, I had let go of the rented buses, which were being used to transport the media. It didn't look like we would need them since the Reagan entourage wasn't traveling to the arena that night.

Shortly thereafter, Steve Studdert — a political wild man who was senior advance man with press responsibilities at the convention — radioed me and told me to get the motorcade ready. Reagan had suddenly made his vice-presidential choice and would shortly go to Joe Louis Arena with him.

I felt a blast of ice shoot down my spine. "I let the buses go," I radioed back.

Studdert's voice squawked back immediately. "Well, you better get them back."

I called the bus companies, but the drivers were long gone. Without buses, the press might have to walk to Joe Louis Arena. The arena was only a few blocks away, but Studdert was adamant.

"I want buses," he shouted at me over the radio.

"There *are* no buses," I shouted back.

Studdert told me to worry about the rest of the motorcade, and he would find buses. A short time later, he triumphantly rode over to the motorcade staging area with Detroit city buses. He had run out into the streets of downtown Detroit and somehow stopped city buses in their routes and commandeered them for use by the Reagan campaign entourage. I could only imagine what he'd told the passengers as he ousted them from the buses and talked the drivers into bringing their buses to the Renaissance Hotel for a Reagan motorcade!

But that was Steve Studdert. He would do whatever it took in a campaign. I was awe-struck. The man was a genius at political advance work and deserved his legendary status.

With the motorcade ready, we waited for Reagan and his mystery choice to descend from Reagan's suite. A dozen of us waited in the garage and watched a small television. Chris Wallace, then with NBC, reported from the floor of the convention that Reagan had chosen Ford as his running mate. I wanted to shout "You guys are wrong!" at the TV set. Reagan wouldn't have asked Ford to do it because it wouldn't have worked.

Then the Secret Service detail waiting with us got word that someone was coming down in the elevator from the Reagans' sixty-ninth-floor suite to the garage. It wasn't Ronald Reagan, they were told.

Then something occurred to me. If Reagan was on the elevator, he would come down to the garage in the same elevator as his running mate.

"So whoever is coming down on that elevator is clearly *not* his running mate," I announced to the folks around me.

We waited for the arrival of the elevator. The tension built. Everyone was wondering, if Kuhn is right, then who is on the elevator? Bush or Ford?

Finally, we heard the elevator's whine and click as it landed on our floor. The doors opened.

Out walked former President Gerald Ford. Quietly, he got into his small motorcade and pulled out.

The elevator went back up. And we knew who Ronald Reagan had chosen — George Bush.

As it turned out, Reagan never asked Ford to be his vice president. But Ford had gone to him and withdrawn from consideration.

A short time later, Ronald Reagan and a jubilant George Herbert Walker Bush came down to the garage and climbed into their motorcade. The press loaded into the buses that Studdert had commandeered, and we left for Joe Louis Arena.

Gerald Ford's days in national office were over. Now it was Reagan's turn.

"More than anything else, I want my candidacy to unify our country, to renew the American spirit and sense of purpose," Reagan told delegates in his acceptance speech. "I want to carry our message to every American, regardless of party affiliation, who is a member of this community of shared values."

After Reagan's acceptance speech, the entire Reagan family came onstage to acknowledge the cheering delegates. Then the Bush family joined the Reagan family onstage.

The general election campaign against President Carter had just begun.

6

VICTORY

For Ronald Reagan, the 1980 campaign was more than a contest for the U.S. presidency. It was a spiritual and moral crusade to revive the heart of America. Decades of growth in government regulations, heavy tax burdens and repeated humiliations around the world, he believed, had crushed the American spirit. In that summer and fall of 1980, as he continued his 12-year-old quest for the presidency, Ronald Reagan vowed to revive it.

Four years of Jimmy Carter had done nothing but continue that destruction of the American spirit, he charged. Carter had embraced the Soviets too closely, weakened America's military might, deepened America's energy crisis and ruined the economy.

"When the American people cried out for economic help," Reagan said in an oft-repeated refrain that always elicited roars from his crowds, "Jimmy Carter took refuge behind a dictionary. Well, if it's a definition he wants, I'll give him one. A recession is when your neighbor loses his job. A depression is when you lose yours. Recovery is when Jimmy Carter loses his."

But to get to the White House, Ronald Reagan needed more than a vision for America. He had to hang on to his solid support west of the Mississippi River, cut into Carter's Southern base and defeat him in key northern industrial states. That meant attracting swing Democratic voters: some union members, Southerners, and urban and ethnic voters.

As for me, I was glad to get out of Detroit and onto the campaign trail again. My feet were killing me beyond belief after all those days of standing on the concrete floor of the Renaissance Hotel parking garage. For the general campaign, we picked up some outstanding staffers from various other presidential campaigns and previous Republican administrations. The Reagans were never ones to hold grudges, and they welcomed these experts with open arms. Jim Baker, who ran Bush's campaign, joined us. Joe Canzeri, a close aide to Nelson Rockefeller, came on board. We also picked up Ron Walker, a former Nixon campaign staffer, who now oversaw scheduling and advance from Washington and, from Connally's press staff, Jim Brady, Mark Weinberg and Hugh O'Neill — three of the best in the country.

Brady was certainly known for his lively personality. But on his first flight with us, he sat next to me and was pretty reserved. He livened up as the campaign went on, although sometimes too much. At one point, Lyn Nofziger kicked him off the plane temporarily for a joke. On one final approach on the campaign plane, the aircraft flew over a heavily wooded area, and Brady commented about all the "killer trees" — a reference to a Reagan comment that trees caused pollution. That didn't sit too well with Nofziger.

As for the Reagans, they decided to base themselves near Washington for the campaign, and moved into a Middleburg, Virginia, farm called the Wexford House, once owned by the Kennedy family but then owned by Texas Governor Bill Clements, who lent it to the Reagans for the campaign. It gave them a place to rest between campaign swings, and Reagan could squeeze in some horseback riding.

Reagan got a postconvention bump in the polls but by late August, President Carter and Reagan were in a dead heat. It was clear that Bill Casey, who had done such yeoman's work to pull us through the primaries, would not be the man in the general election. So Stu Spencer, who had done such an able job of running Ford's presidential campaign in '76, was brought in.

As chief strategist, Spencer helped turn the ship around so that Reagan could focus on his message and do what he did best — explain who he was, what he believed in and how he would implement those beliefs for the betterment of America. *LeaderShip '80*, as Reagan's campaign plane was known, began to right itself. As the campaign picked up its pace, we had to expand to two chartered planes to accommodate more staff and a bigger press corps.

But were our efforts enough to eat into Carter's Democratic base?

Carter pounded away on a now-familiar theme: that Reagan was a divisive, trigger-happy cowboy who would lead America into numerous, unnecessary armed conflicts. The election, Carter claimed, was about whether the country would be at peace or at war. If Reagan was elected president, Carter charged in a speech in Chicago, "Americans will be separated, black from white, Jew from Christian, North from South, rural from urban."

To win, most strategists agreed, Reagan had to win back four states that Carter had carried in 1976 — Ohio, Pennsylvania,

Texas and Florida. Again, Ohio was critical. No Republican had ever ascended to the White House without winning that major state.

Another big battleground state for Carter and Reagan was Illinois, and I realized how powerful Democratic big-city politics were when we reached Chicago in October.

We planned a walking tour of a Lithuanian neighborhood called Marquette Park. It was the perfect setting for Reagan to stroll along a large, busy block on a closed street in the community and work a big crowd. Along that stretch of the street were family shops — hardware stores, butchers, clothing stores — and we determined that a store in the middle of the block would work well as a backdrop from which Reagan could address the crowd. He would also visit some stores.

But as the date for Reagan's stop came closer, some shop owners became uneasy. The owner of the shop where we had planned to set up the podium suggested that maybe Reagan shouldn't speak in front of his shop.

We were puzzled. Clearly, there was a significant problem here. In dire straits, we finally figured out what was going on.

Democratic ward bosses, we confirmed, had heard about Reagan's visit, and they weren't happy about having a Republican candidate on their turf. We were working to pick up swing voters, and they knew it. So the legendary Chicago Democratic machine had cranked up to full steam. Ward bosses warned store owners that if they were helpful to Reagan or seemed too friendly toward him, there would be "problems." They targeted the shop owner who had agreed to let Reagan speak in front of his store. We heard that he was warned that the next time it snowed, he would find even more snow in front of his business instead of seeing existing snow removed. Trash removal could also be a problem, he was told. It was getting serious, and we worried that the situation could get worse.

The night before the event, I called Mike Deaver and explained the situation. He agreed that we didn't want to make life difficult for these small-business owners, and we canceled Reagan's speech, though not his appearance. In the end, Reagan strolled down the street with Governor James R. Thompson. We had a huge crowd, and Reagan received a rapturous reception from people on the street and got a chance to talk to many Chicagoans — despite the efforts of the Democratic machine.

Reagan's warmth and genuineness were making their marks on the electorate. Earlier in September, I had gotten a chance to see how his authentic personality differed dramatically from some other politicians.

We were at the East Texas State Fair in Tyler, Texas — a critical battleground state for Reagan. Governor John Connally, who had recovered from his disastrous presidential primary run and now supported Reagan, accompanied us. I looked forward to meeting Connally — in fact, I was kind of in awe of him. Like millions of Americans, I'd seen him many times in the historic footage from that terrible day in Dallas in 1963 when he was shot along with President Kennedy. To encounter him close up was almost akin to my first encounter with Ronald Reagan.

After participating in a cattle-judging contest at the state fair in Tyler, the Reagans and Governor and Mrs. Connally walked to an exhibit hall for a rally, greeting and talking to fairgoers along the midway. It was a very hot day and a relatively long walk in that steamy heat but, in true Texas style, people surrounded the couples, embracing them, shaking their hands. The Reagans enjoyed it every step of the way.

But along the way, I noticed that Connally wasn't doing as well. He was getting hot and sweaty. And not just a little sweaty. Quite sweaty. Dark stains were spreading, and he soaked right through his medium blue suit. His face was wet with sweat, his hair saturated. He was a mess. Reagan, in contrast, looked cool and collected. Reagan virtually never sweat.

Finally, we reached the air-conditioned hall where the rally was going to take place and piled gratefully in. While we waited for the press to get into position, we went into a holding area, where the Reagans and Mrs. Connally headed for the restrooms.

When we were alone, Connally turned on me. He was furious.

"Goddamn, you [expletive], [expletive]," he roared at me. He gestured at his drenched suit. "Look what you did to me. You almost killed me. I'm a mess. What the hell were you trying to do?"

His tirade continued. "You don't know what the hell you're doing!"

I had no choice but to take it and apologize. But inside I was thinking that I couldn't imagine Ronald Reagan treating someone like that.

I'm glad we buried you in South Carolina, I told Connally in my mind. You never deserved to be president.

We mopped Connally up so he looked respectable when he went on stage at the rally to introduce the Reagans, and nothing more was said about the incident.

Reagan's speech that day focused on the Carter administration's failed energy and economic policies.

"I know the Carter inflation has hit Tyler, and the families of Tyler know what that means," he told them. "You see it every day in the prices you pay, in the dreams you have had to give up, in the future that looks less and less secure because inflation is eating away at income and savings."

I lost a lot of respect for Connally that day, although I had to remind myself that his support was critical for Reagan in Texas.

In early October, we returned to my home state of Ohio, another key state for Reagan. Reagan had already made inroads in that state in a speech before the Ohio conference of Teamsters in late August when he had accused Carter of plunging the nation's economy into a "severe depression" that had taken out hundreds of thousands of jobs.

"As a result, workers and their families today are suffering more than at any time since the Great Depression of the thirties," he told delegates.

That economic depression was certainly evident in our October visit to Youngstown. The steel industry had declined precipitously during my days of working for Peter Voss in the mid- to late '70s. In Youngstown, we drove past acres of mostly abandoned mills and buildings at the Jones & Laughlin Steel Corp. It made a deep impression on Reagan. He said later it reminded him of a ghost town. At one point, we stopped the motorcade and looked around and then went into one of the rusting factories to meet with a small group of workers who were still left. From the thousands who had worked there at one time, it was now down to a few hundred. It was quite sad. I remember that some workers had posted a sign saying CARTER STEEL WORKS.

Reagan talked to the steelworkers for a while. He listened carefully to what they had to say. I remember one steelworker asking him if he could restore the lost jobs.

"You bet," Reagan said.

"I think we've got a policy in our government for the last few years that is hostile," Reagan told him. "It considers business — instead of part of the community — as an adversary. It's time we got government off the back of industry."

It was a grim time for the country. Carter had used the "misery" index — the combined total of the inflation and unemployment rates — to help him unseat Ford in 1976, but wasn't talking much about it now, probably because it had risen from 15 under Ford to about 19 during the Carter administration.

In all, as we came down the home stretch of the campaign in late October, Reagan gained momentum with voters with his message of getting the economy back on track, cutting taxes, eliminating unnecessary government regulations and standing up to the Soviet Union. But some of Carter's punches were landing — some still thought of Ronald Reagan as an old broken-down actor who parroted what his conservative backers wanted him to say and would declare war on the world if elected president. And there was always concern about an "October surprise," where Carter would announce a major breakthrough in the months-long hostage crisis in Iran. While Americans had rallied around Carter when the hostages were first captured, his failure to get them returned had soured them on him, and some sort of resolution would have boosted his reelection prospects immensely.

Carter reluctantly agreed to just one debate with Reagan, and the October 28 debate in Cleveland was Reagan's best shot at convincing the American people that he could lead the United States into prosperity and, yes, peace.

In the debate, Carter looked tense and tired. Reagan looked relaxed and at ease and Reagan used his age to his advantage.

"I have seen four wars in my lifetime," he said. "I'm a father of sons; I have a grandson. I don't ever want to see another generation of young Americans bleed their lives into sandy beachheads in the Pacific, or rice paddies and jungles in Asia, or the muddy, bloody battlefields of Europe."

But probably the best — and most memorable — moment in the debate came when Carter accused Reagan of trying to decimate Medicaid. Reagan smiled and shook his head. "There you go again."

Carter wasn't nearly as articulate. He clumsily tried to bring his family into the debate in answering a question about arms control.

"I had a discussion with my daughter, Amy [then 12], the other day before I came here to ask her what the most important issue was. She said she thought nuclear weaponry and the control of nuclear arms." Some in the audience at the event groaned.

Reagan wrapped up the debate with compelling questions to Americans. He urged voters to ask themselves, "Are you better off than you were four years ago? Is it easier for you to go and buy things in the stores than it was four years ago? Is America as respected throughout the world as it was? Do you feel that our security is as safe, that we're as strong as we were four years ago?"

Polls taken after the debate found that viewers overwhelmingly thought Reagan had won. And, after that triumphant appearance, we went back on the campaign trail on a real high — Ronald Reagan had done it. He'd shown America what he was really like, instead of the caricature painted by the Carter administration. We felt a great surge in momentum.

★ ★ ★

At the first event after the Cleveland debate, in Texarkana, Texas, the next morning, we had such a large crowd at the hangar at the local airport that we had to open the big doors for the overflow crowd to accommodate everybody. Aside from having the luxury of building the campaign stop with help from both our Texas and our Arkansas Reagan organizations, Reagan's performance in Cleveland had taken him to the highest political echelon.

Deaver had ordered up signs that read AMY FOR SECRETARY OF STATE, which were dominant in the crowd. The sound system conked out but, fortunately, we were able to get Reagan a bullhorn, and he kept going. Carter's conduct, he told the crowd, "has become a tragic comedy of errors."

"He reminds me of someone who can name fifty parts of an automobile — he just can't drive it or fix it!" Reagan shouted.

The next morning, the newspapers carried a photo of a commanding Ronald Reagan, bullhorn to his mouth, roaring his message out to the cheering Texarkana crowd as he came down the homestretch of his campaign to bring hope to America.

* * *

On election night, it was an unbelievable feeling to be in Los Angeles at the Century Plaza Hotel as part of the Reagan campaign and monitor those election-night results. Not only was Reagan resoundingly elected the fortieth president of the United States; he also annihilated Carter and the Democrats. He won 489 electoral votes to Carter's 44. Republicans gained 12 seats in the Senate, taking control for the first time since 1952, and they took 33 seats in the House from the Democrats. In fact, Ronald Reagan was the last presidential candidate to have a real coattail effect on Senate and House races nationwide. Nobody has even come close since then.

It was a landslide in every sense of the word — a complete collapse of the traditional coalition that had elected Democratic presidents since the New Deal. Reagan held on to the West, destroyed Carter's Southern base, including Texas, Florida, Mississippi and North Carolina. He seized the Democratic bastions of New York and Pennsylvania. He took Illinois, Michigan and my home state of Ohio in the Midwest.

Reagan had penetrated the traditional Democratic base — unions, blue-collar voters, ethnics and Catholics, just as he had planned.

Carter managed to win only six states, including his home state of Georgia.

Exit polls of voters indicated that Reagan's message had hit home. His question on debate night, "Are you better off than you were four years ago?," got a resounding no from voters. Thirty-five percent of voters interviewed in a *New York Times*/CBS News poll said their financial situation was worse than a year ago. The biggest issue on their minds was the economy — interest rates, inflation and unemployment.

What's more: At the age of 69, Reagan was the oldest person ever elected to the White House.

Carter conceded earlier than expected, and Reagan ended up accepting his congratulations wrapped in a towel after stepping from the shower in his Pacific Palisades home. He and Mrs. Reagan then dined with friends at the home of Earle and Marion Jorgensen. (The Reagans were to repeat the same routine — dinner at the Jorgensens' with the same dinner guests, same menu and then a victory celebration at the Century Plaza Hotel — on election night of 1984. Superstitious, they figured if that routine had worked in 1980, why change it?)

Carter's early concession created a great deal of controversy because the polls hadn't closed in California. The effect on the final results was probably less than believed but, since then, presidents have been careful not to concede like that until later in the evening after all the polls have closed.

As the Reagans proceeded from the Presidential Suite in the Century Plaza Hotel to their appearance in the ballroom, I couldn't help but recall the years of hard work that had led up to this triumphant night. I thought back to times in my life when I had wanted to win but hadn't. But that's life: Most of us win a few and lose a lot. I thought about how difficult it is to ascend to the highest office in the land — and the world. So few had succeeded or would ever succeed.

I recalled Ohio in 1976, when the Reagan campaign said they were coming, then they weren't, then they were, then the scramble to collect signatures to get petitions filed for all those congressional districts and the large slate of delegates. The days on the road, falling asleep at the wheel of my car at a high rate of speed. My bitter drive home after the Kansas City convention in 1976 when I was convinced I would never see Ronald Reagan elected president. All those hours I spent with him on the mashed potato circuit as he'd worked to keep his dream of the presidency alive. The rocky launch of the '80 campaign in New York City, the horrible defeat in snowy Iowa and seeing Reagan once again written off as politically dead. His comeback in New Hampshire, his rivals — Connally, Baker, Ford, Bush, Anderson, Dole, Crane — who had fallen by the wayside.

7

FROM CALIFORNIA TO THE WHITE HOUSE

"I don't want to go."

Ronald Reagan spoke quietly, but firmly, sitting at his desk in the corner of the bedroom of his Pacific Palisades home, staring out the window. It was December 1980, less than a month before his inauguration as the fortieth president of the United States.

It was hard to comprehend. We had gone to him at the request of Mrs. Reagan to ask about helping him pack what he wanted to take to Washington with him. Instead, we were confronted by a man who appeared to be disinclined to leave California. Maybe he didn't really want to be president. Maybe he just wanted to see if he could beat Carter! That was all we could think of at that moment.

After the election, I had opted to stay in California where the Reagans would remain until shortly before Reagan's inauguration on January 20, 1981. The morning after election night, at a 7:00 a.m. meeting, about 50 campaign advance staff met with Chuck Tyson, our boss during the primaries. He told us that we had done great work and were an integral part of the Reagan victory. A tremendous amount of work needed to be done through the transition and Inauguration Day, he told us, and we had jobs in the Reagan administration if we wanted them. However, he made it clear that we couldn't all work in the White House. At that point, the victory was so fresh that most of us couldn't even imagine working in a Reagan administration.

Tyson asked us to write down whether we wanted to go to Washington immediately to work on the transition or the inaugural. He also said that he needed two people to be with the Reagans for the next two and a half months in California. I decided it would be best to remain in L.A., as did Lanny Wiles, one of the '76 senior advance staffers hired by Nick Ruwe for the 1980 campaign. We were the only two to opt for the West Coast.

I figured there wasn't any rush to get to Washington. By staying with the Reagans, I felt that there would be an ongoing, high level of activity, and I would get the chance to work more closely with them than if I was back in Washington. Besides, it was a heck of a lot warmer in Los Angeles, and there would be plenty of time for Washington later.

In Los Angeles, Lanny and I worked out of a house across the street from the Reagans' home on San Onofre Street, a quiet neighborhood overlooking the Santa Monica Mountains and the Pacific coastline. I signed the lease, renting the house for three months at what seemed at the time to be an incredibly expensive $5,000 a month. The Secret Service and the White House Communications Agency (WHCA), both of which we would become intimately familiar with, rented the house next to the Reagans' and set up operations there.

The Reagans' home was a 5,000-square-foot contemporary-style home built for them in the 1950s, when Reagan worked for General Electric. GE had stocked it with its latest appliances and other products at the time, and the Reagans had appeared in GE commercials with their daughter Patti in the 1950s and early 1960s, showing off the various gadgets in the home. Set into a steep hill, it was reached via a narrow, winding driveway, and it had a sweeping view of the "queen's necklace" — Santa Monica Bay, Los Angeles International Airport and the glittering chain of lights — at night.

Lanny and I went back and forth across the street constantly, working with the small West Coast transition staff consisting of Elaine Crispen, Mrs. Reagan's executive assistant, as well as Joe Holmes and David Prosperi, who were press staff.

Among the three houses and the staff and the support personnel, it was a pre-White House compound. The Reagans made two brief trips to Washington, but mostly Washington came to them. Senior aides like Ed Meese, who was heading the transition, and Deaver, one of his deputy directors, flew in and out regularly from Washington to meet with Reagan. Jim Brady served as transition spokesman. Jim Baker, announced as Reagan's White House chief of staff in November, traveled to L.A., as did potential cabinet nominees who met with President-elect Reagan. Agents with the Presidential Protection Detail of the Secret Service came out, upgrading the Secret Service coverage Reagan had received during the campaign.

There were always members of the media — Sam Donaldson, Leslie Stahl, among others — staked out at the end of the Reagans' driveway. No matter where Reagan went, we put together a motorcade and the media went with us. I grew accustomed to this ritual — wherever the president went, the press corps expected to go, too — in the months and years ahead. But at the time, it seemed unusual to us that even if Reagan went to the barbershop, which he did religiously every two weeks, or met with his kitchen cabinet, the wealthy California businessmen who had helped launch his political career, the press went along for the stakeout.

One day, Reagan went to the dentist with an eight-car entourage — staff and press cars, Secret Service vehicles and police escort. The police didn't shut down the intersections for us, though. The Reagans didn't want that since it inconvenienced other drivers in traffic-clogged L.A. But keeping all the cars together was sometimes a challenge.

On this particular trip, coming back from the dentist, the lead car in the motorcade stopped abruptly at a yellow light. Reagan's limo had to stop fast as well. But the Secret Service vehicle behind the Reagans was caught off guard. I was riding in the staff car directly behind the Secret Service follow-up car, and I saw the driver of that car slam on his brakes so hard that smoke came from its rear tires.

The driver's reaction came too late, unfortunately, and the car slammed hard into the back of Reagan's limo, lifting up its rear with an awful crunch. Reagan turned around to look with alarm through the back window. He appeared fine, but the reporters got out of their cars and ran forward.

The Secret Service ordered everyone back into their vehicles and started again to the Reagans' home. We got through the intersection together this time, but the Secret Service car that had struck Reagan's limo was not in good shape. It was leaking fluid. Then pieces of the bumper fell off on San Vincenti Boulevard. Parts of the radiator were next, coming off with a horrible clanging sound.

The Secret Service stopped the motorcade. Since the Secret Service follow car was now completely incapacitated, I directed the agents in that car to ride in our vehicle, which was a large station wagon. We became the follow-up car behind the limo.

The driver of the Secret Service car remained with the vehicle, and I wondered if that was the end of the poor guy's career.

Rear-ending the president-elect's limousine was, most certainly, not a wise career move.

When we got back to the house, Reagan hopped out of the car and walked with a limp to the front door. Just before going inside, he stopped limping, turned and smiled broadly at the grim-looking Secret Service agents. He was fine. Everyone laughed, even the agents.

That was Reagan. He wanted to make the agents feel better. He knew how tightly wound people could get, and he liked to defuse tense situations with humor. I don't think a lot of other powerful people — let alone the president-elect — would have taken such an easygoing attitude toward a major lapse like that. But Reagan just forgot about it. It was a nonissue.

At Thanksgiving 1980, the Reagans went to Rancho del Cielo, which they did every year and continued to do while in the White House. Reagan had told me so much about the ranch during the trips I took with him in the 1970s that I looked forward to finally seeing it.

The 688-acre ranch was about 25 miles north of Santa Barbara, up in the Santa Ynez Mountains, overlooking the Pacific

Ocean on one side and the Santa Ynez Valley on the other. The Reagans had purchased it on November 13, 1974, at 3:33 p.m. to be precise, Reagan had told me. He liked to say that 33 was his lucky number: His number on the Eureka College football team was 33. He was elected the thirty-third governor of California and, when he signed the papers to buy the ranch, he glanced at his watch and it was at 3:33 in the afternoon. He and Mrs. Reagan were positively superstitious about things like that.

The first time we drove up to the ranch on that Thanksgiving weekend, I was scared to death. Lanny Wiles was a fast driver — and I mean *fast* — and he wasn't taking it easy on the narrowest, steepest road I had ever seen. There weren't any roads like that in Ohio! The narrow road up to the ranch was seven miles of twists and turns up a mountainside, complete with many hairpin turns. Two cars could pass each other, but just barely. It was paved but, again, just barely. On various trips over the years, an opaque fog rolled in, and it would be hard to see more than a few feet in front of you. After I drove the road a number of times, it became routine, and I no longer thought about the danger.

But it was hard those first few times.

Over the eight years of the Reagan presidency, thousands of people went up and down that road, and it's a miracle that no one was hurt or killed.

The first time there at the ranch, I was struck by the impact of the enormous blue bowl of a sky and the vast expanse of land that stretched out once you made your way up the mountain road. The Reagans' home was a small adobe ranch house, more than 100 years old, tucked in a small grove of trees. Reagan had laid the patio in the front of the house himself and, with Dennis LeBlanc and Barney Barnett, had reroofed the house with fiberglass Spanish tiles. With the help of a contractor, they tore off an old porch and built an addition around two sides of the place.

The stable contained Reagan's horses. He loved to ride at Rancho del Cielo, especially when he was president because he could get some real freedom out there in his special environment. He'd been riding since his days in Iowa, where he'd learned by joining the 14th Cavalry Regiment reserve unit in the 1930s.

I remembered the telephone-pole fences that Reagan had once told me about with so much pride on the airplane trip to

Youngstown, Ohio, during the mashed potato circuit years. There they were, surrounding the vast meadow and lining the gravel road leading to the ranch house.

Reagan gave a short tour of the ranch and took me to see the view. We were at the very top of a ridge, overlooking the ocean. It was an unbelievable sight.

"Which direction do you think you're looking?" Reagan asked me.

"Well, west," I said, perplexed by the question.

"I know you think that," he said, "but you're looking due south, straight at San Diego."

I was surprised. "How can that be?"

He explained that we weren't facing west, but stood on the south side of a portion of California that juts out into the Pacific.

Reagan liked to correct nonwesterners' misconceptions about western geography. Once when we were flying to Nevada on Air Force One, he asked: "Jim, have you ever been to Reno?" He pointed to a map on the wall. "Which city is farther west — Reno or Los Angeles?"

I thought I didn't even need to look. "Los Angeles, of course," I said.

"It's Reno," said Reagan. "Look at the map."

I glanced up at it. "Hey," I said, "you're right."

During the Reagan presidency, some famous guests visited the ranch, although for the most part the Reagans were very private about it. Only a few people — the president's doctor, a military aide who carried the "football" and a Secret Service detail — stayed on the mountaintop with them. We all stayed in Santa Barbara, about 45 miles south of the ranch, to let the Reagans have their privacy, and drove up only when we were needed.

He loved the physical work of the ranch. It was strenuous, but he was a big man — strong, in shape and very muscular — and it energized him to get out of the White House and do that heavy labor and to be in the fresh California air. It's impossible to count the number of hours he spent clearing brush, cutting down trees and in other work at the ranch. In fact, it exasperated the news-hungry White House press corps. After eight years of hearing from the White House press office that Reagan was spending another trip clearing brush and chopping wood, they began to ask just how many trees were actually *up* there.

But the press loved going to California when the president went to the ranch.

"This is a paradise," one told me during Reagan's first trip as president-elect. "We've been in Plains, Georgia, for the last four years with nothing but those awful mosquitoes."

As 1980 drew to a close and Reagan's first inaugural approached, he gradually inserted himself into national affairs. On Christmas Eve, he made a statement from his Pacific Palisades living room that caused quite an uproar. Standing next to the family Christmas tree, he extended his holiday wishes but also responded to a press question on recent negotiations between the United States and the Iranian extremists who held the 52 Americans hostage. He referred to their Iranian captors as barbarians.

The hostages, he said in a hard voice, are "still there in captivity, and I think all of us down deep inside have an anger also at the idea that their captors today are still making demands on us for their return, where their captors are nothing better than criminals and kidnappers who have long violated international law totally in taking these innocent people and holding them this long."

Some Reagan staffers winced at the bluntness of the message. The concern was that the statement made it sound like Reagan was living up to the Carter administration's campaign accusations that he was a warmonger. But it was actually a stern warning to those who held the hostages that Reagan wasn't going to adopt what he saw as Carter's more reticent attitude toward the outlaw regime of Iran.

Reagan's rhetoric didn't lighten up, either. As he came out of church a few days later, he was asked about a plan proposed by Iranian officials that required the United States to release billions of dollars in frozen Iranian assets as a "down payment" for the freeing of the hostages. Reagan sternly rejected it. "I don't think you pay ransom for people that have been kidnapped by barbarians."

The comments spurred a furious reaction from the Iranians. They called him a Hollywood cowboy. But I believe that Reagan's firm remarks also had a strong impact on them and helped lead to the hostages' release the following month. Iranian officials now knew they were dealing with someone quite different from Jimmy Carter.

Over the years, other nations — most notably the Soviet Union — would discover that as well.

As Inauguration Day approached, Joe Canzeri, Mike Deaver's top deputy, put in a strong word about Lanny and me with Studdert — whom Deaver hired to run the White House Advance Office. Studdert came out in December to tell us we would officially work in the White House advance operations. We started making plans to move to Washington.

Mrs. Reagan was also busy getting ready. She packed up some personal items she wanted to take and was choosing furniture that she wanted in the White House residence. We helped her by moving things around, putting boxes of belongings that she wanted to take in one area of the house.

She kept getting after the president-elect to do the same — figure out which books, records, furniture and so on he wanted to take with him. "Honey, you've got to start deciding what you want to pack," she'd say. But she just couldn't get him to do anything.

Finally, she asked Lanny and me for help.

"You've got to start working on Ronnie," she said. "He's not getting ready to go, and the moving truck's coming. He's got to decide what he wants to bring with him.

You've got to push him."

Finally, that afternoon in December, we approached him as he worked at his desk.

"Governor," Wiles said. We were still calling him governor then. "You know Mrs. Reagan has all these boxes and is getting everything ready for the move to Washington. You haven't even started, and we've got to get busy. What can we do? Let's start this afternoon."

That's when Reagan looked up and said he didn't want to go. Then he repeated it. "I don't want to go."

It was an amazing statement. At the same time, it was the epitome of Ronald Reagan. Any other newly elected president would have been ready to move into the White House the day after the election. But here was Reagan, reluctant to go. He had shown no outward signs of it until now. He had made key cabinet and staff appointments and was very involved in the other aspects of the transition. But even though he was doing the heavy-duty, substantive policy work, when it came to the actual physical part of putting things in boxes, he was having difficulty.

We asked him what he meant.

He said, "I don't want to leave California."

As much as he wanted to be president, he loved the state so much, it was hard for him to leave — he didn't want to leave behind the beloved state that had been his home for more than 40 years. He would be an entire continent away from his ranch. Many times, I heard him tell audiences, "California is not a place. It is a way of life."

He knew he was ready for the job he was about to take on but, I think, in some sense, he wondered why he had to leave California to do it. However, Reagan knew that he would travel west on Air Force One many times — at least for the next four years.

We decided to leave him alone at the time, rather than press the issue.

The next day, he started to pack.

As president, Reagan liked to say that if the settlers had come from the west — across the Pacific to America instead of across the Atlantic — the White House would have been on the West Coast, instead of in Washington. He would have loved that.

The day the Reagans left the Pacific Palisades house for the last time on January 14, their daughter Patti showed up to say good-bye. She was crying. For some reason, I felt good about Patti's farewell.

Despite their difficulties, there was plenty of love between Patti and her parents.

Tradition has it that the outgoing president sends out an air force plane to pick up the president-elect and the first lady-to-be before the inauguration. There were actually two 707s then that operated as Air Force One. The Carter White House dispatched the newer Air Force One — Tail No. 27000, built during the Nixon administration. Since Reagan technically wasn't president, this flight was referred to as Special Air Mission 27000.

A few days before the flight arrived, I got a call from the U.S. Army aide to President Carter, Jose Muratti, to make arrangements for the flight. He told me that the military would handle the president's, first lady's and traveling staff's luggage while on presidential travel in the United States and overseas. He asked if I wanted assistance on this inaugural flight.

"Of course," I said. I was used to rustling up volunteers during the campaign to take care of it. But I was to learn that these chores, and many more, would now be handled by the military. At first, I had a surprisingly mixed reaction to this. I still had some of that antimilitary prejudice that carried over from my Kent State days, and I found myself slightly suspicious about handing over some of my responsibilities to the military.

It didn't take long, however, once I got to the White House to do an attitudinal about-face. I saw the dedication of the military personnel who worked at the White House, and I started to grow up. Overall, the military support for the president of the United State is extensive, and these were great people, intensely devoted to their missions and doing very important jobs. It was a big wake-up call for me.

Special Air Mission 27000, with a planeload of Reagan's senior White House staff on board, came in from Washington to pick up the Reagans, landing at Los Angeles International Airport. Because the flight was full, Lanny and I had been issued tickets on a commercial flight to get to Washington. But the morning of the departure of Special Air Mission 27000, Joe Canzeri surprised us.

"Get your bags," he told us. "We've got two seats for you" on 27000. "You're flying back with us," he said.

He told us we had worked through the campaign and the transition. "This is your reward — traveling to Washington with the Reagans."

I remember walking onto the soon-to-be Air Force One for the first time and looking down at the impeccably clean blue-gray carpet. There was the smiling air force staff in crisp uniforms. After the crowded commercial flights I had grown accustomed to, this was another world. Telephones sat by the thick, upholstered, first-class-size seats, and there were notepads that said AIR FORCE ONE.

Lanny and I settled into our seats in the general staff area near the middle of the plane. As it accelerated down the runway at LAX, I could hardly believe my whereabouts.

And I had no idea how far that flight would take me.

8

"WE HAVE EVERY RIGHT TO DREAM HEROIC DREAMS"

The presidency didn't change Ronald Reagan. He didn't let the office intimidate him, nor did he permit it to affect his ego. He was totally unaffected by the power of the office.

I remember early in his first term, less than a month after his inauguration, there was a black-tie dinner at the Alfalfa Club. Aside from being a stag event, it was the ultimate in high-powered Washington events — diplomats, senior members of Congress and the rest of official Washington. I filled in for Dave Fischer, President Reagan's executive assistant in his first term. After briefing the president in the holding room, we proceeded to the off-stage announcement area. As we waited for the president to be announced into the ballroom, the U.S. Marine Corps band, as is customary, struck up "Hail to the Chief."

The president turned to me, a bemused expression on his face. "You know, I don't think I'm ever going to get used to the fact that they're playing that song for me," he said.

And over the next eight years, he never did.

Not once did I ever hear him refer to himself as the "president." In fact, he couldn't even bring himself to use the word "I" in referring to the office of the presidency. When it came to issues and policies, it was "we," "our," "we believe" or "we are working to" or "it is our sense."

Neither did he view the perks that came with the office as "mine." I remember when the president and Mrs. Reagan visited syndicated columnist Jack Kilpatrick's Virginia farm, White Walnut Hill outside Washington, for lunch in May 1981 with Jack's family and friends. During lunch, Kilpatrick mentioned that it was the birthday of his son, who was in the navy and stationed aboard a destroyer in the Indian Ocean. As Kilpatrick became familiar with the exceptional communication system that was within immediate reach of the president, he commented to President Reagan that it would be wonderful if they could call his son to wish him a happy birthday. The president quietly got up from the table and came to me in the room designated as the president's holding area. Wherever Reagan went, the WHCA went in advance and set up a White House switchboard, along with other sophisticated communication systems, so Reagan and White House staff always had access, including secure telephone lines, to the White House and beyond.

Reagan told me about Kilpatrick's son and his birthday.

"Do you think it would be all right if I used the phone in there — the phone they provide for me — to call his son and wish him a happy birthday?" Reagan asked me. "Do you think we could do that?"

He couldn't call it "my phone." He described it as "the phone they provide for me."

"Mr. President, I know it would be all right," I said. "You're the president and the commander in chief. You can call anyone you want."

I told him that WHCA would work to get in touch with the ship, and there was the question of how long it would take.

"Why don't you let us work on it?" I said.

I found President Reagan's military aide and the WHCA trip officer, who was in charge of communications for that trip to

Kilpatrick's farm, and told them about the president's request. It took about 45 minutes, but they located Kilpatrick's son. Reagan got on the telephone and wished him a happy birthday and then his dad took the phone and they spoke for a few minutes. Reagan stood by, smiling. It was a big deal for him.

Any other president might have come back and ordered me to get this kid on the phone, knowing full well it was his communication system. But Reagan just couldn't bring himself to view the trappings of the most powerful office in the world as "his." He couldn't do it at the beginning of his first term, and he still couldn't do it at the end of his second term.

Throughout his two terms, he remained as courteous as ever. For the first seven months of his presidency, for example, Reagan could not put his knees under his desk in the Oval Office because the barrel chair that he had brought from California was too high for the desk. Dave Fischer finally asked the president why he sat slightly sideways at the desk, and Reagan confessed that the desk was too low and he couldn't fit his knees under it. But he didn't want to say anything. During Reagan's August vacation, the White House raised the desk two inches.

In his second term, I remember when French Prime Minister Jacques Chirac visited the Oval Office and proceeded to light up a cigarette. No one had ever fired up a cigarette in the Oval Office during Reagan's presidency, and we didn't keep an ashtray around. But Reagan could not have cared less about smoking in the Oval Office and immediately began looking around for something we could use as an ashtray. I finally found a small china dish that served as a temporary ashtray.

When it came to the treatment of women, Reagan was a true gentleman. I remember when we got our first woman to go on the road with the White House advance operation — CeCe Kremer — during Reagan's first term, and she was the site advance person for a fund-raiser in Minneapolis in 1983. When Marine One landed in the back parking lot of the hotel where the president was to speak, Kremer — who was on the ground — was hit with a wind blast by the helicopter's rotors. The president emerged from Marine One and strode over to her immediately, placing both hands on her shoulders. "CeCe, don't ever do that again. Don't ever come out in front of the helicopter like that. You could get hurt!"

As longtime advance men for Ronald Reagan, we were jealous of all the attention that CeCe was getting on her first presidential advance trip!

Once after a meeting, we were walking back from the Old Executive Office Building, next to the White House, accompanied by White House senior staffer Mauri Masseng. The short trip involved going through a few sets of doors. At each one, the president stopped to let Masseng go first. Well, Masseng didn't want to precede the president of the United States through the door, so she also stopped and gestured the president to go first. We ended up with a standoff each time as the president was a gentleman and believed that ladies always went first. Finally, I said to Masseng at the last set of doors, "We'll be standing here all day unless you go first." So Masseng gave in and preceded the president. He beamed.

Reagan rarely asked for a personal favor from anyone, despite his position as president. There was one exception, but the request wasn't for himself. It was for his daughter Maureen. Maureen and Reagan's older son, Michael, had worked hard to get him elected. They were on the campaign trail for weeks, speaking at various rallies and dinners for their father.

During Reagan's first term, he wanted new Republican National Committee Chairman Frank Fahrenkopf Jr. to name Maureen cochair of the RNC. But Fahrenkopf was prepared to resist. Reagan asked Fahrenkopf into the Oval Office and told him that there were a lot of things he couldn't do and couldn't ask for as president. But, he said, this was one request that he knew he could make. Fahrenkopf graciously accepted his new colleague.

Along with remaining the same warm-hearted, down-to-earth man he always was, Reagan never strayed from his core beliefs. His policies as president were, in many ways, extensions of the ideas that he had presented in his famous 1964 Goldwater speech. Reagan's speeches emphasized his policies while rallying support from the American people.

"You have to keep pounding away with your message, year after year, because that's the only way it will sink into the collective consciousness," he said in his book *Speaking My Mind*, a collection of his most famous speeches, published shortly after his presidency. "Because if you have something you believe in deeply, it's worth repeating time and time again until you achieve it."

His inaugural address on January 20, 1981 was a reflection of this philosophy — and also a shimmering statement of his faith in the American people and his boundless optimism for the future. It was a marked contrast to the message Americans had been hearing for the previous four years. Democrats, Reagan believed, had lost faith in the American people, telling them there was a "malaise" in the United States, that America had to resign itself to a slow, relentless decline in its power, its wealth, its prestige. It was up to him to convince them of their greatness again.

"It is time for us to realize that we're too great a nation to limit ourselves to small dreams" was one of his most famous lines from his inaugural address.

"We have every right to dream heroic dreams," he told Americans that day. "Those who say that we're in a time when there are no heroes, they just don't know where to look."

Highlighting American heroism became a favorite theme of Reagan's in his State of the Union speeches as well. In his first such address in 1982, he hailed the heroic spirit of Lenny Skutnik, who had dived into the frigid Potomac River in Washington just a few days previously to rescue victims of an airplane crash. Skutnik sat with Mrs. Reagan during the address and was the first of many American heroes invited to sit with the first lady to be introduced by Reagan in his State of the Union addresses.

At Reagan's 1981 inaugural, he announced the fulfillment of one dream that he and all Americans had nurtured for the previous 444 days. He told Americans at the traditional luncheon in Statuary Hall in the Capitol after the inaugural ceremony that the Americans who had been held hostage in Iran were on their way home.

"Some thirty minutes ago," he told members of Congress and special guests, "the planes bearing our prisoners left Iranian airspace and are now free of Iran." Ringing applause greeted his remarks.

I remember standing in Statuary Hall hearing the announcement and thinking about the significant impact he had on their release with his statements while president-elect letting the Iranians know that they certainly weren't going to get any better deals from Ronald Reagan than from the Carter administration.

After the lunch in Statuary Hall, it was time for the inaugural parade down Constitution and Pennsylvania avenues to the White House. Steve Studdert and I watched as the Reagans got into the limo on the east side of the Capitol, and the motorcade pulled out. Then we realized *we* had no way of getting to the White House. As the motorcade slowly departed, the quick-thinking Studdert spied an empty sedan in the procession. Signs on the exterior of the car said it was for House Majority Leader Howard Baker, but Baker was not in sight.

"Get in the car," Studdert ordered.

I was horrified. "We can't do that," I said. "It's Baker's car!"

"Yes, we can," Studdert said. "Baker's not coming." Baker was skipping the parade to convene the Senate to confirm Alexander Haig as secretary of state and Caspar Weinberger as secretary of defense.

We climbed into the car, and the motorcade headed down the hill from the Senate side — both sides of Constitution Avenue jammed with cheering spectators — with us labeled as Senate Majority Leader Howard Baker. Steve, ever the showman, hot-dogged it a bit at first, leaning out the open window and waving to the crowd. I just sat hunched down and tried to be inconspicuous. When I heard someone in the crowd shout my name, I told Steve that was enough, and we both reached out our respective windows to remove the Baker signs from the car.

Political consultant Ed Rollins once told presidential candidate and millionaire businessman Ross Perot that the only days on which a president has "fun" are his Inauguration Day and the day he dedicates his presidential library. Well, Reagan wore the mantle of power more easily. I can't say that a lot of days were fun for him, but he didn't let the routine burden him unduly.

He was firmly a conservative — and had been for 40 years — but he was pragmatic. He had no hesitation in hiring former adversaries or going against his most passionate supporters if he could achieve his ultimate goals and fulfill the promises he had made to the American people. For his staff and cabinet choices, he chose the best people for the job, even though some of those choices didn't win kudos from his most committed supporters. His choice of James Baker as his chief of staff instead of longtime loyalist and conservative Ed Meese was controversial in some circles because Baker had worked against him in 1976 in Gerald Ford's campaign and again in the 1980 primaries, when he managed George Bush's campaign. But Reagan didn't bear grudges, and he believed that Baker was the best man for the job. And he was.

Jim Brady, who served as Reagan's White House spokesman until he was wounded tragically in the March 1981 assassination attempt on Reagan, had worked for Connally during the primaries.

But once he'd hired them, Reagan hated to fire people, and he displayed a loyalty to staff that, at times, caused problems, as we saw later in his presidency. Former NATO Commander Alexander Haig, Reagan's choice for secretary of state, for example, eventually found himself on the outs with Reagan, but Reagan gave him many opportunities to redeem himself before Haig was finally forced to resign in 1982. White House Chief of Staff Don Regan ended up in a similar position in Reagan's second term.

In my new job, I worked out of the Old Executive Office Building, an ornate but definitely dated, century-old structure located just to the west of the White House. It wasn't the most glamorous office, but it was part of the White House complex, known internally as the 18 Acres. In President Reagan's first term, I worked in the advance operation as I had during the campaign — working as the president's representative with host governments and domestic entities, everything from corporations, charities and other organizations to political groups — setting up events before the president's appearance to make sure that every detail was impeccable. It was infinitely more complicated, though certainly not less hectic, than on the campaign trail because we now had to manage the military, WHCA and the Presidential Protection Detail of the Secret Service.

One unique aspect of the presidential operations now was the constant presence of a military aide carrying the black attaché case called the football. The president carried the nuclear-launch command codes on a plastic card. On flights on Air Force One, he kept it in his briefcase, but he always retrieved it when we landed and slipped it into his pocket.

One of the most traumatic events in Reagan's two terms occurred in the eleventh week of his presidency when he was struck down and almost killed by an assassin's bullet. I was in Springfield, Illinois, at the time preparing for the first in a series of speeches he planned to make to state legislators to sell his economic recovery plan for the country. Reagan was scheduled to give a public speech on the steps of the Illinois state capitol to about 10,000 people, address a joint session of the state legislature and conclude with a reception.

On March 30, 1981, Reagan was at the Washington Hilton, a hulking building not far from the White House, giving a speech to 3,500 members of the AFL-CIO's Building Trades Association.

At midday on March 30, I was in the Illinois state capitol meeting alone with Governor Jim Thompson. While I talked to Thompson, his press secretary burst into the room and said there had been a shooting at the Washington Hilton. Three people had been shot, he said. The president was not hit, and he was fine, he told us.

"Who was shot?" I asked.

A Washington, D.C., police officer, a Secret Service agent and the president's press secretary, James Brady, was the answer.

"Oh, my God," I said. "Jim Brady."

Jim Brady was from Centralia, Illinois, and a friend of Governor Thompson's, so Thompson was deeply concerned. Thompson and I tried to resume our meeting while waiting for further word on the shootings when his chief of staff came in less than 10 minutes later.

"The president was hit," he told Thompson. We immediately turned on Thompson's television. We saw chaos. The president was at George Washington Hospital, television reporters were saying. There was no report on his condition.

I tried to call the White House to find out more. WHCA had already established a switchboard in Springfield in preparation for the president's arrival the next day, but even that Springfield switchboard couldn't reach the White House. All the circuits were jammed. Governor Thompson and I then headed to the governor's mansion to work the phones. Studdert reached me from an air force plane and directed me to the home of Brady's father. The governor secured two state planes — one to fly Brady's family to Washington and the other to fly me to Centralia to be with Brady's dad, who was not well enough to travel.

I found Mr. Brady's block surrounded by police, but I showed my White House commission book — our identification —

and went in to see him. Earlier that day, Dave Prosperi of the White House press office had gotten erroneous information that Jim Brady had died, but it was later corrected by Lyn Nofziger at the hospital.

Mr. Brady was watching the TV coverage with neighbors, family and friends.

"Please don't die, Jimmy," he quietly pleaded as we watched the replay of the shootings over and over again. "Don't die, Jimmy."

The camera swung back and forth as the gunman fired off six shots in two seconds. The president, wearing a new blue suit, waved and then suddenly hunched over, a look of surprise and pain spreading across his face. Secret Service agent Timothy McCarthy jumped in front of the president, taking a bullet and falling, wounded in the stomach. D.C. Police Officer Thomas Delahanty lay on the ground; a bullet had pierced his neck and shoulder. Jim Brady was on the pavement, bleeding from the head, grievously wounded. Secret Service Agent Jerry Parr grabbed the president by the shoulders and shoved him headfirst into the presidential limo. The gunman — later identified as John Hinckley, a blond-haired young man wearing a tan raincoat who had invaded the press area — was shoved up against the hotel's wall.

We saw the back of the president as he emerged from the limo and walked into the George Washington Hospital emergency room, a Secret Service agent on each side. The first lady arrived a short time later and virtually sprinted into the hospital.

And while Vice President Bush was flying back to Washington from Texas after the shooting, we watched as Al Haig made a historic, but bizarre, appearance on television later in the afternoon to declare that he was "in control here in the White House."

It was a long, confusing, draining afternoon. In the end, it was a close call, but we knew that President Reagan would make a full recovery.

Years later, the president used to tell portions of the story to Oval Office visitors. Even though photos appear to show the president in some pain after he was shot — a bullet had ricocheted off the presidential limo and pierced the president's left chest, stopping within an inch of his heart — Reagan always said he experienced just a tingling from the actual shot. The president said that after Parr jumped on top of him in the limo, he could barely breathe. After he began coughing up blood, he assumed that Parr had broken his ribs, and he had to ask Parr to get off him so that he could breathe. Parr ordered the limo to George Washington Hospital.

Once inside the hospital, the president collapsed and was loaded onto a stretcher, his new blue suit soon cut off him. He was severely wounded, but his first instinct was to put everyone at ease. Lifting his oxygen mask, dried blood around his mouth, he whispered, "Honey, I forgot to duck," to the first lady when she arrived, shortly before he was wheeled into surgery for a two-and-a-half-hour operation to retrieve the .22-caliber bullet.

"I hope you're Republican," he joked to the doctors.

"Today, Mr. President, we're all Republicans," one replied.

Later, with tubes running down his throat, he kept up his commentary. "All in all, I'd rather be in Philadelphia," he wrote. Another note he scrawled, however, displayed his concern about his future health. It said: "Will I be able to do ranch work, ride, etc.?"

In ensuing years, some commentators tried to claim that the assassination attempt triggered a long, slow decline in Reagan. But as all who were truly close to him and who worked with him every day knew, Reagan did make a full recovery. In his second term, when I worked with him virtually seven days a week, I saw absolutely no hint of any decline in his capabilities. He had the same energy, the same mental sharpness that I had observed in the 1970s when I first met him.

While Reagan was recovering from the assassination attempt, his travel was naturally curtailed, which meant a break for his advance operation. Lanny and I settled into a rented town house in nearby Georgetown, a short cab ride from the White House, where we had moved two weeks prior to the shooting. We knew we had to live near the White House because, even with the recovery period, the hectic schedule would soon return.

It did shortly after that. The president's first major event was a triumphant visit to Capitol Hill for a speech to Congress on April 28, 1981. Characteristically, he opened his speech with a joke about his recent experience. "You wouldn't want to talk me into an encore, would you?"

In the nationally televised address, he refuted those who had claimed that his assassination attempt was evidence of a "sick society."

The president told Americans, "Sick societies don't make people like us so proud to be Americans and so very proud of our fellow citizens."

Reagan was back on track.

9

JELLY BEANS AND FORMER PRESIDENTS

Less than a month after Reagan's assassination attempt, he redoubled his efforts to end the deadly nuclear arms race with the Soviets. Against the advice of Secretary of State Al Haig, he lifted the Carter administration's grain embargo imposed after the Soviet invasion of Afghanistan. And on a legal pad, he wrote out a letter to Soviet leader Leonid Brezhnev, also over the strenuous objections of Haig.

In his letter, Reagan tried to reassure Brezhnev that the United States was not seeking world domination and wanted only peace. The people of the world, said Reagan, "have very much in common. They want the dignity of having some control over their individual destiny. They want to work at the craft or trade of their own choosing and be fairly rewarded. They want to raise their families in peace without harming anyone or suffering harm themselves. Government exists for their convenience, not the other way around."

Reagan, who had met Brezhnev a decade earlier after Brezhnev's meeting with then-President Nixon in San Clemente, California, said he hoped the lifting of the grain embargo would "lead to a meaningful and constructive dialogue which will assist us in fulfilling our joint obligation to find lasting peace."

Haig had the State Department rewrite Reagan's letter, but Reagan didn't like that version and, in the end, Reagan's handwritten version went to Brezhnev on the presidential letterhead, along with a more boiler-plate typed State Department letter.

Brezhnev rejected the overture. But it was only the beginning of Reagan's efforts to engage the Soviets and end the nuclear weapons race.

The assassination attempt in 1981 didn't deter Reagan on any front. He lobbied heavily for his economic recovery package and was rewarded with its passage that summer. On a fog-enshrouded August day at the ranch, he signed the Economic Recovery Act of 1981 into law, smiling from ear to ear. It was the largest package of tax cuts in U.S. history.

In July, he fulfilled a campaign promise by nominating the first woman in history to the U.S. Supreme Court, Arizona Judge

Sandra Day O'Connor.

He also faced down the air traffic controllers, who had threatened to go out on strike. After repeatedly warning their union, the Professional Air Traffic Controllers Organization, Reagan fired them in August. To virtually all the Reagan appointees, like me, the PATCO firings were a turning point in his first term from a domestic policy standpoint: They were a decisive action that the American people could see, understand and relate to.

In October, Reagan announced the U.S. strategic weapons program to rebuild our armed forces — part of his "peace through strength" initiative. "The U.S. does not start fights," he said in a speech. "We maintain our strength in order to deter and defend against aggression — to preserve freedom and peace."

Not everyone saw it his way, of course. We were dogged by protesters who repeated the accusation that had followed Reagan for years — that he was a warmonger bent on sending the U.S. military in whenever and wherever he wished.

On the personal front, however, President Reagan's security became a huge concern in the White House because of the assassination attempt.

The first lady, deeply affected by the shooting, pushed the Secret Service to drastically tighten security around the president. Every precaution needed to be taken. For the first time, screening devices, like the ones utilized in airports since hijackings erupted in the '70s, began to be used in ballrooms, outdoor areas, auditoriums, conference rooms — wherever the president went. For most outdoor events, he wore a bulletproof vest. This made life more difficult for the White House advance operation. Now, in building events, we also had to factor in time to get people, sometimes thousands of them, through metal detectors.

We were always battling with the Secret Service over the number of metal detectors they brought to events. The Secret Service had a large budget, but it hated shelling out money for more metal detectors and personnel than it absolutely had to. If we had an event in a ballroom with, say, 2,000 people, the Secret Service brought two metal detectors, which was fine. But if 5,000, 10,000 or more people were expected, it was usually a real battle to get the Secret Service to provide a sufficient number of metal detectors. Sometimes we had long lines, and people got impatient and left. Of course, if the Secret Service had its way, the president would never leave the Oval Office. Presidents have to get out, and after Reagan was shot, dealing with his Presidential Protection Detail was a constant issue.

Then in October 1981, Egyptian leader Anwar Sadat was assassinated while inspecting a military parade in Cairo. In my mind, that changed our lives even more than the Hinckley shooting and certainly affected the first lady. Unlike the Hinckley shooting, the Sadat killing was an organized plot. His assassins planned the attack — infiltrating a military parade, jumping off the vehicles as they rode past Sadat, running into the pavilion where Sadat was standing and massacring him and others.

What exacerbated the security situation for Reagan even more was that, shortly after the Sadat shooting, Reagan had a similar event coming up. He was supposed to review a military parade in Williamsburg for the two hundredth anniversary of the Battle of Yorktown. Granted, the troops would be in Colonial uniforms, but no one was happy about the parallels. We ended up having to build a large bulletproof reviewing stand for him there, a practice that would continue at large public events for the rest of his presidency.

Sadat's funeral was scheduled for a few days after his assassination. While many world leaders were attending, taking the U.S. president to the Middle East in the aftermath of a horrible assassination for Sadat's funeral would have been extremely dangerous. In the end, it was decided to put together a delegation of former presidents — Carter, Ford and Nixon — led by Secretary of State Haig to make the trip and pay their respects. Despite Nixon's troubles, Reagan always had a deep respect for him. They had a decades-long relationship and maintained a substantive dialogue throughout Reagan's presidency. Nixon called the president every three or four months because he wanted to be helpful, and Reagan appreciated his input.

The Sadat funeral was a chilling event. I had flown out ahead of the three former presidents and met them in Cairo. Hundreds of foreign dignitaries followed Sadat's coffin, trudging along the same dusty street taken by Egypt's military forces and Sadat's assassins just four days previously. They were guarded by thousands of soldiers, policemen and special security agents who lined the streets and carried automatic weapons. Helicopters circled overhead. Most foreign leaders brought their own security forces as well, and the American delegation was guarded by Secret Service agents.

At the end of the procession, a reception was held in a building behind the pavilion where Sadat was killed. En route to the reception, we paused briefly in front of the site of the assassination. Dark bloodstains were still visible, bullets were lodged in the concrete and wood was still heavily splintered where bullets had struck. Even with this horrible sight, it was nearly impossible to comprehend the carnage that had taken place just a few days earlier.

That evening, I flew to Washington with Presidents Ford and Carter while Nixon planned to leave on his own to fly to Saudi Arabia. We climbed aboard the backup Air Force One for the trip back, tired and relieved to be on the aircraft. It was frightening to be in Cairo, with all its reminders of the violence that had ripped through it. We wanted to get back to Washington.

That day must have been especially difficult for Carter, who had brought Sadat and Israeli leader Menachem Begin together just three years earlier to forge the historic Camp David peace agreement.

That's the only way I can account for his

behavior on the flight home. On the plane, we tried to settle Carter and Ford in the executive lounge, but Carter refused and seated himself behind the executive lounge in the senior staff area with us, where seats faced each other. I sat across the aisle from him, startled to find him there. But, I figured, he was always a different kind of guy and maybe he just didn't want to be with Ford, whom he had defeated for the White House in 1976.

On the tables in front of us were the ubiquitous Air Force One notepads, but also small jars with the presidential seal on them, filled with Jelly Bellies, Reagan's favorite jelly beans. The jars were attached with Velcro to the tables to keep them from sliding around during takeoffs and landings.

Carter sat down in his seat, looking grim. Just as we began to take off, one of the jelly bean jars caught his eye. With a look of irritation, Carter grabbed the jar, pulled it off the table and tossed it on the floor. I was appalled. What was his problem? First, he didn't want to sit with President Ford. Then he threw President Reagan's jelly beans around! I had heard that Carter wasn't very friendly but this was ridiculous. I wanted to say something, but restrained myself.

After refueling in Madrid, we started on our last leg of the trip home, to Andrews Air Force Base in Washington. On the flight to Andrews, Jack Kightlinger, a veteran White House photographer, suggested that we get some photos of the two presidents with the staff. It was a historic occasion, Jack said, and it would be nice to have photos to commemorate it. I thought it was a good idea and checked with Ford's aide and Carter's aide, who was Jody Powell. Ford liked the proposal. Carter gave a terse okay. He moved, reluctantly, to the executive lounge and we brought in the first staff person. Everyone wanted an individual photo with the two ex-presidents but Carter complained that it would take too long.

"I'm not going to stand here and do all these people on this plane one by one," he said irritably. "That's going to take forever."

I was startled. There were only 45 or so people on the plane, and we were prepared to move quickly.

"Bring in four at a time," ordered Carter. So we did, and Kightlinger clicked away as fast as he could. But while Ford smiled genially, Carter looked more and more unhappy. Finally, I thought we'd done everyone, but then I remembered I'd forgotten about the air force galley people. I didn't want to leave them out. I explained the situation to Ford and Carter and ran to get them. Carter shot me a hostile look and threw his arms up in exasperation.

After assuring the former presidents that we were done, a staffer who had been in the bathroom walked in, so I took him to have his photo taken. It wasn't a big deal, I figured, and Ford gracefully complied. Carter looked thunderous. And then one *more* person emerged from somewhere. I apologized again and asked for one more photo and assured them this was the last photo.

"You're right," snapped Carter. "I don't care who else is on this plane, I'm not doing any more photos." He turned on me, raising his voice. "Do you understand me?"

"Yes, sir, I do," I told him. Carter stormed out of the executive lounge.

I was devastated. The thirty-ninth president of the United States had just taken me apart. The photos hadn't seemed like such a big deal and, in fact, Ford hadn't objected.

Throughout much of the Reagan presidency, Carter was harshly critical of Reagan. Even so, the Reagans attended the dedication of his presidential library in 1986, and I know he was grateful to them for that. Five years later, he reciprocated by attending the dedication of Reagan's library, and I know the Reagans were touched by that gesture.

But I still believed Carter's behavior was inappropriate no matter how hard the trip was for him. I couldn't help but compare Carter's actions with the behavior I'd seen from Reagan under different but challenging circumstances. The contrast was night and day. Reagan was always able to separate his emotions from the events of the moment. Tragedies during Reagan's presidency — the bombing of the marine barracks in Lebanon, the explosion of the space shuttle *Challenger* — proved this. Presidents can't become overwhelmed with emotions; they must be able to switch gears emotionally. Reagan could do that. Even as he dealt with heart-wrenching crises, he always remained courteous to his staff and others.

After Carter stormed out of the executive lounge, I stood there for a moment next to Ford in semishock, asking myself why this had gone so horribly wrong.

"I really screwed this up for President Carter," I said to Ford.

"No, you didn't, young man," Ford said warmly. "That worked fine." He grinned at me as if he were confiding a secret.

"I've always said," he told me, "that you can't make chicken salad out of chicken shit."

With that, he shook his head. President Ford made me feel human again.

10

TOUGH TIMES IN THE PRESIDENCY

The papal library in the Vatican was warm and stuffy, and the pope droned on in a soft monotone. It was June 1982, and we were in the midst of our first presidential trip to Europe. I looked at the president, who was sitting in a high-back chair next to His Holiness. With a stunned sense of helplessness, I realized that Reagan's eyes were closing. Good Lord, I thought, he's falling asleep in front of the pope and the whole world.

And there wasn't a damned thing we could do about it.

That year, 1982, was not an easy year for the Reagan administration. Even though Reagan had signed the Economic Recovery Act in August 1981, it had not yet taken effect, and the economy was still mired in the Carter recession. Many — including some on Capitol Hill — blamed Reagan for it. Even Republican candidates running for office tried to distance themselves from the president.

Battles over the federal budget raged.

President Reagan's critics argued that if he would consent to cuts in the defense buildup, there would be more money for domestic spending. But Reagan was determined to stick to his guns, so to speak. He believed that only by demonstrating to the Soviets our determination to build up our military could we drive them to the bargaining table. Then, and only then, could the two countries negotiate a reduction in nuclear arms and an end to mutual assured destruction (MAD), which had both counties aiming nuclear weapons at each other as some kind of bizarre deterrence from using them.

Amid this environment, the Reagans went to the Caribbean at Easter to visit longtime friend actress Claudette Colbert, who lived in Barbados, and for bilateral meetings in both Jamaica and Barbados. While the president and first lady were in Barbados, a nasty blizzard hit Washington that buried the city in snow, and when the Reagans got to Colbert's home, the president went swimming from her private beach. Unfortunately, network camera crews were filming from a nearby hotel, so the pictures from that trip on the nightly news and in newspapers around the nation featured Reagan splashing in the Caribbean surf while Americans suffered in unemployment lines, Capitol Hill was immersed in budget battles and Washington was trying to dig itself out of a snowstorm.

Once again, Reagan had substantive policy discussions with leaders of Jamaica and Barbados to discuss subjects such as the Caribbean basin initiative to stimulate economic development in the region, and the encroachment of Communist forces in Central America.

Some press coverage wasn't any kinder for that trip to the Vatican in 1982. It was one stop on our first major international trip — a grueling 10-day journey — first to France for an economic summit, then on to Rome, Great Britain and Germany, where we saw giant demonstrations against Reagan's decision to place intermediate-range nuclear force (INF) missiles there.

The president made a five-hour visit to Rome to meet with Pope John Paul and Italian leaders. But he had been up until early that morning for a closing ceremony at the economic summit in Versailles, and it showed. Reagan and the entire traveling entourage were also very tired.

In fact, the Vatican trip was difficult in other ways, too. The White House advance team established its presence in Rome three weeks before the president and Mrs. Reagan arrived, but it was almost impossible to write a schedule for their Vatican visit because of the trouble in working with Vatican officials. We couldn't get answers from them. Bill Wilson, Reagan's ambassador to the Vatican and the first U.S. ambassador to the Holy See, was a member of Reagan's kitchen cabinet and a close friend of the Reagans. However, in my opinion Wilson was so concerned about looking good to the Vatican that he sometimes sacrificed the president's best interests.

We finally hammered out a schedule, but that wasn't the end of it. The day before the president and first lady arrived, Vatican officials changed around our schedule, which added 45 minutes to the itinerary. That's a lot of time in a presidential daily schedule, let alone on a foreign trip where everything is timed down to the last minute.

Mike Deaver, who was in charge of the president's travel, was literally shoved around by Vatican officials. At one point, he went to check in on the Reagans while they were alone in a holding room. For some reason, our chief liaison, a Vatican monsignor, took umbrage at this and refused to allow him into the room.

Deaver was annoyed.

"This is crazy," he said. "I'm going in." He headed for the door, but the monsignor threw himself in front of it, spread-eagled, to prevent Deaver from entering. Deaver grabbed the door handle and tried to go under the monsignor's left arm. The monsignor went down on his knees to block him.

Deaver gave up. "That's it," he shouted. "I've had enough of you guys." He stormed off.

The president met privately with the pope for about 45 minutes. I'm sure they had a lot to talk about: They both headed large, powerful institutions, had been in power for relatively short periods of time — Reagan for 18 months and the pope for just two years — and they both had survived assassination attempts.

After the meeting, the president and the pope emerged so each could make statements from the papal library. The media were there, and the event was broadcast live around the world. Reagan spoke first, then the pope took his turn. In his statement, which he made in slow, halting English, the pope called the ongoing warfare in Lebanon "a grave crisis," and he repeated his appeals against the nuclear arms race by warning against "ever more sophisticated and deadly weapons."

Right there in his chair, I saw Reagan's eyes close. He opened them briefly, but then they closed again. He dozed only for a couple of minutes but, of course, the press caught it, and it was the story of the day.

Though the incident didn't raise the issue of Reagan's age again — at least not right then — it wasn't the impression we wanted to make to the world. If he had it to do over, the president and Mrs. Reagan would have spent the night in Rome, as we had considered. In fact, we had reserved 900 rooms in Rome for the previous evening. In not bringing the president and Mrs. Reagan in the night before, we did a major disservice to the president, and it was simply one of those unfortunate things.

In 1987, the president and Mrs. Reagan returned to the Vatican, and Reagan dozed off *again* during statements in the papal library. Senior White House photographer Bill Fitzpatrick, who was standing next to me, and I both noticed it. Thinking quickly, Fitzpatrick deliberately dropped his camera. It landed with a hard crash against the hardwood floor, and it snapped the president awake.

The president and Mrs. Reagan felt horrible that it had happened again. But I felt strongly about something, which I conveyed to the Reagans.

"For some reason," I told the president and Mrs. Reagan as we flew to Venice on Air Force One, "the pope's voice has a hypnotic effect on the president. It's not his fault. If he was to meet the pope again, the same circumstances would prevail. There's nothing you can do about it, Mr. President."

I sensed my words helped the Reagans to feel slightly better about the incident. Despite the occurrences, the president's missions to the Vatican in '82 and '87, as well as his meetings with Italian officials, were productive.

The first Italy trip in 1982 also marked the end of Al Haig's tenure in the Reagan administration. Haig had irritated the Reagan administration by continually claiming that other members of the administration were undercutting his authority and taking over foreign policy matters. Haig attempted to formulate his own policy, which, of course, irritated those close to Reagan. Haig's rash comments after the Reagan shooting, however well intentioned, didn't sit well with anyone, either. He clashed often with other Reagan officials involved in foreign policy, such as Secretary of Defense Caspar Weinberger and national security advisers Richard V. Allen, his successor William P. Clark and U.N. Representative Jeane Kirkpatrick. In other words, he butted heads with just about everybody who mattered.

Haig — although he had a distinguished record of government service — was a mistake from the beginning, I believe. He wasn't a team player; he always seemed to have his own agenda and his own interests in mind, not the president's. He failed to realize as a member of the cabinet that the administration's policies are the *president's* policies, not cabinet members' initiatives. But Reagan had a legendary distaste for firing people. So the ground was being laid to "encourage" him to resign.

To get around Rome on our 1982 visit, we used White House helicopters and, normally, the secretary of state has a seat on Marine One on international trips. But on all of our helicopter movements throughout Rome, Haig was not assigned a seat on Marine One. He ended up with a seat on a helicopter transporting midlevel staff and press people who were further down in the pecking order.

It turned out to be a dirty trip in more ways than one for Haig. On the last leg of the Rome trip, we flew out of an old Italian army base in downtown Rome that housed mounted troops. After the first wave of helicopters carrying the president and Mrs. Reagan, senior staff and Secret Service had lifted off, the second set of helicopters landed on the pavement for the rest of the staff and the press. These helicopters were decidedly inelegant — giant Chinooks with rotors in the front and back that blew up a veritable storm when they touched down and took off. Ours dropped down its back hatch, and we dashed up the ramp and into the helicopter, but not before we were pelted with dust from dried horse manure kicked up by the Chinook's massive rotors. I ran in, brushed myself off and turned around just in time to see Secretary and Mrs. Haig clambering in after me. Haig had his handkerchief out and was wiping his forehead.

"I'll be a goddamned son of a bitch," he said, shaking his head.

Wow, I thought. They must want him out of here very badly.

Less than three weeks later, Haig resigned, ending his stormy career in the

Reagan administration. Reagan nominated George Shultz as his next secretary of state.

After the trip to Rome, the president and Mrs. Reagan flew to Great Britain, where Reagan's visit was more trouble free. The Reagans stayed at Windsor Castle, and the president went horseback riding with the queen. He also delivered a major speech before the British Parliament, which he considered one of the most important speeches of his presidency. He used the now famous term consigning communism to "the ash heap of history."

Praise greeted Reagan's powerful speech to Parliament but criticism against Reagan was mounting in other countries.

In a trip to Central America in December 1982, Reagan was denounced by the president of Colombia, Belisario Betancur, during an exchange of toasts at a luncheon in the presidential palace in Bogotá.

Betancur told Reagan that the United States should shift its Latin American policies to reflect "the reality of the continent as it is."

"We cannot deliberate calmly over abstract problems in our hemispheric organizations when in certain parts of Central

America," said Betancur in a sharply worded toast, "bonfires are lit by social injustice or provoked by foreign hands that do not belong in the area."

There was no doubt that Betancur's "foreign hands" reference was aimed at the United States. He also told Reagan that relations between the United States and Latin America "have deteriorated considerably."

But Reagan kept his composure. The American ambassador had given me a copy of the remarks the night before, and I had alerted Mike Deaver, so Reagan was prepared.

Colombia was a frightening place. The M-19 drug organization was rampant, and crime was epidemic. Before we left, Ed Hickey, assistant to the president and director of the White House military office, warned us that it was so dangerous in Bogotá that it was said that a driver making a left turn shouldn't stick his hand out the window to signal because thieves would chop it off to get his watch.

Anti-Americanism was also strong. Along the route of Reagan's motorcade from the airport to downtown Bogotá, we could see scrawled anti-Reagan slogans on the walls of buildings. Some in the crowd jeered the motorcade as it sped by, and there were shouts of "Go home!"

During a wreath-laying ceremony at the statue of Simón Bolívar, a nineteenth-century hero of Latin American independence, an anti-American demonstration was so close it seemed almost on top of us. We could hear the echo of hundreds of voices, so loud that it seemed to rattle the area where we stood. It was the only time in eight years that I was actually afraid that something bad was going to happen to the president.

Those types of obstacles — big protests, sharp words from foreign leaders — didn't bother Reagan. He just shrugged them off. His staff was always up and down — off the Richter scale — when the waves of criticism and praise over the performance of Ronald Reagan rolled through. But Reagan was always able to stay focused on the big picture, control his emotions and not let the critics get him down. He was steady in the best of times and the worst of times.

In 1982, we also faced the off-year elections and the concern that the Republicans could lose control of the Senate again. Because of the poor economy, some Republican candidates were distancing themselves from Reagan, despite his 1981 landslide that had carried so many Republicans into office.

In September, for example, we went to Columbus, Ohio, for a rally for Republican statewide candidates. Congressman Bud Brown was in a tight race for governor there. But some Republicans made statements to the press that they weren't happy about Reagan's appearance in their state. In fact, the Republican mayor of Columbus, who was running for state auditor, complained publicly that the president was going to hurt Republican candidates in Ohio more than he helped them.

We were livid. This guy was trashing a president who had led so many Republicans into office on his coattails in 1980! But 1982 was a different year. Granted, we had inherited a bad economy from Carter, but we knew that Americans blamed their current president for the lingering problems and demanded that he fix them. Reagan was working hard, but it would take time for his policies to impact the vast American economy. In the meantime, it was rough going, and Reagan was the man at the top.

But Reagan was always willing to help out a fellow Republican.

House Minority Leader Robert H.

Michel, who had represented the area around Peoria for 28 years, did ask for Reagan's assistance in his reelection bid, and the president agreed immediately. The United Auto Workers had put up a Democratic candidate, G. Douglas Stephens and was marshaling all its muscle behind him. Michel and Stephens were dead even in the polls. But Bill Henkel, who now ran the advance office, warned me that putting together an event in Peoria would be difficult. Peoria was a mess economically, and there was a lot of anger at "Reaganomics," which laid-off workers in the city blamed for their plight. A lot of presidents would have avoided the event all together, but Reagan did it out of loyalty to Michel.

I had to lobby Michel to get him to move the main campaign rally from a 12,000-seat coliseum to a smaller facility that we could more easily fill on a Wednesday night, which could likely be the night of the seventh game of the World Series between the St. Louis Cardinals and the Milwaukee Brewers — both popular teams in this midwestern town. On top of that, the Michel campaign was selling tickets to the political rally — practically unheard of in politics. Most rallies are free. If the facility was only half filled, it would look very bad for Reagan and Michel. I finally succeeded in getting Michel's sign-off to move the event to a smaller facility, although Michel was not very gracious about it.

We ended up having a great campaign rally. The room was packed with more than 6,000 people, all cheering Reagan and Michel. On Election Day, Michel eked out a win — squeaking by Stephens by less than one percentage point. According to Ed Rollins, director of White House political affairs and a longtime political strategist, the president's campaign appearance in Peoria to support Michel was one campaign stop in which a president actually won the election for the candidate.

Even though Reagan knew he was going into the middle of the fray in Peoria, he didn't worry about the political fallout. He had made a promise to Michel, and he intended to keep it. We were to come up against Reagan's unparalleled loyalty again and again. No matter how hard we tried to persuade Reagan to do the more expedient thing politically, we always failed. He never broke a promise.

That isn't to say he didn't have some loyal support in Congress at the time. When I was in charge of another campaign stop in Casper, Wyoming, just before the '82 election, I got a visit from Senator Alan Simpson and the state's congressman at large, Dick Cheney. Simpson loved the president — and vice versa — partly because Simpson told great jokes. Reagan loved good jokes, and when he and Simpson got together, they would trade them with great delight.

Both Simpson and Cheney said they didn't want anything from Reagan. They just wanted to know how they could be helpful. I wanted to hug those guys. While some Republicans were jumping ship, people like Cheney and Simpson were offering to do anything they could to help the president.

In '82, however, it seemed that Cheney and Simpson were the exception, not the rule. In Casper, Reagan went to an airport rally for Senator Malcolm Wallop, who was also up for reelection. The event was a great success, and then Reagan flew to his next stop. I stayed behind to finish up and watched network correspondent Sam Donaldson interview Senator Wallop.

As Air Force One took off in the distance behind them, Donaldson asked Wallop why he had invited Reagan to Casper to speak at a campaign rally with the economy in such bad shape and Reagan's popularity falling.

Wallop denied inviting Reagan, claiming that the White House had *asked* him if the president could come!

I was shattered. Why say that? It was uncalled for and just vicious. Reagan would have never made such a statement or allowed such a statement to be made by his people.

But I had to remember that I worked for Ronald Reagan, and I couldn't hold grudges.

In the end, the Republicans weathered the midterm elections well, maintaining control with thc same margin in the Senate that they gained in the Reagan landslide of '80. But the year ahead would bring joy, and much sorrow, to the country and to the president.

11

TRIUMPH AND TRAGEDY

Even royalty isn't immune from unpleasant people. I learned that the hard way when Queen Elizabeth and Prince Philip came to the United States for a state visit in early 1983. Normally, the State Department handles the U.S. visits of heads of state, but Mike Deaver decided that the White House Advance Office, which was under Deaver's direction, would handle the queen's 10-day visit to the United States. He said the royal couple had taken care of the Reagans so well during their visit to England the previous year that the White House should handle the queen's trip to the United States.

I drew this two-and-a-half-month assignment from Advance Office Director Bill Henkel and, at the outset, I was not happy about it. From my perspective, I was at the White House to serve at the pleasure of the president, not the queen of England. However, I had my mandate, and the upside was that the president and Mrs. Reagan would be with the queen and Prince Philip at various points in California, including the Reagans' ranch.

President Reagan looked forward to the queen's visit to the ranch in late February. He had very much enjoyed riding with the queen during their stay at Windsor Castle the previous June and he wanted to reciprocate by riding with her at Rancho del Cielo.

But when the queen and Prince Philip arrived in California for their tour of the United States and Canada, the weather initially ruled the day. It rained. And rained. And, accompanied by high winds, it rained more and more. Along the coast of California, the tide was so strong that home owners opened their doors facing the ocean and their doors on the opposite sides of their homes so the water could literally flow in and out to alleviate the scale of damage. The royal yacht *Britannia* was docked at Long Beach and was supposed to sail to Santa Barbara with the queen and Prince Philip, but the seas were too rough. Instead, the royal party spent the night on the *Britannia*. The next morning, the piers were flooded so much that the Secret Service limo could not drive up to *Britannia*, and we ended up using a U.S. Navy-supplied bus to transport the royal party to Long Beach Airport. It was not as luxurious as a yacht or a limo, but it sat higher off the ground, so it could ford the water we plowed through. We got a photo of the queen and Prince Philip sitting in the front seat of the former school bus, painted navy gray, looking almost like school kids.

Getting them to the ranch proved another challenge. Thick streams of water flowed across the mountain road leading to the Reagans' ranch, making a regular motorcade impossible. So we brought in SUVs to get them up.

At the ranch, the weather was even worse, so Reagan and the queen were not able to get their ride together. Reagan — who rarely let things bother him — was very disappointed that he couldn't go horseback riding to show the queen his beloved ranch. But nothing could be done about it; at midday, with the rain and heavy fog, you couldn't see five feet in front of you. Instead, the Reagans and the royal couple settled for a shorter visit and a California-Mexican lunch of tacos, burritos and refried beans. Later, I was amused to learn the queen had said that she'd never had "reused beans" before!

We took the royal couple, their entourage and Mrs. Reagan down into Santa Barbara to tour Santa Barbara's historic old Spanish mission. It was still raining buckets, and it took us awhile to load all the limos after the tour. Later, a Secret Service agent told me that Prince Philip had become enraged at the delay. He lambasted the Secret Service personnel at the holdup and demanded that the motorcade depart.

"Get this [expletive, expletive] car going," he roared at the Secret Service, in front of the queen and Mrs. Reagan, who were also seated in the limo with him. I was shocked. Ronald Reagan was the ultimate gentleman and never swore in the presence of women.

The queen, oddly, didn't react to Prince Philip's outburst at all. She remained sitting, staring ahead as if nothing had happened. Mrs. Reagan, tactfully, took the same approach. It was clear the queen was used to such temper tantrums from her husband.

After Santa Barbara, we headed for San Francisco, where the royal couple was to host a small dinner and reception with an expanded guest list of about 80 people in honor of the Reagans' thirty-first wedding anniversary on March 4. The president and Mrs. Reagan would spend the night on *Britannia* as well. Driving in from the San

Francisco airport, we saw a lively and large demonstration with a big banner proclaiming the demonstration QUEENS AGAINST THE QUEEN. Ironically, it wasn't until we arrived in the foggy city of San Francisco, our sixth day of the overall tour, that we saw sunshine.

Because of the yacht's size, the royal couple remained in the dining room for the reception, and the Reagans went into the drawing room. Guests were supposed to move back and forth. During the reception, however, I noticed quite a contrast between the two rooms. In the dining room, where the royal couple received guests, it was somber, quiet, formal — and rather empty. Relatively few of the guests stayed more than a few minutes with the stiff royals. They seemed almost afraid of them. Instead, guests crowded into the drawing room with the Reagans, screaming, laughing and chatting. It was noisy and upbeat, and the Reagans were enjoying themselves immensely.

The next stop for the queen and Prince Philip was Yosemite National Park, where we had a rather embarrassing mishap. We flew out of San Francisco International Airport, where there were airplanes all over the tarmac because the president and Mrs.

Reagan were also departing separately at the same time as the royal couple. I accompanied the queen and Prince Philip on the Air Force One backup plane for the flight to Merced Air Force Base. From there, we drove to Yosemite. I got a call on the phone next to my seat. It was Rick Ahearn, the White House advance man in San Francisco.

"Jim, you've got a problem," he said.

"I do?" I said.

"Don't you realize who you left behind?" Ahearn asked me. "The queen's footmen are still here at San Francisco Airport with all her luggage, and they're livid."

I couldn't believe it. "You've got to be kidding me!"

"I'm not kidding," said Ahearn.

As it turned out, the military aide in charge of the military support for the royal couple's U.S. trip had gotten impatient and had ordered the flight to depart, even though he knew the queen's footmen hadn't yet loaded the trunks holding her belongings, clothing and royal jewelry.

I explained the situation to Robert Fellows, the queen's private secretary, who was sitting next to me, that the queen's footmen and her precious belongings were still sitting on the tarmac of San Francisco Airport.

Fellows shook his head. "This has never happened before," he said.

"It shouldn't have happened *this* time," I said. "Let me try to figure out what to do."

Fellows said he would have to go into the 707's stateroom and explain the situation to her majesty. The queen had been delightful the entire trip but, having seen the behavior of her husband after a minor inconvenience, I wondered how she would react to such a major screwup. But Fellows came back smiling.

"She's laughing," he reported. "She took the news very well."

In the end, I flew back to San Francisco after leaving off the queen and her party at Merced and retrieved the luggage, crown jewels and two very unhappy royal footmen. During the entire plane ride to Merced Air Force Base, they sat in chilly silence.

The trip wasn't over yet, however, and Prince Philip treated us to his royal disposition one more time.

We flew to Seattle after the Yosemite visit, and the queen and Prince Philip toured a local hospital, took a ride on the monorail and attended a reception hosted by Washington Governor John Spellman. Her majesty also gave an address at the University of Washington.

We were loading the motorcade for the 10-minute trip across town to the pier where the royal yacht was docked when we heard from his highness again. The plan was for Governor Spellman and his wife to ride with the queen and Prince Philip to *Britannia.* Unfortunately, we didn't have a stretch limo available in Seattle, and the queen and Prince Philip were in a regular armored limo. The seating was more confined than in a stretch, but there was still room for four passengers. The door to the royal couple's limo was already closed, so I had the Secret Service open it to let in the Spellmans. When I did, Prince Philip glared at me from the car.

"Can I help you?" he asked icily.

"Yes, Your Highness," I said politely. "I have Governor and Mrs. Spellman."

Prince Philip was still glaring.

"For what?" he demanded.

"The schedule calls for the governor and Mrs. Spellman to ride with you and her majesty to *Britannia,*" I explained, confused by the prince's demeanor.

"They're *not,*" Philip said shortly. "They

can't ride in here. There isn't enough room."

I explained that it was just for a short ride to the harbor. I noticed that the queen shot him a mildly exasperated look but she said nothing as Philip lit into me.

"I don't give a *goddamn*," he snapped. "They're not riding in here."

At that, I gave up. I told the Secret Service to shut their door, even though I felt like slamming it in his face. Maybe when someone has to play second fiddle for decades, it's easy to become that unpleasant.

I immediately apologized to the governor and Mrs. Spellman for Prince Philip's behavior and found a staff car near the end of the motorcade that could accommodate them.

The trip did end on a high note in Seattle: The queen called President Reagan to bid farewell as *Britannia* sailed out of Puget Sound toward Canada. Two days after the trip, Deaver's office called me and told me to be in the Oval Office at noon. It was my first visit to the Oval Office in the presence of the president.

In the Oval Office, a smiling Reagan complimented me on my handling of the royal visit.

"I want you to know how much it meant

to me, and I appreciate all of your hard work," he told me.

Yet again, I was struck by the contrast between Reagan and some other public figures. Courtesy to his own staff was as important to Ronald Reagan as paying honor to a queen. When events went awry, Ronald Reagan wasn't one to lay blame.

I remember another episode when we were at Ford's Theatre for the theater's annual gala fund-raiser in September 1982. The president and first lady attended the performance, but then the complicated logistics of getting them in one way and out of the theater another way for security reasons became confused. To the amusement of some audience members after the performance ended, I was pointing the Reagans in one direction while they were headed in the other direction. Eventually, we ended up in our unusual exit route, which was a dark corridor on the right side of the theater. I apologized to the Reagans for the confusion. But it was absolutely no problem from their viewpoint.

"Well, Jim," the president joked, "I bet this is the way that John Wilkes Booth left that evening."

He had a way of making you feel better even when you'd messed up.

Compared with his unending courtesy to others, President Reagan's rhetoric toward the Soviet Union seemed uncharacteristically tough. But he was shrewdly laying the groundwork for progress on ending the cold war.

In March 1983, he gave a speech to the National Association of Evangelicals in Orlando that spelled out his "peace through strength" approach to the Soviet Union.

"I intend to do everything to persuade them of our peaceful intent," he told the gathering, adding, "At the same time, however, they must be made to understand we will never compromise our principles and standards. . . . If history teaches anything, it teaches that simpleminded appeasement or wishful thinking about our adversaries is folly."

But the speech was most famous for his labeling the Soviet Union the "evil empire."

In discussing nuclear freeze proposals, he told the group, "I urge you to beware the temptation of pride — the temptation of blithely declaring yourselves above it all, and label both sides equally at fault, to ignore the facts of history and the aggressive impulses of an evil empire. . . ."

Also in March, he proposed the ambitious strategic defense initiative, immediately dubbed "Star Wars" by its opponents, a defensive system that would intercept and destroy nuclear weapons before they reached the United States. The system, he said, was essential in helping the United States negotiate with the Soviet Union from a position of strength while at the same time pursuing real reductions in nuclear arms.

The Soviets, he warned in his speech to the nation on March 23, 1983, have "increased their military power [and] been emboldened to extend that power. They're spreading their military influence in ways that can directly challenge our vital interests and those of our allies."

At the same time, the president liked to leaven all kinds of speeches with jokes about the Soviets. One frequently repeated was "Question: What are the four things wrong with Soviet agriculture? Answer: spring, summer, fall and winter." Another joke he often told was about a farmer who told a Communist official that the harvest was so bountiful that if the potatoes were stacked on top of each other, they would reach the foot of God. "But this is the Soviet Union," the official responded. "There is no God here." "That's all right," said the farmer. "There are no potatoes, either."

Also in 1983, Reagan became the target of the growing worldwide nuclear freeze movement, in which his daughter Patti became an activist. She even brought antinuclear activist Helen Caldicott into the White House to meet with Reagan. But Reagan remained steadfast in his opposition to a nuclear freeze, arguing that it would reward the Soviets for their military buildup and make the United States less, not more, secure.

I remember 1983 as a tumultuous year in terms of protests for, and against, the president. The president's "peace through strength" approach, his support of contra rebels in Nicaragua and the anti-Communist El Salvador government and his decisions on weapons systems like the MX and Pershing-2 missiles were bringing praise and condemnation worldwide. He seemed to generate passionate feelings among many.

One example of the kind of praise he could receive was a high-spirited reception he got in Miami when we went there in May 1983 on Cuban-American Day for a celebration of Cuba's independence from Spain 81 years previously. Reagan, whose strong stance against communism made him a hero in the Cuban-American community, had lunch in a small restaurant in Little Havana with guests invited by the Cuban-American Committee before giving a major speech at the Dade County Auditorium where, unfortunately, the audience had to be limited due to space restrictions.

Because of heavy media coverage in Miami about his visit and with such a small number of people having a chance to see him, we determined that we needed to do something to make President Reagan more visible.

I came up with the idea of establishing a parade route from the restaurant to the auditorium. I asked our host committee whether they thought people would come out to see Reagan along the one-and-a-half-mile route. You will have a *fantastic* crowd, they predicted. The Secret Service was apprehensive and didn't want publicity about the motorcade route in the media. So I suggested that we publicize it only on Spanish-language radio. The Secret Service was fine with that, figuring that publicity wouldn't draw a significant crowd, which is what we wanted them to think.

They were wrong. Tens of thousands of people lined the parade route in Little Havana, crying, shouting and waving Cuban and American flags, welcoming the president back to their community. *"Viva el presidente!"* they shouted as Reagan slowly went by in his motorcade.

"This is the big man. After Lincoln, Reagan is the best," Al Fernandez, a Cuban-born aircraft mechanic told the Associated Press as he leaned out the window of an open-air café trying to catch a better glimpse of the president's motorcade. Along the parade route was parked a flatbed truck with a long dummy rocket pointed up that had a sign on it reading MX-YES! The *Miami Herald* reported the next day that upward of 100,000 people lined the parade route to see President Reagan.

We couldn't help but be pleased with the way the parade went. As the motorcade pulled up to the Dade County Auditorium, Deaver came over to compliment me — the only time in four years that he personally did so.

"Well done," he said. "That was unbelievable."

During Reagan's speech in the auditorium, people clustered around radios, listening to a simultaneous Spanish translation of his remarks. And Reagan didn't pull any punches. He ridiculed the Cuban government of Fidel Castro as a "grotesque joke."

"You know," he said, departing from his prepared text, "they say that there are only two places where communism works: in heaven where they don't need it, and in hell where they've already got it."

The next month, our reception in Minneapolis could not have been more different. And the same went for Seattle in August. In Minneapolis, where the president was attending a fund-raising dinner for Senator Rudy Boschwitz and promoting his Excellence in Education initiative, the wife of the St. Paul police chief led thousands of demonstrators protesting against Reagan. As we left Minneapolis, the crowd threw rocks and bottles at our motorcade. I was in the lead car, and the debris crashed down around us as we got into our vehicles.

In Seattle in August, Reagan spoke to 5,000 American Legion delegates at their national convention. He didn't disappoint them, attacking the "so-called 'peace movement' " as waging "peace by weakening the free. That just doesn't make sense."

Outside, thousands demonstrated against him again, protesting his military buildup and the administration's foreign policy in Central America. They blocked traffic and shouted "No more Reagan!" Some protesters slashed the tires of two of the press cars in our motorcade, and we had to scramble for other automobiles. The Seattle police had a reputation for being very lenient with demonstrators.

When Reagan's limo pulled out, demonstrators launched a model of an MX missile made out of fruit at his limo. Bananas, apples and other fruit hit the armored vehicle, but no damage was done.

We thought it was pretty funny, actually. And protests never bothered Reagan, which was fortunate since he experienced them worldwide throughout his two terms. I remember in 1988, late in his second term, we were driving to a doctor's appointment in Los Angeles. We hadn't publicized the visit but, somehow, word must have gotten out because a spontaneous protest sprang up along the motorcade for a couple of blocks. People, some sitting on the shoulders of others, shouted disdainfully and some shook their fists at our cars. One bare-chested man beat his chest defiantly at us.

When we were waiting in the doctor's office, the president commented on the reaction.

"Did you see those people back there?" he asked.

"I sure did," I said.

"They were certainly upset about something, weren't they?" the president said with a little smile.

"Yeah," I said, grinning, "you."

The president pretended to look surprised. "Me? What did I do?"

"Who knows?" I said. I reeled off a list of the usual suspects — Central America, Iran-contra, the military buildup, his economic policies. "You're the president, and they just wanted to squawk a bit," I said.

He laughed. "I know. But I didn't think I'd see anything today."

Despite the protests, the president was doing well in 1983; the economy was recovering and his popularity was heading up.

But then triumph and tragedy struck on the same weekend in October 1983.

It was supposed to be a quiet weekend; the Reagans went to the Augusta National Golf Club in Georgia at the invitation of Secretary of State Shultz for a weekend of golf. Treasury Secretary Don Regan was there, as was former Senator Nicholas Brady, who later became Treasury secretary. I had been down twice beforehand to look over the golf club and where they would stay. It was secure; the golf club was closed and looked peaceful.

But the quiet weekend started to unravel in the middle of Friday night when the president was awakened with news that six Caribbean countries had asked the United States to help oust radical Marxists from the island of Grenada, about 90 miles north of Venezuela. They had executed the prime minister the previous week, and neighboring countries were concerned that the Cuban-sponsored leftists would attack them shortly.

Another concern was closer to home for the United States: 800 American medical students were in Grenada attending St. George's University Medical School and were in danger of being held hostage by the insurgents. In his pajamas and robe, Reagan met with his advisers and approved an invasion force.

The next day, he and his golfing party were only a few rounds into their golf game when a gunman crashed his pickup truck through a gate on the course and took two White House staff and the golf-course manager hostage at gunpoint in the pro shop.

I was in Dallas at the time, but caught the news on television when ABC News broke into the Michigan-Iowa football game. I called the Augusta White House switchboard to find out who the two White House staffers were. I knew that Dave Fischer, Reagan's executive assistant, was on the trip, in addition to Lanny Wiles, my former roommate and college friend who had worked with me for 18 months in the White House Advance Office before going into the private sector. An avid golfer, Lanny did the lead advance for the Augusta golf trip as a volunteer.

The television report said that the Reagans had been taken away, so they were safe. I had the Dallas White House switchboard connect me with Augusta.

"It's Lanny and Dave, right?" I asked the operator. He said yes.

The gunman demanded to speak to President Reagan, who called him several times, but the gunman hung up on him. In the end, Lanny and Dave freed themselves. They talked to the gunman, plied him with liquor and escaped with the golf course manager. The gunman was arrested.

As frightening as it was, Lanny's and Dave's ordeal turned out to be just a sideshow to the nightmare that erupted a short time later.

Early the next morning, on the other

side of the world, a young suicide bomber smashed a truck loaded with dynamite into the U.S. Marine barracks at the Beirut airport. Witnesses said he smiled as he drove by. The massive explosion dug a crater in the heart of the building 30 feet deep and 40 feet across.

Two hundred forty-one brave marines, who were part of a peacekeeping mission in Lebanon, died as they slept.

Reagan made a statement in Augusta and returned to the White House. I was called back to Washington to help plan a memorial service at Camp Lejeune in North Carolina in early November.

It was one of the saddest days of the Reagan presidency. It poured rain on that dreary, cold November day — a fitting testament to the devastating mood at Camp Lejeune, where many of the young marines had been based. For security reasons, the Secret Service had wanted to drive Reagan right up to the outdoor stage from which he would speak, but we decided that Reagan would walk in like everyone else and that he would sit in the chairs with the marines and mourners. It was a terrible day, and Reagan needed to be with the people who grieved.

On the sloping lawn in front of Lejeune's

brick headquarters, families of the dead marines and some of the survivors, wrapped in cloaks with their wounds and casts, wept.

Despite the downpour, Reagan refused an aide's offer to hold an umbrella over him as he addressed the mourners. He wanted to withstand the elements just like everyone else. Standing in the chill and rain, he tried to comfort the 5,000 present. "These gallant Americans — and, yes, they were gallant — they understood the danger they faced, yet they willingly went to Beirut," he said. "They were attacked because they represented *us*. . . . But free people are not deterred by such cowardly acts of terrorism, and we will not be diverted from the honorable endeavor of promoting peace, security and freedom, which is the reason for our presence in the troubled country of Lebanon."

After the memorial service, the Reagans met privately with family members inside the headquarters. People were so wet from the rain that there were pools of water everywhere, dripping off raincoats, off umbrellas. Relatives sobbing with grief were slipping and falling on the wet floor. We would pick them up, and they would collapse again.

But Reagan remained composed. He always managed to do that in situations like that, where it would have been easy to come apart emotionally. Even when those around him were losing it, he knew how to remain strong and compassionate.

The mood was more joyous a few weeks after Camp Lejeune, when we held a welcome-home ceremony on the South Lawn of the White House for the medical students rescued from Grenada.

It took two days for 5,000 U.S. Marines and Army Rangers to capture the Grenadian prime minister's killer and take the island. Sadly, 19 American members of the military were killed.

When the medical students returned to the United States, some knelt and kissed the ground as they got off military cargo jets in Charleston, South Carolina.

Ann Higgins, the White House director of correspondence, went through letters from the medical students to President Reagan, and we viewed videotapes of the homecoming in South Carolina to find the most eloquent students to speak at the South Lawn celebration.

At the event, one of the students told reporters that the evacuation had changed his liberal political views.

"It's one thing to view an American military operation from afar and quite another to be rescued by one," he said.

Reagan addressed the students waving small American flags: "What you saw ten days ago was patriotism," he told students.

Shortly after the South Lawn event, I was back in my office in the Old Executive Office Building when a volunteer answering the phones told me I had a call from the president on the White House administrative line. I thought it was a joke. Reagan didn't call the staff often, nor did he need to. Even when I heard a familiar voice calling me "Jim," I still wasn't sure it was really Reagan.

"Yes," I said warily and then was embarrassed to realize that it was, indeed, the president.

He told me he was touched by the event for the medical students and thanked me for it. "It couldn't have been more meaningful," he said.

I immediately brought up Ann Higgins, telling the president that she had done much more than I had and that she deserved all the credit.

Reagan's voice lit up. He told me about a plaque he kept on his desk. THERE'S NO LIMIT TO HOW FAR ONE CAN GO IF

THEY DON'T MIND WHO GETS THE CREDIT.

It was an important motto for him. Reagan didn't take credit for much. If he got kudos, fine, but he never looked for them. He lived by that motto on his desk, and he really believed in it.

Raised in a big Catholic farm family in Ohio, I never thought I would one day be traveling around the world with the president of the United States, meeting historic figures such as Pope John Paul II, on his 1987 visit to Miami.

As President Reagan prepares to fire a snowball at the Old Executive Office Building next door to the White House, I'm (*far left*) cheering him on. Whether he was shaping events on the world stage, as he did in bringing down communism, or just horsing around in private, Ronald Reagan always exuded the same warmth and genuine spirit.

British Prime Minister Margaret Thatcher just lit up around Reagan, and he lit up around her. Their unique rapport is captured in this 1985 picture of them, taken while we were in Bonn, West Germany, for the G-7 economic summit.

Mikhail Gorbachev is someone you can talk to, Margaret Thatcher counseled Ronald Reagan before the two superpower leaders ever met. After Reagan "won" the first round of the 1985 Geneva summit by going coatless — and looking younger and more fit than the bundled-up Gorbachev — the Soviet reformer always asked, "Mr. President, coats on or coats off the next time we meet?" Here the two are in Geneva, coats on.

President Reagan's 1984 trip to Normandy to commemorate the fortieth anniversary of the D-Day invasion was marked with his characteristic emotion and personal connection. Addressing a group of the World War II Army Rangers, he said, "These are the boys of Pointe du Hoc. These are the men who took the cliffs. These are the champions who helped free a continent. These are the heroes who helped end a war."

First Lady Nancy Reagan was at his side for that stirring trip to Normandy and to visit the gravesites of the brave men who are buried near Omaha Beach. Always sensitive to the feelings of others, the Reagans received strong assurances by the White House staff that it was appropriate for them to walk among the headstones, with their feet touching the soil covering these heroes.

Ronald Reagan played college football, but was humble enough to admit he needed a warm-up before throwing the pigskin in front of the press one day in 1988. I was shocked when he suggested we practice right there in the Oval Office. Not too shocked, thank goodness, to catch his perfect passes.

One of the greatest perks of working as Ronald Reagan's executive assistant was the opportunity to include my family in such a historic place and time. White House staff worked an immense number of hours per week, but he always made my family welcome when they visited. Here I am with (*left to right*) my son, Greg, daughter Caitlin, daughter Alyssa, and wife, Carole, in the Oval Office.

Just six months after this picture of my carrying Caitlin and walking with the president was taken, the president stopped me in this very spot on the Colonnade that leads from the White House residence to the Oval Office. He told me how aware he was of the fact that so many of America's women were pro-choice and that he was sensitive about imposing his will upon them. He never wavered in his pro-life position, but his compassion for both sides of the issue surprised and impressed me.

It's quite a thrill to be chauffeured by the president of the United States, even if it is only in a golf cart, and even if it looks in this picture like his eyes aren't where they should be! This photo was taken at Camp David, the weekend retreat for presidents located in the Catoctin Mountains of Maryland, 80 miles from Washington, D.C.

My family accompanied me to Camp David on nearly every one of the 91 weekend trips I made there with the Reagans. So did the Reagans' dogs. Here is Mrs. Reagan outside Laurel Lodge walking Lucky, the Bouvier des Flanders whose weekend exploits at Camp David included an attempt at eating a box of chocolates set out for guests while the Reagans were enjoying a movie.

Mrs. Reagan was so proud of her husband for everything he did to end the cold war. Returning from Moscow aboard Air Force One in 1988, we all joined in a toast to the president's successes, offered by Chief of Staff Howard Baker (*center, striped tie*).

Notice the glass jar of Air Force One jelly beans behind my folded hands in this picture? It's very similar to the one President Jimmy Carter picked up and threw on the floor in disgust when he was coming back from Egyptian Prime Minister Anwar Sadat's funeral aboard the presidential jet with President Ford and me.

The first lady was an infrequent visitor to the Oval Office, preferring instead to watch from afar and manage her own affairs. But on the rare occasions when she did stop in, the president and I would enjoy many light moments like this one.

President Reagan understood he was a temporary custodian of the White House Oval Office, and he never let the power affect him. As he exits the Oval Office for the last time on January 20, 1989, a couple of hours before George H. W. Bush was sworn in as his successor, I reflected in wonderment about how down to earth Ronald Reagan remained throughout his eight years in office.

12

HEADING FOR A SECOND TERM

By 1984, life in America had improved significantly since Reagan took office. We were officially out of the recession, and the economy was booming. Inflation had dropped from more than 13 percent to less than 4 percent, and the prime rate had been sliced almost in half. Unemployment had come down significantly. Reagan was riding a crest of popularity; some polls found that as many as 80 percent of Americans thought they were better off as a result of Reagan's four years in office.

Those who had confidently predicted that Reagan would be a one-term president had fallen silent, and Reagan laid out the themes of what he hoped would be his second term in his State of the Union on January 25, declaring that America stood tall again.

"The cynics were wrong," he said. "America never was a sick society. We're seeing rededication to bedrock values of faith, family, work, neighborhood, peace and freedom — values that help bring us together as one people, from the youngest child to the most senior citizen."

Now he just had to fend off whatever the Democrats threw at him.

Our first big campaign event after the State of the Union was the next day — a "Spirit of America" rally in Atlanta with 18,000 people. We had so many people that we had to create an overflow facility in a nearby exhibit hall for 2,500 more.

Rich DeVos, cofounder of Amway Corp. and one of Reagan's biggest financial supporters, introduced Reagan, who gave a rousing speech. Congress had been pressing Reagan to support a tax increase but, he told the Atlanta crowd, he refused to "balance the budget on your backs" by raising taxes.

During the '84 campaign, I stayed on the White House payroll, and the time that I spent on political travel was billed to the Reagan-Bush '84 campaign. But I was starting to contemplate a change in jobs. I was married now, and my wife, Carole, was pregnant with our first child. The grueling, unpredictable travel and long hours of advance work nationwide and overseas were wearing, and I wanted to find work with a more predictable schedule. But I was committed to putting my full effort into getting President Reagan reelected.

In February, I started planning for President Reagan's visit to France for the fortieth anniversary of D-Day. The president would go to Normandy on June 6 to honor the U.S. and Allied soldiers who had landed that day in the largest seaborne invasion in history. I met with our embassy people in France in February and traveled to the windswept beaches of Normandy to figure out where the president would go there. With the approval of Deaver and Henkel, we settled on Pointe du Hoc, a spike of land that juts into the English Channel where 225 U.S. Rangers assaulted the 100-foot cliffs at dawn on D-Day, June 6, 1944. We also decided on a Reagan visit to Omaha Beach, part of the crescent-shaped coast where 50,000 men from the U.S. First Army attacked Nazi troops. The French chose Utah Beach for a closing Allied ceremony.

Reagan started his European trip on June 5 with a sentimental visit to Ireland to the little village of Ballyporeen, where his great-grandfather Michael had lived before emigrating to the United States in the 1800s. But the heart of the journey came when the president and Mrs. Reagan helicoptered across the English Channel the next day, June 6, to Normandy. Marine One landed right on time for many Americans on the East Coast to watch the beginning of the D-Day events on the morning network news shows.

We had located 27 survivors of the Army Ranger troops who had climbed the sand-colored cliffs in the face of withering German fire. They were seated next to Reagan at the top of the cliffs by a monument commemorating their harrowing feat — a rough granite dagger piercing a German concrete bunker.

Overlooking the rugged cliffs in the bright sun, the gray English Channel lapping quietly below us, Reagan recounted the exploits of the Rangers on that climactic day. Anyone who heard those eloquent words will never forget them.

The rangers "shot rope ladders over the face of these cliffs and began to pull themselves up," Reagan told the assembled guests. "When one ranger fell, another would take his place. When one rope was cut, a ranger would grab another and begin his climb again. Soon, one by one, the rangers pulled themselves over the top, and in seizing the firm land at the top of these cliffs, they began to seize back the continent of Europe.

"These are the boys of Pointe du Hoc," he said. "These are the men who took the cliffs. These are the champions who helped free a continent. These are the heroes who helped end a war."

It was almost as if we were back there on June 6, 1944. The rangers were in tears, many wiping their eyes. Reagan, old pro that he was, kept his composure.

For many months, we had believed that the fortieth anniversary of D-Day was made to order for Reagan. There was perhaps no president more appropriate than Ronald Reagan to commemorate that day in Normandy. He served in the military in World War II, though not in a combat role, and he believed strongly in the lessons of that great war. He lived through the war and he lived by it, applying that experience going forward better than anybody I knew. Totalitarianism brought only misery, he believed, and he believed strongly in freedom, in self-determination and, most important, in peace through strength. It was this singular vision that drove much of Reagan's presidency and led to later breakthroughs such as the INF treaty and the fostering of democracy around the world. Somehow, Reagan was able to look past his opposition — sometimes including members of his own party — to initiatives that he believed would further his ultimate goal of making the world safer.

In Normandy, the Reagans helicoptered from Pointe du Hoc to Omaha Beach and walked among the white marble crosses that marked the graves at the American Cemetery, where 9,380 men are buried. The rows and rows of crosses that stretched across the landscape carried an impeccable beauty, and I knew that the Reagans felt honored to be able to pay tribute to those who had made the ultimate sacrifice. I was concerned they would object to walking through the cemetery because it might seem disrespectful to step on the graves, but their executive assistant Dave Fischer reassured them that it was appropriate to do so, and the Reagans put flowers on the grave of the grandson of Teddy Roosevelt.

For Reagan's speech, Ann Higgins unearthed a letter from a woman whose father, Private First Class Peter Robert Zannata, of the 37th Engineer Combat Battalion, had been one of the first troops to assault the beach. Higgins gave the letter to Reagan's speechwriters. Zannata had died of cancer in 1976, but his daughter, Lisa Zanatta Henn, said in the letter that her father had described the assault to his family and had spoken of his desire to see the beach, the bunkers and the graves once again.

In his address, Reagan read from Lisa Zanatta Henn's letter about how her father watched many of his friends die and about how he died inside a little each time. Henn's father explained to her, " 'You did what you had to do, and you kept on going.' "

Lisa Zanatta Henn ended her letter to President Reagan by quoting her father when she told him she would go to see the beaches, the barricades, the monuments, and the graves and that she would put flowers there like he wanted to. "I'll never forget what you went through, Dad, nor will I let anyone else forget. And, Dad, I'll always be proud."

Reagan's voice cracked as he read the speech, his eyes shimmered with tears. Lisa Zannata Henn, who was in the front row, had tears streaming down her face. French President François Mitterrand, uncharacteristically, embraced Reagan after he spoke.

After the Allied ceremony at Utah Beach, it was 7:00 p.m. and we were done.

The Reagans' helicopter lifted off, and they went back to London. Our advance team was exhausted from the emotion and the exertions of the day. It was the hardest work I'd ever done, including laboring on my family's farm, working in a factory and on construction projects. At the same time, people would pay to have such a White House job.

Reagan's ability to capture the emotions of the moment, along with his tremendous personal appeal, was what made him the Great Communicator. Through his spoken words, he could connect emotionally with people in a way that was unparalleled. I saw it again later that year during the Los Angeles Olympics. In April, Deaver, Bill Sittman, Deaver's deputy, and I had met with L.A. Olympics chief Peter Ueberroth in the L.A. Coliseum, where the opening ceremonies of the Games would take place in late July. Reagan would make the traditional 16-word announcement that opens the Games from an enclosed, bulletproof press box high above the L.A. Coliseum. But the president wanted to do more than just recite a few words, and we searched for a way for the president and Mrs. Reagan to be more a part of the Olympics without exposing them to security risks and creating major logistical headaches for the athletes and the L.A. Olympic Organizing Committee.

Reagan never worried about the risks to himself, yet he was very concerned that his presence could endanger those around him. He said to me many times, "I'm a security threat to other people," and, for this reason, the president and Mrs. Reagan didn't participate in "normal" activities like millions of other Americans, such as attending church or going to restaurants for dinner. The day before he was shot, the president and the first lady had walked across Lafayette Park to attend a Sunday-morning service at St. John's Church. But after the shooting, they decided to forgo these visits, with only a few exceptions. Reagan didn't want to expose other churchgoers to the increased security risk caused by the presence of the president of the United States and the first lady, and he didn't like the disruption it caused others. Going through metal detectors, submitting to Secret Service searches — Reagan hated to inflict that inconvenience on those around him for those types of events.

For the Olympics, we settled on an event with the Reagans and the U.S. Olympic team, and we located an area on the campus of the University of Southern California, site of one of the Olympic villages, for the gathering. Greeted exuberantly with shouts of "U.S.A.! U.S.A.!" by the athletes, Reagan talked about the "new patriotism" as a "positive force, an attitude toward those things that are fundamental to America — that draw together our freedom, our decency, our sense of fair play as people."

He got a great response from the athletes when he urged them to "do it for the Gipper" — a reference to his movie role as George Gipp, a Notre Dame football player who died of cancer. Olympic sprinter Carl Lewis, unfortunately, snubbed the Reagans by skipping the meeting. But Ronald Reagan always understood.

Somewhat surprisingly, given his age, Reagan had a strong rapport with young people. As a former athlete himself, he loved spending time with athletes, even though he didn't watch sports on television, and he didn't like to go to games because they caused such security problems for other spectators. He was the first president to make it a regular tradition to have various athletic champions — World Series winners, Super Bowl champions, NCAA winning teams, U.S. Olympians — into the White House.

At one get-together with the Los Angeles Dodgers after they won the 1988 World Series, we brought owner Peter O'Malley, manager Tommy Lasorda and the entire team into the Oval Office before a congratulatory ceremony in the Rose Garden. In there, second baseman Steve Sax startled us all by doing Reagan impressions. Reagan just busted up laughing. He loved that sort of stuff.

In fact, as humble as Ronald Reagan was about being president, he was very proud of his athletic background and loved to show it off.

In December 1988, we were at a dinner honoring Congressman Jack Kemp, a former NFL quarterback. Kemp presented Reagan with a football. Immediately, Reagan looked around for someone to pass to. Oh God, I was thinking. Just put the ball down. But Reagan looked over, saw me in the wings of the stage and fired a bullet over to me.

In the '88 presidential campaign, on a campaign stop in Cleveland, we went to see the Cleveland Browns practice facility at Baldwin-Wallace College nearby in Berea, Ohio. We had an expanded press pool with us, and we had set it up so Reagan would throw a football to Ozzie

Newsome, the Browns' Hall of Fame-to-be tight end. Newsome got into position and waited for the ball from Reagan. However, our advance guy had screwed up. Newsome was supposed to run, and Reagan would throw a pass, but Newsome — as instructed by our site advance man — just stood there. Later, Reagan let me know that his visit to the Browns had fallen flat. He wanted to hit Newsome on the run.

After the 1984 opening ceremonies at the L.A. Olympics, we flew to Santa Barbara as the Reagans would begin their August vacation at Rancho del Cielo. I was on the second helicopter and was surprised to see Roosevelt "Rosie" Grier, legendary tackle for the Los Angeles Rams, on board. I had thought he was a stalwart Democrat — in fact, he had subdued Robert Kennedy's assassin, Sirhan Sirhan, in 1968 at the Ambassador Hotel in Los Angeles. I found out later that Grier had recently switched parties and had become a strong Republican and Reagan supporter. That certainly topped off a great weekend.

I was brought back down to earth shortly before the Republican National Convention in mid-August, when I managed to get tangled up in controversy during a campaign stop in Cincinnati. We had planned a big campaign rally in Fountain Square in downtown Cincinnati. But the day before the rally, I started getting phone calls from representatives of various fringe groups that said they planned demonstrations against Reagan at the rally. I was surprised that they were calling to tell me about their intentions and also that the Secret Service intelligence division had not picked up on any of this.

I called my boss, Bill Henkel, who was flying on Air Force One back from the Missouri state fair that Sunday afternoon, to tell him about the impending problem and to suggest that we ban signs from being brought into the event, to make the protesters less visible. We couldn't just forbid anti-Reagan signs, so even pro-Reagan signs would be confiscated at the entrances. Volunteers had already made hundreds of signs that we could give to people once they got past the Secret Service magnetometers into the rally site.

Henkel agreed, and we deployed teams of strong-minded volunteers to take away signs as people came to the rally. More than 20,000 people showed up for the rally on a beautiful, sunny day, and the protesters were lost in the large sea of support.

You could actually feel the vibrations at Fountain Square that day: people screaming "Four more years!," bands playing, tremendous enthusiasm.

Unfortunately, our event was tainted afterward when the Ohio Civil Liberties Union sued the Reagan-Bush '84 campaign and me for denying the protesters their First Amendment rights. We mounted our defense, and the White House press office dealt with the media onslaught while Reagan continued to forge ahead in the campaign.

Despite such adoration in Fountain Square — and traveling around the United States and the world, for that matter — Reagan stayed the same person he always was. At a stop in Nashville during the campaign, we went to the Grand Old Opry to celebrate legendary country singer Roy Acuff's eighty-first birthday. The plan was that Reagan would go onstage with Acuff and cut the ceremonial first slice of a birthday cake for Acuff. I met with Acuff the day before the event, and he was thrilled that the president would be there to celebrate his birthday with him.

But backstage, Reagan objected to cutting Acuff's cake. It wasn't his birthday, he insisted, it was Acuff's, so Acuff should cut the cake. David Fischer asked me to talk to Reagan about it. I tried, but Reagan maintained that, while he would stand there when Acuff cut the cake, it was rude for him to take the honor away from Acuff. "It's not right," he said. It was Acuff's day, and Reagan believed the attention should go to Acuff, not him. Typical Reagan.

I could tell that Reagan was going to remain firm about this. And when Ronald Reagan dug in his heels, there wasn't much that could be done. But he was right; it would look thoughtless if Reagan got all the attention at an event that was really for Acuff.

The event turned out to be a great undertaking — a flag-waving, raucous celebration. There was something magical about being onstage at the Grand Old Opry, where so many legendary country singers had performed. We got the picture of the day, Acuff cutting his cake with Reagan standing by. Country singer Greenberg Greenwood came out at the end and led the 3,500 people in a roof-raising rendition of "God Bless the U.S.A.," and at the crescendo, confetti showered down from the catwalk high above. Reagan even got a ringing endorsement from Acuff, who told the crowd,

"This feller, Mr. Reagan, has put our country back in order where it should be."

As the campaign wound on, Dave Fischer approached me in the summer of '84 with a proposal. We were waiting in a Winnebago, the president's holding room, for Reagan to finish a speech at the National Campers and Hikers Association outside Bowling Green, Kentucky. Fischer asked me what my plans were after the campaign. I told him I was thinking of doing something else in the administration that wouldn't involve so much travel. I'd been married for a little over a year, and our daughter Caitlin was only five months old.

"I've got a job for you," said Fischer.

"What?" I asked. "One of the federal agencies?"

"No," he said. "I'm leaving at the end of the year, and this job requires somebody who knows the Reagans. More important, we need somebody whom the Reagans can trust. I don't know anyone other than you who could do this. What do you think?"

"Of course," I said. "What do I need to do to apply for it?"

"Nothing," Fischer told me. "I'll talk to the Reagans, Deaver and Jim Baker."

Fischer pointed out that the hours were

long and there was plenty of travel, since the president's executive assistant travels everywhere with the president. But I would have a predictable schedule built around the president's. Also, some of the president's schedule was planned up to six months in advance (barring unexpected events, of course) and many domestic trips were usually day trips. Foreign trips were longer, of course, but I would travel with the president, instead of spending weeks in far-off locations planning those visits.

I kept quiet about my conversation with Fischer and waited. First we had to get the president reelected.

Reagan was renominated at a triumphant August Republican National Convention in Dallas, at which he talked about a "springtime of hope for America." Our official campaign kickoff was a Labor Day rally in Orange County, an area of bedrock Reagan support, with a subsequent event the same day in Silicon Valley in northern California. We had aimed to have 35,000 people at the Orange County event in Fountain Valley, but the turnout far exceeded even our greatest expectations. In a massive show of support for President Reagan, more than 80,000 people showed up — so many that they overwhelmed the

Secret Service metal detectors, and the newspapers reported the next day that 20,000 people had to be turned away. That night on the evening news in a twist of irony, NBC correspondent Chris Wallace even described the Orange County celebration as a "Woodstock-like setting."

With political support like that, we were confident that Reagan and Vice President Bush would power past Democratic candidate Walter Mondale, who made the monumental mistake of promising at the Democratic National Convention in San Francisco that he and his running mate, Geraldine Ferraro, would raise taxes.

But we hit some bumps along the way.

Reagan's first of two debates with Walter Mondale in Louisville in October came up short. Dick Darman, assistant to the president and staff secretary, led the debate preparations, but he stuffed the president full of microdetails about policies, issues and what-all. So in the debate, instead of presenting the big-picture perspective of his optimistic vision for America, the president was clearly thrown off-stride.

The postmortems were not kind. Reagan's age — 73 — suddenly became a factor in the campaign. The networks showed footage of Reagan's falling asleep on the pope, a headline in the *Wall Street Journal* read IS THE OLDEST U.S. PRESIDENT SHOWING HIS AGE? and the *Washington Post* reported that Congressman Tony Coelho, chairman of the Democratic Congressional Campaign Committee, said Reagan "looked old and acted old." The president's poll numbers slipped.

Both the president and Mrs. Reagan were upset about Reagan's debate performance and its aftermath. Reagan's strength lay in his ability to articulate his big vision and convey that vision to Americans, and he clearly hadn't done that during the Louisville debate. Also, although the president and those of us close to him knew the speculation that he was too old for the job wasn't true, it really bothered Reagan this time. After the debate, at Chicago-area campaign appearances that I was in charge of, Reagan, after disembarking from Marine One, waved off the limo that was supposed to drive him the short distance to one event — a speech at a suburban Chicago high school. Rather, he told the Secret Service, he would walk. On his way, he jumped a rail fence in front of the press, showing them he wasn't too old to be president. Reagan also refused the limo after

Marine One landed at the third Chicago stop that day, a political rally at DuPage County Community College.

Before the next debate later that month in Kansas City, Mrs. Reagan and Deaver stepped in and made sure that Reagan wasn't so loaded up with facts that he lost sight of what he wanted to communicate. This time, the real Ronald Reagan returned. He took the age issue and slammed it into the mat with a superbly delivered one-liner when a debate moderator, journalist Henry Trewhitt, asked him if he had any doubts about his ability to function as president.

"Not at all, Mr. Trewhitt," Reagan replied, "and I want you to know that also I will not make age an issue of this campaign. I'm not going to exploit, for political purposes, my opponent's age and inexperience."

The debate audience roared with laughter, and even Mondale chuckled. Later, polls showed that voters overwhelmingly believed that Reagan had won the debate, and his performance renewed voters' faith in the president and allayed their fears that Reagan was over the hill.

Election Day proved to be the triumph we had hoped for. That afternoon, presidential pollster Dick Wirthlin gave the Reagans a winding analysis of the campaign and various mundane scenarios on how Reagan could beat Mondale. But Ed Rollins, longtime senior political adviser and campaign director, was more decisive.

"It's a fact," he told the Reagans. "You're going to win forty-nine states, but you're going to lose Minnesota."

Mrs. Reagan, who always worried, challenged him. "How can you say that so confidently?" she asked.

The Reagans didn't leave the results to chance. To keep their good luck flowing on election night '84, the Reagans repeated the same routine as they had on election night '80. They dined at the home of Earle and Marion Jorgensen again, with the same guests and the same menu as four years earlier, and planned a victory rally with supporters again for later in the evening at the Century Plaza Hotel while utilizing the same stage as '80. This time, of course, there were some differences because Reagan was president. The White House Communications Agency had a switchboard set up in Los Angeles. Also, Mondale didn't concede as early as Jimmy Carter had, so Reagan was at dinner, rather than in the shower, when he got the concession call. I was at the Jorgensens' that night, and Dave Fischer invited me to come into the presidential holding room for Mondale's call. It was brief. Mondale was cordial. Reagan thanked him, and that was that.

Both of the Reagans were very superstitious. I remember in Reagan's second term, I was telling the president about the prospects of a key vote on Capitol Hill. "Hopefully," I said, crossing the fingers on both hands, "the votes will be there."

He recoiled. "Don't do that!" he said.

"Do what?" I said. I was perplexed.

"Cross the fingers of both hands," he said. "If you cross both, it cancels out the luck."

For election night '84, so many people wanted to cram into the Century Plaza that the fire marshal's office threatened to shut us down.

Campaign advance men live in fear of fire marshals. Fire marshals dislike overflowing crowds crammed into rooms, and advance men love them. Fire marshals see the fire hazard. We see great footage and photos.

At the Century Plaza, the fire marshals not only limited the number of people to about 1,000 — from upward of 3,000 that we had planned — they also tried to ban the balloons and confetti. It was absurd! I figured I couldn't appeal to Los Angeles Mayor Tom Bradley, because he was a Democrat and singularly uninterested in helping us out. So for help, I called Lyn Nofziger, who was back in California and planning to attend the election night events. But Nofziger wasn't optimistic.

"You're in a Democratic world out here," he said. "The city isn't going to do much to help Ronald Reagan."

I pleaded with the fire marshal, telling him that Reagan's supporters deserved to see him that night. "They've worked hard," I said. "It's a big night for them." In the end, the fire marshal's office relented a bit, but we still had to shut out many people who wanted to come in. When Reagan came out for his victory speech, I could see some gaps in the crowd in the back — the worst sight for an advance man. But it was still a significant event, and a monumental evening, with much more on the Reagan agenda.

In late 1984, I began making the transition to executive assistant to President Reagan. Getting the job had been the one time in my life when I didn't have to do anything to get something that I very much wanted. Dave Fischer started bringing me over to the West Wing to show me the ropes until he departed in early 1985.

In December of '84, I did my first solo trip to Camp David — my second time to Camp David but my first without Dave Fischer.

The Reagans loved Camp David and, in Reagan's second term, I spent 91 weekends at the presidential retreat with them. The bucolic, 250-acre compound sits on top of a small mountaintop in the Cacoctin Mountains, 80 miles north of Washington. President Franklin Roosevelt, the first president to use it, called it Shangri-La.

Camp David is in a wooded, rustic setting and it is guarded and, thus, the Reagans enjoyed much more freedom there than at the White House. In fact, in President Reagan's exit interviews as his second term neared its end, Reagan always said that the only part of the presidency he would miss would be Camp David.

In Washington, the president and Mrs. Reagan didn't go out much for impromptu dinners or evenings out with friends because they didn't want to inconvenience anyone, and such occasions were always a logistical issue for staff and Secret Service.

Intersections had to be closed off. Tents had to be put up so the presidential limo could pull up to a facility and not be seen by the public. They socialized more when they went to Los Angeles, when they could go to friends' homes, such as Betsy Bloomingale's, Charles and Mary Jane Wick's or the Jorgensens', among several others. While in Washington, they relied on Camp David for rest and recreation.

At Camp David, the Reagans stayed at Aspen Cabin, which had a living and dining area, a bedroom suite, a guestroom and a large kitchen. Reagan had an office, but he preferred to work in a cushioned, low-back chair near the big living-room window that overlooked the swimming pool. On a clear night, you could see the lights of Emmettsville, Maryland, sparkling miles below.

Over the years, Reagan had developed an undeserved reputation for being anything but a workaholic. At one press conference, he cracked, "Mike Deaver said that I have a short attention span. I was going to reply to that but, what the hell, let's move on to something else."

But, jokes aside, Ronald Reagan was definitely not a slacker. He was always busy with something important. I never saw him when he wasn't working — reading, writing, dealing with significant issues or policy matters — whether it was in the White House residence or Oval Office, on Air Force One or Marine One, at Camp David, in hotel suites in the United States and around the world. He was a voracious reader, and he also loved to write. At the end of the workday at the White House, he always went upstairs with a stack of briefing material to get through that evening, and he always came down the next day having read everything and knowing it all. Every time I saw President Reagan over the four years of his second term, he was working. He never just relaxed or watched television, and I never saw him take a nap. At Camp David, the television was usually on just for Sunday-morning talk shows or various other news shows.

Some critics unfairly contrasted Reagan's work habits to those of Carter who, it was claimed, came downstairs to the Oval Office at 4:30 or 5:00 a.m. during the Iranian hostage crisis to work at his desk. When you work in the White House, you learn much about its previous residents, and I was told by reliable sources that Carter would actually retreat to his study and go back to sleep on the couch. However, the press would report that President Carter was hard at work in the Oval Office before dawn. I'm not trying to take a swipe at Carter here. I just believe that Reagan sometimes got a bum rap.

At Camp David, the Reagans liked taking long walks on the paths that wound through the retreat, and the president enjoyed riding horses there. The U.S. Park Police transported horses from its stables in Washington for the president, Mrs. Reagan and their security detail. But Reagan was sensitive about the inconvenience to the police and the strain on the horses of making that 80-mile trek up to Camp David. So if the weather forecast was in any way iffy, he always asked me to cancel the horses for the weekend. The camp commander used to insist to me that the Park Police should always bring the horses to Camp David just in case the weather cleared up, but Reagan would rather give up a weekend of riding than cause an unnecessary burden.

On weekends that the Reagans were going to Camp David, we used to leave about 3:30 p.m. on Fridays. On those days, the president generally worked in the Oval Office — he always wore a suit and tie to the Oval Office on weekdays and never took his suit coat off, out of respect for the office of the presidency — and changed into casual clothes before departure, although he hated changing clothes in the middle of the day.

During most of my tenure as Reagan's assistant, Navy Commander Jim Broaddus ran Camp David. Reagan told me he was the best commander out of the five who had run the presidential retreat during Reagan's terms in office. Broaddus was responsible for many improvements in the naval facility, including the construction of a fitness center and also raising private funds for the construction of a chapel on the grounds. The Reagans participated in a small groundbreaking ceremony when construction of the chapel began, although Reagan was out of office by the time it was complete.

Only a few White House individuals stayed at Camp David for the weekend — me, the White House doctor, assistant press secretary Mark Weinberg, and the military aide. The Reagans graciously invited the families of the executive assistant and doctor to Camp David, so my family was there virtually every weekend that I was. First, it was just my wife, Carole, and our daughter Caitlin. Then with the additions of our son, Greg, in '86, and our daughter Alyssa in '88, all five of us spent weekends there. We stayed in Red Oak Cabin, about 150 yards from the Reagans' cabin.

Normally, I flew with the Reagans on Marine One — about a 30-minute trip — while Carole drove up with the children and met us there. But midway through Reagan's second term, when the threats of terrorism increased dramatically, he asked me to travel with Carole and the children instead of taking Marine One with him because of the increased risk.

"I want you driving up with your family," he told me. "I would feel better about it. I just think you ought to be with them instead of me with the new level of terrorist threats from Iran."

So for about three months, Carole fought rush-hour traffic to get into Washington from our home in Alexandria to pick me up, and we drove out of Washington and headed north to Camp David together. Finally, it got to be too much. One Saturday at Camp David, after his radio address, the president asked Carole how the Friday drives were going.

Carole gave it to him straight.

"Mr. President, it's not going so well,"

she said. "He's never ready, and the traffic is always bad. And it's like having another kid in the car. Would you please put him back on the helicopter?"

"Really?" said Reagan. "That would be easier for you?"

"Yes," Carole said. "Take him back . . . please!"

So I returned to traveling on Marine One, and our journeys went more smoothly.

The Reagans loved having children around. One time, Greg was playing on the floor right behind Mrs. Reagan, and she backed up and almost fell over him. I apologized, but she just laughed.

"Jim," she said, "enjoy them now. They'll be twenty tomorrow."

"What do you mean?" I asked.

"You'll find out," she said. "They're going to grow up so fast."

Now that my children are almost grown, I know what Mrs. Reagan meant. She couldn't have been more correct.

If we were at Camp David on Saturdays, then Reagan did his live weekly radio address from there, promptly at 12:06 p.m. As a former radio broadcaster, he took great pride in doing his radio addresses live instead of prerecording them. In fact, he only taped them if he was traveling, and the time change made it impossible for a live broadcast. If we were in the White House, he did the broadcasts from the Oval Office. At the ranch, he broadcast from one of the small, temporary "huts" set up there by the Navy Seabees during his presidency. At Camp David, he did them from Laurel Lodge.

The radio addresses were supposed to run five minutes, and although the radio networks could always adjust if they ran slightly short or slightly long, Reagan made it a formality to get them to come out at exactly five minutes. In order to do that, he rehearsed the written remarks beforehand, looking at his watch to time himself and then marking the script at each one-minute mark.

Then, when he delivered the remarks live, we timed him with a stopwatch and signaled at every one-minute mark. He checked the marks on his script to make sure he was on pace. If he was slightly behind, he sped up, and if he was ahead, he slowed down. He always came in at five minutes and was never off by more than a second or two. As simple as it sounds, it was important for him to get it right. I guess broadcasters never break their former habits.

On Friday and Saturday nights at Camp David, the Reagans usually watched movies and always invited the small support team to join them. Mark Weinberg always brought chocolates. One evening, however, the Reagans' big dog, Lucky, whom the Reagans had received as a gift in 1984, stuck her nose in the candies and began lapping them up. Saying, "No, Lucky, you can't have these!," the president pulled her back before she attempted to polish off the box.

For movies, the Reagans liked films from their Hollywood era, and over the years, we watched movies like *African Queen*, *The Maltese Falcon* and *Roman Holiday* and some of the Reagans' movies, including *The Winning Team*, *King's Row* and *Hellcats of the Navy*. We also screened contemporary films, including *Prizzi's Honor*, *Top Gun* and *Ferris Bueller's Day Off*, but they really preferred the golden oldies. In the first term, Dave Fischer once made the mistake of suggesting *The Big Chill*, a movie about a weekend reunion of a band of baby boomers, and Mrs. Reagan disliked it. Too much drugs and sex, she said.

One evening in Reagan's second term, we watched *Kiss of the Spider Woman*, the story of a cross-dressing transvestite and his roommate in a Mexican prison. Mike Deaver, who had left the administration by then, had recommended it.

After the movie ended, there was silence for a moment. Then the president stood up from the couch, with a look of irritated disbelief.

"Well," he said, "I would like to know one thing — what the hell has gotten into Mike Deaver since he's gone into the private sector?" He shook his head.

Over the years, history had been made in the relatively modest cabins that dotted the Camp David retreat. In Jimmy Carter's administration, Egyptian President Anwar Sadat and Israeli Prime Minister Menachem Begin agreed to their historic peace accord there in 1978.

But the Reagans preferred it as more of a private retreat. Aside from Reagan family members and some close friends, relatively few others — mostly just a handful of world leaders — visited. I remember flipping through the guest book near the end of Reagan's second term and found that in eight years, the numbers of overnight guests who'd signed it had filled up just a few pages.

One world leader who visited Camp

David was Japanese Prime Minister Nakasone in 1986. He presented the president with Sony's latest handheld TV and audio device, which hadn't yet arrived in U.S. markets.

"We are going to invade your markets with this product," the quiet prime minister told Reagan with a broad smile.

Reagan happily accepted the gift. It was at a time when the Japanese economy was booming, and Japanese products were pouring into U.S. markets and Japanese investors were snapping up prominent American assets. But none of this bothered Reagan.

"I don't have a problem with countries like Japan that see the United States as a very good investment," he told me.

At times, Reagan conducted other business at Camp David as well. In 1987, for instance, then-General Electric CEO Jack Welch came to Camp David to discuss the imminent airing of an NBC News segment on the U.S. Navy's secret "hydrophone" system — extremely sensitive underwater listening devices that were used starting in the '60s to track Soviet submarines in the North Atlantic, Pacific and Mediterranean. It was highly sophisticated and very effective. The president was concerned about the effect the revelations by NBC would have on the U.S. intelligence capabilities. GE owned NBC, and Vice President Bush and Welch were close friends, so Bush arranged for a meeting between Reagan and Welch at Camp David to discuss the matter. Bush alerted us that Welch liked martinis and suggested we offer him one when he came up. Later that same day, Welch helicoptered from GE headquarters in Fairfield, Connecticut, to Camp David. I met him at the Camp David landing zone and rode with him to Aspen Cabin. President Reagan was waiting for us and played the gracious host.

"I've been told by a close friend — and you know who I mean — that you're a martini drinker, and we're here to fill that order," he said.

Welch smilingly turned him down. "Mr. President, I'm here to discuss a serious issue with you. I don't think I can do that and drink a martini at the same time," he said. "But thank you, though."

They met for about an hour, and Reagan told me later that it had gone well and that Welch understood the implications of running the story and would discuss the matter with others. In the end, NBC delayed the story and then ran a toned-down version that didn't reveal as much as we had feared.

On my first weekend working solo as the president's executive assistant in December 1984, Prime Minister Margaret Thatcher came to Camp David for a Saturday meeting and lunch. I found her to be rather cold and officious, but President Reagan adored her. They had met in the 1970s, before each came into office, on a trip Reagan took to England. They discovered they shared the same philosophy when it came to smaller government and expanding economic freedom.

Thatcher just lit up around Reagan, and he lit up around her. She made two visits to Camp David; the other was in November 1986 when the two discussed nuclear deterrence and a host of bilateral issues. At that time, they met one on one and then joined their advisers in Laurel Lodge for a plenary session. Thatcher dominated the first half of the expanded meeting. She rambled on for 45 minutes about the Soviet Union, the world economy, trade and aviation issues. Reagan just listened. During the break, I got the president alone and asked him about her lengthy remarks.

"Mr. President," I said, "I know you

have a great rapport with the prime minister, but you haven't said anything. You have lots of points you need to make."

The president just smiled. "Jim," he said, "you've got to understand that Maggie and I are old friends, and I just couldn't step in like that. She's much too dear of a friend."

But in the second half of the talks, the president managed to get in all his points. He had his own effective way of handling her.

At that weekend in 1984, however, Thatcher brought the president some intriguing news. She had recently met with an up-and-coming Soviet Union government official who, she told Reagan, was likely to become the leader of the Soviet Union once current U.S.S.R. leader Konstantin Chernenko passed on.

This fellow, Thatcher told Reagan, was different from the usual brand of Soviet Communist leaders. He was someone with whom Reagan could engage, she said, more forward-looking, more open to the West and intensely aware of the economic problems of the Soviet Union.

His name was Mikhail Gorbachev.

13

EXECUTIVE ASSISTANT TO THE PRESIDENT

We were in Portugal, the last stop on an eventful European trip in 1985. When we arrived at the old presidential guesthouse in Lisbon where we would spend two nights, the drapes were drawn, but we could hear the muffled sounds of a demonstration taking place across the street from our residence. Reagan and I were upstairs together, and he was eager to catch a glimpse of the protesters. We tried to open the thick, floor-length curtains, but they had been pinned shut by the Secret Service. Suddenly, Reagan spied a door leading to a small balcony overlooking the demonstration.

"Let's go out there," he suggested.

I was floored. "You can't go out there," I said. "The Secret Service would go crazy."

Reagan grinned at me. "Watch me," he said, and opened the door and stepped onto the rooftop deck. Shirtless, he leaned over the short wall to gaze below at the hundreds of shouting protesters demonstrating against him in the streets.

I entreated him to come back into the room. "They might *see* you."

"So what?" shrugged Reagan.

Fortunately, none of the Lisbon demonstrators looked up or they would have glimpsed the bare-chested president of the United States surveying them!

This was the Ronald Reagan I got to know in my four years as his executive assistant in his second term. When he was visible — whether it was in meetings in the Oval Office or in the cabinet room, events in the Rose Garden, at press conferences and speeches in front of the nation or on the other side of the world — he was bigger than life as the president of the United States. He looked, spoke and breathed the part. But when you were alone with him, he was the nicest, most regular guy in the world.

When I took over from Dave Fischer shortly after the president's second term began, Fischer gave me some wise advice.

"He's so unassuming and so completely unaffected by the power of the presidency," Fischer said, "that you're going to have to keep reminding yourself that he's president."

Fischer was right. In the White House, I discovered, Reagan was the same man that

I came to know in the 1970s. He was not driven to be the star of the show and had no temperamental displays to which some public figures are prone when not on public display. At the same time, he had enormous respect for the office of the presidency and took it very seriously. But he never took himself too seriously.

I remember one time, also in 1985, we were in Quebec City to meet with Canadian Prime Minister Brian Mulroney. Reagan and Mulroney, two delightful Irishmen, had always hit it off. Mulroney called Reagan Ron, and Reagan always called him Brian. They liked to exchange jokes and some light banter when they got together.

Both leaders were scheduled to speak at an event at the beginning of the Quebec City trip, which required Mulroney and Reagan to walk into the event together. But, I earnestly explained to them, protocol dictated that they wait until the others in the U.S. and Canadian delegations had taken their places in the room first, which seemed to be taking a long time.

Reagan looked at Mulroney and grinned. "Brian, it's protocol — spelled bullshit."

Mulroney just about fell down laughing.

Inevitably, presidents of the United States make faux pas from time to time, but Reagan never let his faze him. After the 1985 World Series, Reagan called the world champion Kansas City Royals' locker room to congratulate the Royals on beating the St. Louis Cardinals. Relief pitcher Dan Quisenberry had played a pivotal role in the series, and Reagan praised the pitcher to manager Dick Howser by pointing out the great relief pitching by "Jim" Quisenberry. But Quisenberry's first name was Dan.

When thc Royals came to the White House later that fall, Reagan apologized for mixing up Quisenberry's name when he was shaking hands with him in the Rose Garden. I didn't catch Quisenberry's reply, but I suddenly saw Reagan double over with laughter. When we returned to the Oval Office after the ceremony, I asked the president what was so funny out there. He said that when he apologized to Quisenberry for calling him by the wrong name after the World Series, Quisenberry looked him straight in the eye and said, "That's all right, Don."

Ronald Reagan loved to joke around with people and when he made a goof, he thought it was as funny as everybody else did.

At a campaign rally at the University of Oklahoma for Senator Don Nickles in 1986, I was reading along with a written copy of the president's speech as he delivered it. When it came to Nickles's name, I heard him say "Don Rickles," the famous comedian. I looked around, hoping nobody else had heard it. There was no visible reaction from the crowd or from the press, except Sam Donaldson, who was jumping up and down in front of the podium. I could hear him say: "He called him Don Rickles! He called him Don Rickles!" I told the president about the slip-up later. He thought it was hilarious.

In 1987, in the midst of the Iran-contra madness, we put together a surprise seventy-sixth birthday for the president with Mrs. Reagan and 200-plus White House staff and guests in the Old Executive Office Building. To get Reagan to the party, we devised a ruse of telling him he was going to speak to a business group, and we even put together a speech for him, which he reviewed and marked up. When the president entered the room, we kicked off the birthday celebration. Then Mrs. Reagan came out on the stage and surprised the president. But, sure enough, after cutting the cake, Reagan approached the podium and took out the notes for his speech. Mrs. Reagan grabbed him. "No, honey," she said, and told him the event was just a cover for his birthday party. The president threw his speech over his shoulder, laughed and went on to enjoy his party.

As president, Ronald Reagan drew neither emotional sustenance nor his sense of self from the attention and admiration of others. He knew himself very well — his strengths and his weaknesses. For example, when he met with a head of government, he carried small cards with notes on them in his pockct to remind himself of key points he needed to make with the leader. The White House press office staff — Larry Speakes and Mark Weinberg — always went crazy when he displayed his note cards during photo ops, when the White House and visiting press photographed him and the international leader.

"He just pulled the cards out," one of them would say to me in exasperation as photographers clicked away. "Can't you get him to put them away? We don't need photos of him with his note cards." So in between photos, I would go over and whisper in his ear, "Mr. President, could you put the cards back in your pocket until you might need them?"

Reagan would always shoot me a mildly perturbed look. He didn't much care if the press saw the note cards. His attitude was that if he had to refer to his notes in order to refer to the finer points of an issue, so be it. He didn't mind if anyone — a head of government, his staff, the press, the public — knew it. Reagan was never worried about the loss of any mystique he had as president.

But as President Reagan's executive assistant, it was my job to worry about such details. That job, more than anything, was to protect the president. Not from physical harm, of course. We had the Secret Service for that formidable task. My job was to safeguard him from all the other forces at work around the office of the president. After all, I was with him all day, every day — the one constant in a churning sea of faces, issues and policies.

The given was that Ronald Reagan wasn't a detail person. His strength was maintaining a vast perspective. Throughout his political career, he was accustomed to having a right-hand person to help him manage the myriad details of his life and his job. That became even more important when he was president because of the enormous competing demands on his time.

On weekdays, after the 8:00 a.m. meeting with the White House chief of staff and other senior White House staff, my day with the president started when I met him at the bottom of the elevator on the ground floor of the White House residence. From there, accompanied by his ever-present Secret Service detail, we walked to the Oval Office in the West Wing. In those days, the only route from the White House residence to the Oval Office was outside, around the back of the White House on the Colonnade, a columned walkway that wound past the Rose Garden and the press room in the West Wing of the White House.

On the walk, I briefed the president on the highlights or changes in the day's schedule, although with constantly changing world and domestic events, it was always a work in progress. Within just a couple of hours, for example, the president could find himself greeting a group of Girl Scouts, meeting a visiting foreign dignitary, convening a meeting with his national security team to discuss a fast-breaking world crisis, congratulating a championship sports team, meeting with corporate leaders, discussing issues with various members of his cabinet and negotiating with congressional leaders over legislation. There could be phone calls, Rose Garden ceremonies, drafts of upcoming speeches to be reviewed, maybe a trip to the Old Executive Office Building or a local hotel to deliver remarks at a luncheon or conference. He was constantly switching gears — from domestic to foreign policy, from engaging with the press to legislative affairs. Along the way, there were crises, disasters and what all.

On our daily Colonnade walk, I had to talk fast because as soon as Reagan reached his desk, he was ready to go. On mornings when I had a lot to cover, I met the president upstairs in the residence. Once the president was in the Oval Office, I used one of his phones to call the vice president and chief of staff to let them know that the president was in and ready for their daily morning meeting.

As president, Reagan retained his dislike of tardiness, his own or others'. In the spring of 1985, for example, at one of our first outdoor events of the season, the president and I were in the Oval Office as the White House staff started bringing people into the Rose Garden for a signing ceremony about a half hour before the event. From the Oval Office, the president could see the growing crowd and grew agitated as we tried to complete some paperwork before going out to the ceremony.

"Look at them," he said impatiently, pacing up and down. "They're all waiting for me."

"You can't go out, Mr. President," I said, "until the press is ready and everything is set."

The president didn't like to keep anyone waiting. So from then on, we asked the White House staff to bring people into the Rose Garden for an event just five minutes to 10 minutes ahead of time because when the president saw them, he would want to go out and get things going. He had a big heart, and he hated to put people out by forcing them to wait for him.

When others were late for meetings with him, the president could get upset because it threw his schedule off, meaning subsequent meeting participants or guests would have to wait for him as the day went on. For example, Bob Dole — Senate majority leader, and later minority leader — was late virtually every time for the president's regular Tuesday 9:30 a.m. meeting with Republican congressional leaders in the cabinet room when Congress was in session. We couldn't start the meeting without Dole, so the president would work at his desk in the Oval Office until everyone had gathered. But Dole's lateness really bothered Reagan. He would grimace, look at his watch, then glance up at the grandfather clock on the other side of the Oval Office and throw his pen down impatiently.

"Everybody else is in there waiting?" he would ask. "Let me know when Bob gets here. We've got a full day to get through."

One day in his second term, a number of foreign ambassadors were coming through to present their credentials to the president. We were running late, and the president was anxious to get to his 4:30 p.m. haircut appointment downstairs in the White House barbershop. As the clock ticked toward 4:30, we still had two ambassadors to go.

"Jim, you'd better get these next two guys in here fast," Reagan told me, "or they're going to have to go downstairs and present their credentials to me while I'm in the barber's chair."

Fortunately, we hustled them through quickly.

Of course, there were times when we simply couldn't stay on schedule. On the days when there were lots of moving pieces, I'd just tell him: "Right now, we have to tear up your schedule for the day, and we're going to be rolling with the punches all day long." That would be just fine with him as long as he knew what we were dealing with.

Along with my duty to keep the president on schedule and ensure he knew what to expect, and what was expected from him in every situation into which he went, I also felt it was my job to try to safeguard him from other people — members of Congress, foreign leaders, business leaders, the media, White House staff, members of his cabinet, occasionally even the first lady.

I was constantly on the lookout for people who wanted something they shouldn't be asking for. Once they had an audience with the president, they would seize the opportunity to take advantage of the nicest human being I have ever met.

In 1987, Secretary of State George Shultz got the president to sign a memo requiring top White House staff with national security clearances — the White House chief of staff and the national security adviser — to always travel on military aircraft so they could stay in secure communications with the White House at all times. Shultz came up with the policy after the White House Office of Administration challenged his request for a plane to fly him to the San Francisco area in order to go to Stanford University on homecoming weekend. He presented this "decision memorandum" directly to the president instead of sending it through the clearance system at the White House that was supposed to vet every document that ended up on the president's desk. Reagan approved the memorandum, which later led to the demise of President George H. W. Bush's chief of staff, John Sununu, for use of military aircraft on personal trips. Ultimately, Shultz knew that if those who ranked below him, such as the chief of staff and the national security adviser, always had military planes, then he would no longer be challenged again on his use of aircraft.

Some particular individuals used to meet with the president in private, but as they almost always asked the president for some favor, these meetings had to be staffed in order to prevent such occurrences. And staff members learned to be skilled at deflecting requests to the president. At the end of 1987, long-serving Reagan speechwriter Dana Rohrabacher was leaving to run for the House of Representatives. He came in to say good-bye to the president, but asked for a favor. Would the president ask Walter Annenberg, a longtime friend of the Reagans' and a billionaire businessman, to do a fund-raiser for him? Reagan hated to say no to Rohrabacher, but he was uncomfortable with calling Annenberg up and asking for a favor himself, even though Annenberg would have done it in a New York minute! Reagan handed it off to Deputy Chief of Staff Ken Duberstein, but the fund-raiser did not become a reality. But Reagan himself made a campaign appearance in California, which included Rohrabacher, who had devoted many years of service to him, and Rohrabacher was easily elected as a congressman from Orange County, California. At the same time, if you were going to make an exception for individuals, then Rohrabacher led that list.

In my eight years of service to the president, I did ask for one small favor from the president, and — typical Reagan — he said yes immediately. In September 1987, we were in Miami where the Reagans were having a private meeting with the pope upon his arrival in the United States. Normally, anyone in the official party — and that included senior White House staff — could greet the pope after the president's meeting and get their picture taken. But that day, there was no official party, and it was understood that no one except the Reagans would have contact with the pope. It occurred to me that Mark Weinberg and I had never actually met the pope, even though we had been to the Vatican twice during the Reagans' meetings with His Holiness. Both of us wanted to meet him and have our photos taken with him. We probably wouldn't get the chance after Reagan left office.

After we got to Miami, I talked to the president about it when we had a few minutes alone. I told him that it had been determined that only he and Mrs. Reagan would see the pope, and I asked him to make an exception for us. He smiled and said: "I would be delighted to present you and Mark to the pope."

So at the appropriate time, Reagan introduced us to Pope John Paul, explaining to him that we had worked for him since the beginning of his presidency. "Your Holiness, I would like to present to you Jim Kuhn and Mark Weinberg," he said.

The pope, who had also been informed that he would meet only the Reagans on this stop, was very gracious, smiling at us warmly. In fact, he reminded me of Queen Elizabeth — easygoing and pleasant despite his worldwide fame.

But I think the hardest part of my job was protecting the president from himself. While there was no one better to work for, Reagan could also be the most obstinate. Sometimes he would decide on what course of action, and there wasn't any way in hell we could talk him out of it even if it was against his best interests. It was like trying to win a tug-of-war with a horse. At times, even Mrs. Reagan lost.

One key area of Reagan's stubbornness was that he always kept his promises, consequences be damned.

Nowhere was that tendency more evident than in the Bitburg controversy in 1985. It all started when West German Chancellor Helmut Kohl invited the president and Mrs. Reagan for a state visit to his country after the Bonn economic summit in May. The Reagans accepted. It was decided that President Reagan and Chancellor Kohl, at Kohl's request, would lay a wreath at a Germany military cemetery as a gesture of reconciliation with the Germans on the fortieth anniversary of the Allied victory in Europe, although there was concern in the White House about whether it was politically safe to visit such a site, even 40 years after war with Germany. The Germans selected a cemetery near Bitburg, in western West Germany, where 2,000 Germans were buried. Mike Deaver led the survey team to Europe in early 1985 to get an overview of each meeting and event site for the entire European trip. In Bitburg, unfortunately, snow covered some of the graves and the White House team, including senior U.S. embassy representatives, didn't see that some members of Hitler's elite Nazi SS troops were buried there.

The press found them soon after that, however, and a firestorm of criticism hit the president. War veterans' groups and dozens of Jewish organizations implored Reagan not to visit Bitburg. Several state legislatures sent resolutions to President Reagan asking him to call off the visit. In April, 82 senators approved a resolution urging Reagan to reassess the stop, and more than 250 House members wrote Kohl asking him to withdraw the invitation.

Many in the White House and the world community wanted Reagan to take Bitburg off his schedule. But Ronald Reagan had given his word to Helmut Kohl that he would go to Bitburg with him and nothing short of Chancellor Kohl himself could change that.

The controversy just wouldn't go away, but Reagan held fast. The bottom line for Reagan was that when he made a commitment, it was set in stone, no matter the consequences.

In late April, matters got worse for us when author Elie Wiesel, a survivor of two Nazi death camps, came to the White House. Reagan and Wiesel met privately in the Oval Office, where Reagan explained his rationale for visiting the Bitburg cemetery. But when they spoke to a select audience and media in the Roosevelt Room, Wiesel slammed Reagan for his decision. "That place is not your place," he told Reagan, who was standing next to him. "Your place is with the victims of the SS."

We were caught completely offguard by Wiesel's attack. We had thought he was coming in to give an endorsement to Reagan because of the president's strong stance in favor of Jewish emigration out of the Soviet Union. Instead, Wiesel ripped into Reagan in front of the White House press corps. But Reagan just took it. He never expressed anger about Wiesel's comments. But neither did they dissuade him.

Several weeks before the trip, Reagan and Kohl, who was also getting torn apart in his own country about the visit, spoke by phone — one of the longest phone calls of Reagan's presidency. They discussed the trip, and the White House senior staff was hoping that Kohl would pull the plug. I didn't think there was much chance of that, however.

After Reagan got off the phone, I asked him, "Any new developments?"

"Nope," the president said. "We're going."

"I know," I said. "You committed to go. You gave him your word."

The president nodded. "He still wants to do it and so be it."

That was Reagan. He never believed in doing anything for political gain, but rather because it was the right thing to do in terms of the national interest or, in this case, not going back on his word. He used to tell his advisers that he didn't want to know how he was going to gain or lose politically from any policy decision. In the case of the Bitburg trip, Reagan was convinced that keeping his promise was the right thing to do.

In the end, a former U.S. Army general, 90-year-old Matthew Ridgeway, stepped forward and offered to lay the wreath for Reagan. He would have a German counterpart perform the same role for Chancellor Kohl.

The day of the event, on May 5, we were all very emotional. As I briefed President Reagan in the presidential guest residence outside Bonn where the president and first lady stayed during the Bonn summit, Mrs. Reagan listened in. When I got to the part about placing the wreath, she interrupted.

"Wait a minute," she said. "That's not what Mike [Deaver] told me. Ronnie and Chancellor Kohl are not supposed to be a part of the wreath-laying ceremony. They'll just witness it."

She was upset, and I immediately called in Mike Deaver to straighten it out. When Deaver walked into their room, he and Mrs. Reagan gave each other a long, warm hug and just held each other. I could tell by his body language what Deaver was telling her: *Nancy, don't worry. We'll get through this. Everything is going to be all right.* This was the last White House overseas trip that Deaver would make with the Reagans. Deaver had announced that he was leaving the White House, and I think this made the trip even more difficult for Mrs. Reagan. She and Mike were very close.

"Look, Nancy, this is what we've got to do," Deaver told her. The two leaders would be at the site, but they would not actually place the wreath, he said. They would watch the two generals do it. "They'll be in the picture, though," he warned her. "That's what the Germans want to do."

Mrs. Reagan accepted it.

When Marine One landed near the cemetery, and I saw it for the first time, I was surprised. It was small — not much larger than a large suburban lawn. But this patch of land on a hilltop had dominated the world media for months.

Reagan handled the event gracefully. He and Kohl spent only eight minutes at the site, walking slowly through the narrow cemetery ablaze with flowers — tulips, marigolds, pansies. Neither made a speech. General Ridgeway, who fought in the Battle of the Bulge, and Lieutenant General Johannes Steinhoff, a retired West German Air Force officer, laid the wreath at the base of a brick cemetery tower. The German "Taps" was played, and as the last lonely notes echoed out over the hilltop the two generals clasped hands in a gesture of reconciliation.

Earlier that day, the president and Mrs.

Reagan had visited the Bergen-Belsen concentration camp, in northeastern West Germany, where they walked in the early morning mist amid the mass graves where 64,000 Jews and others died, including young author Anne Frank.

The president's voice was thick with emotion as, with the first lady looking on sorrowfully, he read from Anne Frank's diaries: ". . . I still believe that people are good at heart. I simply can't build up my hopes on a foundation consisting of confusion, misery and death. I see the world gradually being turned into a wilderness. I hear the ever-approaching thunder which will destroy us, too; I can feel the suffering of millions and yet, if I look up into the heavens, I think that it will all come right, that this cruelty, too, will end and that peace and tranquillity will return again."

At the end of that emotional day, Reagan was applauded as he boarded Air Force One. He had done a magnificent job at quelling the criticism and anger exploding around him.

And Ronald Reagan had delivered on his promise.

Returning from Europe, the Reagans had to deal with Deaver's departure. Deaver had worked for the Reagans for most of the last 20 years, except for the short stretch at the beginning of Reagan's 1980 campaign when he walked out in a clash with campaign director John Sears. Before Reagan's first term, there had been talk that Deaver would be named chief of staff, but Mrs. Reagan played a big role in selecting Jim Baker for the job. Deaver became assistant to the president and deputy chief of staff, part of the "troika" supporting Reagan in his first term, which also included Baker and Ed Meese as counselor to the president. But Deaver had some of the most valuable real estate in the White House — an office in the West Wing with direct internal access to the Oval Office — and he remained the Reagans' closest adviser.

In the second term, the troika split up: Meese became attorney general, and Baker and Treasury Secretary Don Regan switched posts. Baker became secretary of the Treasury and Regan took Baker's post as chief of staff. After Deaver left, we turned his office into a larger study for the president.

We held a farewell reception for Deaver in the Rose Garden — a rarity. Deaver came in for it with his wife and children and talked to the president and Mrs.

Reagan in the Oval Office for a short while before the reception. I remember he told the president, "When we go into the Rose Garden, we'll have none of this," and he grabbed his own throat.

Later, I asked the president what Deaver had meant by the gesture. Reagan said he had meant, "Don't choke me up out there."

People have said that Ronald Reagan was emotionally distant. I didn't think that was so. I found him one of the most generous, compassionate people one could know. But I think that he always kept a part of himself hidden. It's been said that actors have a way of holding part of themselves back when they're offstage, that they keep something in reserve for the next time. For Reagan, it may have been partly that. He had tremendous personal appeal and an uncanny ability to attract people to him and to listen to him, but I think he always kept something tucked away.

He was far more comfortable writing letters than talking on the telephone. In fact, he was an enormously prolific letter writer and found it enjoyable to convey his thoughts on paper. In fact, as eloquent as he was verbally, his writing was just as articulate. He penned hundreds of letters a year — to supporters, opponents, world leaders, Hollywood friends and ordinary citizens who wrote either to praise or to criticize him. Also, Reagan wrote numerous letters to children who wrote him when he was president, including one in which he gently let down a boy hoping to receive federal cleanup funds because his mother had declared his room a "disaster area."

Another young child he wrote to regularly for almost five years was his pen pal — Rudy Hines, a student at Martin Luther King Jr. Elementary School in Southeast Washington. Reagan visited the school, then called Congress Heights Elementary, in 1983 after the White House had adopted the school as part of a program to encourage private-sector involvement in education. During his visit, Reagan suggested that a student from the school become his pen pal, and the principal selected Rudy, who was six years old.

The president took his assignment very seriously and wrote Rudy regularly. In 1984, the boy invited Reagan to his house for dinner, writing, "You have to let us know in advance so my mom can pick up the laundry off the floor."

The White House contacted Rudy's

mother, Stephanie Lee, in September 1984 and asked her to host the dinner as a surprise for Rudy. I was in Iowa at the time, completing three campaign events for the president when Bill Henkel called me back to Washington to advance the event the next night, September 21. The event was off the record, meaning it wasn't listed on the president's official schedule, so the security precautions could be low key.

The afternoon of the twenty-first, I went to Rudy's neighborhood with a Secret Service agent and walked around near Rudy's home, which was a two-story brick apartment house where Rudy lived with his mother. His father lived a short distance away. But even though the dinner was an off the record event, we must have tipped off some people that afternoon because by the time we returned that evening with the president and Mrs. Reagan, there were more than 100 people waiting outside Rudy's home. The Reagans, carrying gift-wrapped jelly beans, came to the boy's apartment, and Rudy opened the door, giving a big smile when he saw the president and first lady, and then we left them alone.

The Reagans, Rudy and his parents ate

fried chicken, salad and rice from TV trays. The Reagans also brought a present for Rudy, some of his classmates and the school principal — front-row tickets for a Michael Jackson concert that night at RFK Stadium in Washington. Afterward, Rudy wrote the president a gracious thank-you note, thanking him for the visit, the jelly beans and the concert tickets.

Several months later, the president invited Rudy and other children from the school to attend the circus with him. Rudy sat next to Reagan, and the president gave him the whistle he used as honorary ringmaster of the circus that day.

Experiences like that gave Reagan a lot of joy. But the summer of 1985 marked a new crisis: the terrifying ordeal of the passengers of TWA Flight 847. On the morning of June 14, a plane filled with mostly American tourists departing from Athens and headed to Rome was hijacked by two Arabs armed with grenades and handguns. In a deadly game of Ping-Pong, the hijackers forced the plane to fly back and forth between Beirut and Algiers. Along the way, they released 40 passengers, mostly women and children. But on June 15, they brutally beat, then shot, navy diver Robert Stethem in the head and threw his body onto the tarmac of Beirut International Airport.

During the crisis, Reagan met privately with some of the families of the 40 remaining hostages. The meetings had a profound impact on him; the thought of any American being held against his or her will really bothered him, but he always vowed that the United States would not negotiate with terrorists, as this would only validate their vicious acts.

In a speech to the annual convention of the Lions Club International in Dallas on June 21, he was blunt. "We consider these murders, hijackings and abductions an attack on western civilization by uncivilized barbarians," he told the crowd of several thousand.

It was a difficult time for the White House, and the country. Terrorism had struck home. On June 19, Salvadoran guerrillas killed 14 people, including four U.S. Marines, at a sidewalk café in San Salvador, and a bomb in the Frankfurt airport in West Germany killed three people.

During the TWA hostage crisis, the president canceled a planned trip to the ranch, but otherwise stuck to his schedule. He didn't want the terrorists to think they were disrupting the process of the U.S. government.

The captives were ultimately released in late June, and President Reagan addressed the nation from the Oval Office on July 1, saying the remaining 39 hostages were "free, safe and, at this moment, on their way to Frankfurt, Germany."

His anger at the terrorists became evident, however, less than five minutes before he went on the air with his Oval Office address. The Reagans and friends had screened the movie *Rambo* the previous evening, and he told the White House staff, WHCA and network pool technicians in the Oval Office that having seen *Rambo* last night, "I know what to do the next time this happens." The microphone was inadvertently left open, and the remark was transmitted to the White House press center. Reagan got tagged again as shooting from the hip. A similar incident had occurred in 1984 when the president was asked to do a microphone check at the ranch before his weekly radio broadcast. He quipped that he'd just signed legislation outlawing the Soviet Union forever and "the bombing begins in five minutes." In Reagan's defense, these were technical errors by WHCA and not mistakes by President Reagan.

Reagan had a way of keeping things interesting.

In his '85 Oval Office speech after the TWA hijacking, he noted that it wasn't a moment for celebration because seven Americans were still being held captive in Lebanon, and the murderers of Stethem and the marines in El Salvador were still at large.

The next day, the president and Mrs. Reagan laid a wreath on Robert Stethem's grave at Arlington National Cemetery, then drove to Andrews Air Force Base and greeted 30 of thc former captives still onboard the TWA plane. The plane erupted in applause when Reagan vowed to bring Stethem's murderers to justice.

"None of you were held prisoner because of any personal wrongs that any of you had done to anyone," Reagan told them. "You were held simply because you were Americans. In the minds of your captors, you represented us."

It was an emotional time for the president and, despite his joy over the release of the 39 TWA captives, the Americans still held hostage in Lebanon were constantly on his mind. They included CIA Beirut Station Chief William Buckley, journalist Terry Anderson, the Reverend Lawrence

Jenco, head of Catholic Relief Services in Lebanon, and David Jacobsen, an administrator at American University in Beirut. Reagan met with Jenco's family in conjunction with one of his private meetings with the families of the TWA hostages. Reagan remained very concerned about the fate of the seven. He asked almost daily for updates on their status during his intelligence briefings.

A new, more personal, concern arrived for the president in July 1985. He had gone to the Bethesda Naval Hospital for a routine physical, which included a colonoscopy. Doctors discovered a large mass, about the size of a golf ball, on the lower right side of the colon, large enough so that a section of his colon would have to be removed. They didn't find out until shortly after the surgery that the mass was actually malignant, but doctors felt they had removed enough of the colon to catch the cancer before it spread.

On the day of the surgery, the president invoked the Twenty-fifth Amendment and signed over his presidential powers to Vice President Bush and then signed them back to himself that evening. He was in the hospital for seven nights, but he never complained about anything. Naturally, we cut down on the number of people who could see him, but we brought him plenty of paperwork. National Security Adviser Bud McFarlane seemed especially eager to get in to see the president. We put him off for several days — Reagan was already receiving his daily international security briefing in writing with the Presidential Daily Brief (PDP) — but finally McFarlane got his audience with the president. (It turned out to be a rather momentous one, as we were to learn later.)

The president was upbeat, in great spirits and, despite the ordeal, never lost his composure. Most people would have wanted sympathy, but he didn't. He also didn't slow down. A short time later, in August, when the Reagans were at the ranch for their regular August vacation, the big issue was whether or not the president could ride a horse so soon after his surgery. Reagan assumed he would be able to get to the ranch, just climb on a horse and take off. Mrs. Reagan had other ideas, and it got to be a source of friction between the first lady and the president, with White House doctor John Hutton stuck in the middle. The first lady would go to Hutton and tell him that "you have to tell Ronnie he can't ride." And the president would go to Hutton and say, "You have to tell her it's okay to ride."

Finally, everybody worked out a compromise where the president could get on a horse, but only for walking. No trotting or cantering. Well, Reagan was a proud man, and he had this macho side to him — not as president of the United States, but as a horseman and former athlete. He thought he could do anything. He complied with the doctor's directive — for a few days. Then one day during the August ride with Mrs. Reagan, he took off in a cloud of dust at a full gallop. Mrs. Reagan was quite upset with her "roommate" as she humorously called him.

As time went on, when the press asked the president about the surgery, Reagan always insisted that he'd never had cancer.

"There was a growth that was cancerous," he would explain. "But they got it all. But *I* didn't have cancer."

During his round of media exit interviews in late 1988, he was asked about it frequently. After one exit interview when the topic came up again, Reagan turned to me and said, "They keep asking me about cancer. Hell, I never had cancer!"

I used to think, Gee, Mr. President,

that's a stretch. But that was his way of blocking it out. Reagan was the eternal optimist.

One of the reasons that Reagan could stay the course amid a storm of controversy was because of this relentless optimism. His favorite phrase was "Never say never." He always believed that things would work out in the end. I think his positive attitude was the main reason for his powerful impact on the American consciousness, then and now. Ronald Reagan could see the sunny side to just about any situation, even if it meant viewing it slightly differently from the rest of the world.

14

GENEVA AND THE BATTLE OF THE COATS

No one said much as we stood behind the glass front doors in the atrium of Château Fleur d'Eau, an imposing lakeside château in Geneva, on that overcast, chilly November morning in 1985. The president seemed calm, but preoccupied. His foreign policy team — Secretary of State George Shultz and National Security Adviser Bud McFarlane — and White House Chief of Staff Don Regan stood uneasily nearby. Reagan clearly wasn't in the mood to make one of his well-timed jokes that had so often diffused a tense situation.

Soviet General Secretary Mikhail Sergeyevich Gorbachev, we had been told, was en route from the Soviet diplomatic mission in Geneva, where he was staying. So much depended on this encounter between the cold war warrior and his younger Soviet counterpart. It would be the first top-level U.S.-Soviet meeting in more than six years. For weeks, there had been speculation about the first meeting between the 74-year-old Reagan and his 54-year-old counterpart, who had come to power in the Soviet Union the previous March. Many wondered whether Reagan would be able to hold his own with this dynamic new breed of Soviet leader, who had been winning raves worldwide, even from Reagan's friend British Prime Minister Margaret Thatcher.

The plan was for Reagan to greet Gorbachev as he stepped out of his limo, shake his hand, escort him up the short flight of stairs and then the duo would pause for photographs before entering the château. Once inside, they were scheduled to meet privately for 20 minutes before being joined by their negotiators to discuss U.S.-Soviet relations.

Gorbachev's motorcade was 10 minutes away, we were told. President Reagan asked his chief valet, Eddie Serrano, for his coat and scarf. Hearing the president's request, I suddenly got a sick feeling in my stomach.

We had a problem.

We had arrived in Geneva just after 10:00 a.m. on November 17 for the three-day summit. Flying over on Air Force One, what I remembered most were the high spirits of the first lady. Usually tightly wound, Mrs. Reagan was in the best mood I had ever seen her in: She was relaxed, even joyous. For years, Reagan had been making overtures to the Soviets, and he had told his foreign policy advisers to let him know when the Soviets were ready for a constructive dialogue. But Mrs. Reagan had also privately urged her husband toward the goal of ending the cold war, saying that he couldn't wait for the Soviets to get fully ready. She had lived through enough of the cold war to believe passionately that it had to end and that her husband could play a major role in ending it. She wanted that to be part of the legacy of the Reagan presidency. It was my sense that on the flight to Geneva, she could see her hopes and dreams starting to come to fruition.

The president had prepared thoroughly for the meetings with Gorbachev. He had been briefed for many hours and reviewed mountains of materials in the White House residence and at Camp David in the evenings and on weekends.

Usually, from an overall domestic and foreign policy standpoint, Reagan believed his aides gave him too much paperwork. "Jim, they're telling me more than I need to know," he would say in exasperation to me. He didn't need all the details, he told me. Since he had a very clear vision of where he wanted to take the country, he always knew what the outcome should be, and he wanted to stay focused on the implementation of his domestic and foreign policy agendas. Reagan also believed that change was good, especially if it came to the role of the federal government.

"That's why we're here," he frequently reminded members of his cabinet and others.

But this time was an exception and Reagan recognized that detailed information was important in terms of negotiating with the Soviets.

Throughout his presidency, Reagan had been making overtures to the Soviet leaders through personal letters, but as he said, "They keep dying on me." Gorbachev, the fourth Soviet leader in less than two and a half years, had replaced President Konstantin Chernenko. Gorbachev, Reagan was told, was different from the previous generation of Soviet leaders. He was confident, impatient, media savvy, vigorous. Thatcher had spoken highly of him to Reagan at Camp David.

Gorbachev appeared to recognize that the Soviet Union's closed society was in serious trouble, and he might be more willing to consider opening up the Soviet Union to the rest of the world. But as upbeat as the first lady was about the Geneva summit, the president was more cautious. He was willing to look Gorbachev in the eye to see if they could begin a dialogue. But he was suspicious of the Soviets and, after all, they still had the nuclear stalemate of mutual assured destruction. While many on his staff, including me, were optimistic about the prospect of this historic encounter, Reagan kept his expectations low.

That morning, we traveled to the U.S. meeting venue from our residence, La Maison de Saussure, an eighteenth-century château a few miles north of Geneva and the home of the Prince Aga Khan and Princess Salida and their young son. The boy had left a note for the president asking him to feed his goldfish in his second-floor bedroom. The president was faithfully following his instructions.

At Château Fleur d'Eau, I was uneasy as Gorbachev's motorcade got closer and closer and Reagan donned his blue cashmere coat and white scarf. So much rode on this first encounter. Why did the president need to wear a coat? He simply needed to step outside, walk maybe 25 feet to greet Gorbachev and then escort him up the stairs for the official photo.

I was thinking fast. Thousands of the world's press were covering this historic meeting, and it could be a major mistake to have the president all bundled up. What if Gorbachev got out of his car without a coat? Then the world would see a younger, more vigorous man greeting an old and feeble man, dressed as if he couldn't be out in the cold for just a few minutes.

As the president was donning his coat, I spoke up.

"Mr. President, I'm not so sure you're going to need your coat," I said. "You're only going to be outside for a couple of minutes. Plus, Mr. Gorbachev may not be wearing his coat."

Shultz, who had heard me, looked at me as if I were crazy.

"Mr. President," he said, "don't worry about it. Gorbachev will have his coat on."

I fired back. "I'm not so sure." My experience as an advance man had kicked in. Perception was everything, especially at a historic moment like this. "We don't know what Gorbachev is going to be wearing. These details haven't been discussed."

Then McFarlane spoke up. "Jim," he

said, "don't worry about it. He'll have his coat on. It's not a concern."

I thought Regan might back me up, but he joined in: "Jim, it's not going to be a problem."

The president finished buttoning his overcoat and adjusting his scarf around his neck. Five minutes to go. Shultz, Regan and McFarlane moved into their positions outside at the arrival. It was just the president and me.

I had this intense fear of the world perception of this first encounter if Reagan was seen as old and weak. It would be a bad start to the summit, a setback that would be very difficult to overcome. I took a deep breath and tried again.

"Mr. President, I know you've got a lot on your mind, but I need to talk to you again," I said. "We both heard what Shultz, McFarlane and Regan said. But they don't have any idea what's going on with the coats. None of us focused on this until now, but it could become a major thing when you step outside for the first greeting."

Reagan dismissed my concern.

"Well, don't worry about it, Jim," he said. "I'm fine, and we're ready to go."

Two minutes until Gorbachev's arrival.

We were just a few feet from the front door, ready to step outside. I kept seeing a vision of a heavily bundled-up Reagan greeting Gorbachev, who would appear in his business suit. I had to protect President Reagan. I tried yet again.

"Mr. President, this is the last thing I'm going to say."

The president, who rarely got angry, was getting irritated.

"What is it now?" he said. "It's not the coat again, is it?"

"Yes, sir. But let me ask you one final question," I said.

"What?" Now the president was definitely irritated.

"Suppose I'm right about the coat," I said. "And Mr. Gorbachev gets out of the car with just his business suit on, looking strong and ready to go. And you're all covered up the way you are as if you can't be outside for a few minutes without this heavy wrap on. If that's the case, then who's going to look stupid before the whole world? You or Gorbachev?"

The president gave in.

"All right, damn it, Jim," he said. "Have it your way." And he ripped off the scarf, pulled off his coat and tossed it into my arms.

"There, is that what you want?" he said.

"Yes, sir," I said. "Now you're ready to go."

Almost immediately thereafter, we heard distant sirens of the Soviet motorcade. One minute later, the motorcade pulled up, and I opened the door for Reagan. He stepped outside to the top of the stairs until Gorbachev's limo crunched to a halt on the gravel drive. The windows of Gorbachev's limo were dark, so we couldn't see inside. Reagan then descended the stairs and approached the limo as the Soviet leader emerged.

Gorbachev wore a dark overcoat. A scarf was tightly wrapped around his neck.

As Gorbachev climbed out, he snatched his dark fedora off his head and held out his other hand to the president.

The two men greeted each other and then turned to climb the stairs. As they did, Reagan reached out and gently placed his hand on Gorbachev's elbow. It was a warm and welcoming gesture, but it also looked like he was trying to assist the much younger Gorbachev.

At the top of the stairs, they stopped and turned for photographers. And that was the photo that ran on the front page of every newspaper and newsmagazine and in every news telecast. Ronald Reagan, dressed in his finely tailored blue suit, towering over the stocky Gorbachev, who looked like something out of central casting — a stodgy Russian who had just arrived from snowy Moscow.

We had ended up rolling the Soviets big time. Without intending to, we had hit them hard. We got off to a great start.

The Soviets were not at all pleased about it and talked about it far after the summit. "I felt like we lost the game during the first movement," said Kremlin press official Sergei Tarasenko years later.

That day, the coat incident bothered the Soviets so much that as we broke for lunch at the end of the first session to head back to our respective venues, Gorbachev's last words to Reagan were, "When we meet again, will it be coats on or coats off?" And at every point over the next three days, whenever there was an upcoming departure, Gorbachev invariably asked the president the same question. "The next time we meet, will it be coats on or coats off?"

Inside Château Fleur d'Eau after their first meeting, Reagan and Gorbachev sat for a photo op for the waves of world press that rolled through and then met privately for their scheduled 20-minute meeting.

Well, 20 minutes came and went quickly. Then it was 40 minutes, and Don Regan approached me. He said that the meeting had gone for twice the scheduled time. As executive assistant to the president, it was my job to signal to the president that a meeting needed to end. Regan suggested I do so now.

I disagreed. "It's their first meeting," I said.

"What about the schedule?" Regan asked me.

"I don't think it matters," I said. "I think we need to leave them alone."

Ten minutes later, the Soviets and the American team were still hovering outside the meeting room.

"What do you think?" Regan asked me.

"Don," I said, "I don't think anything different. They've got to go on. We can't cut off this meeting. It's too important."

At the one-hour mark, Regan and Bud McFarlane approached me. They said that I had to end the meeting so the plenary session could begin.

I was still holding fast. "I don't think I should go in there," I said. "The president wouldn't want that. I think he'll want to continue. We need to leave it up to him."

If the president wanted to end the

meeting, I argued, he would have. It would be a mistake for anyone to enter that room. From our standpoint, I said, Ronald Reagan had control of this, and he would emerge at the appropriate time.

The doors to the meeting room still hadn't opened. I was trying to watch the door and at the same time stay away from the increasingly impatient Regan and McFarlane. Ten minutes later, they approached me again.

"Anybody who knows Ronald Reagan knows he's doing just fine," I maintained. "It would be absolutely wrong for us to end it."

McFarlane suggested that I ask Shultz. I wasn't inclined to talk to any more people since I felt we already had our answer, and Shultz was the last person I wanted to ask, but I reluctantly agreed to consult him out of respect for Regan and McFarlane.

I found him in another room, meeting with Soviet Foreign Minister Eduard Shevardnadze. I entered and leaned over Shultz and quietly explained the situation.

"Bud and Don are concerned about the Reagan-Gorbachev meeting," I told him so Shevardnadze couldn't overhear. "They think the meeting has gone on long enough. I don't agree with them, but they wanted me to ask you whether I should go in and end the meeting."

Shultz lashed out at me, his voice booming around the room.

"If you're stupid enough to walk into that room and break up the meeting between those two leaders, then you don't deserve the job you have," he said.

Shevardnadze shot Shultz a look as if saying, "What's your problem?" As hard as it was, I kept my composure with Shultz and said nothing. I went back to communicate with McFarlane and Regan.

They rushed over when they saw me, asking me what Shultz had said.

"He's in total disagreement with you guys," I told them. "He just ripped my neck off in front of Shevardnadze. Leave the president alone. Nobody goes in. The president and the general secretary will end it when they want to end it."

After an hour and twenty minutes, the president and Gorbachev emerged, wreathed in smiles, and we went into our abbreviated plenary session. After that, we broke for lunch and went back to La Maison de Saussure for lunch.

The president was upbeat about his one-on-one marathon with Gorbachev. He said they'd talked about big-picture issues regarding the United States and the Soviet Union. This guy is different, he told us over lunch. We're going to be able to continue to talk with him.

During the afternoon plenary session, we'd worked it out so that Reagan would invite Gorbachev to go for a walk down to a little lakeshore boathouse a short distance from the château while their negotiators continued their dialogue. Gorbachev accepted and the two leaders, seated in front of a roaring fire, chatted through their translators as Eddie Serrano served coffee.

It was at that juncture that Reagan pointed out to Gorbachev that they were probably the only two men in the world who might be able to bring about peace. He also indicated that if there continued to be an all-out arms race between the two countries, the Soviet Union would never win. The United States, he said, would always have the ability to outspend the U.S.S.R.

When they arrived back at the château, I asked the president if he wanted to go back in since the plenary session was still going on. Reagan asked Gorbachev if he was ready to end for the afternoon, and the two leaders agreed to adjourn. They were scheduled to get together again that night for a dinner at the Soviet mission. The two leaders stood in the gravel driveway as we sent word to the U.S. and Soviet delegations that Reagan and Gorbachev were ready to depart. Reagan invited Gorbachev to a summit in Washington. Gorbachev accepted immediately and reciprocated with an invitation to Moscow. Reagan, also, instantly agreed.

They parted, but not until Gorbachev asked: "Coats on or coats off?" when they met again for the dinner that evening.

When we got out of our motorcade at La Maison de Saussure, the president told Shultz, Regan and McFarlane that he and Gorbachev had agreed to meet again. They were taken aback by the ease with which this had been accomplished. It had been one of the major goals of the Geneva summit, and the president had taken care of it by the end of the first day of the summit.

Mrs. Reagan arrived back at the residence shortly after we did. She gave the president a hug and a kiss, and he asked her how her day had gone. She had been having tea with Gorbachev's wife, Raisa, a vibrant, intelligent — but pushy — woman who had managed to break out of the mold of the anonymous Soviet leader's wife.

Clearly, the first ladies' encounter hadn't gone nearly as well as their husbands' had. Mrs. Gorbachev was given, it turned out, to lecturing virtually everyone.

"That Raisa Gorbachev," said Mrs. Reagan with a thin smile, "is one cold cookie."

She asked the president about his day. He told her it had gone very well and that the two men had agreed to two more summits. Mrs. Reagan gave a big smile.

The second day also proceeded well for the Americans. This time, the talks were held at the Soviet mission, and Gorbachev invited Reagan for another private meeting at the outset. At that meeting, Reagan gave Gorbachev a list of Soviets who were being prevented from leaving the U.S.S.R. It was a ritual he would repeat every time he and Gorbachev got together. It used to make Gorbachev's blood boil! But it was Reagan's idea. He cared a lot about the issue of people being held against their will. Gorbachev used to retaliate when they got together by railing against American society, pointing out our homelessness and crime problems. Yes, you have an open society, he would say, but you have people sleeping on the sidewalks, under bridges, and murderers who kill innocent people. Reagan would respond by pointing out that even these people live in a free society.

Reagan had been faithfully feeding the fish belonging to the son of the Aga Kahn, but later that afternoon he suddenly noticed that one of them was, clearly, quite dead. It was floating belly up at the top of the boy's fish tank. The president felt terrible about it. I wondered what we were going to do and then decided that we would replace the fish. I asked two of our advance team to go out and purchase two fish (one for backup) of the same size and breed. We got the replacement fish but, unfortunately, our advance guys had told enough people about the dead fish, so the story got out that the president had killed the little boy's fish. The president left the boy an apologetic note. "I don't know what could have happened," the note said. He told the boy he'd replaced the fish with two other fish. "I hope this is all right." He signed the note: "Your friend, Ronald Reagan."

That evening at the official dinner, however, I discovered a horrible mistake that dwarfed the fish episode. Three of Gorbachev's aides — although we knew they were KGB agents — had been placed in a holding room upstairs, right next to the room the president was using as a study, where all his briefing materials for the summit were spread out!

To make matters worse, the Secret Service agent stationed upstairs was located outside the Reagans' bedroom but couldn't see the study. So the KGB agents could have easily slipped into the study, photographed materials and been back out before anyone ever knew. It was an appalling screwup. I grabbed all the president's briefing materials and hid everything in my bedroom, which was just down the hallway.

I then located Ray Shaddick, director of the White House Presidential Protection Detail, and explained the situation.

"You've got three KGB people upstairs next to the president's study, with full access to it. There's an agent up there outside the bedroom, but nobody is watching the study," I said. "The KGB have been up there for forty-five minutes. Why in the hell are they upstairs? They could have read anything, photographed anything, planted audio or video bugs, and nobody would have known."

Shaddick said he didn't know why they'd been placed there. "Your advance team worked it out with the Soviets," he said.

I found our site advance man, Andrew Littlefair. "What were you doing?" I asked. Littlefair said it was the Secret Service's fault; they hadn't posted their agents correctly.

"They shouldn't have been upstairs in the first place," I told Littlefair. "You've got to move them somewhere downstairs. For all we know, they've already done their damage."

Andrew went back upstairs and explained to the Soviet aides that they would have to move downstairs. They weren't happy, and I had to get involved. I told them we'd found a better holding room for them, but they knew we didn't want them upstairs. They were offended and didn't want to move. I apologized profusely, but they still just sat there. I finally asked them respectfully, but firmly, to follow me. They did, but rather sulkily.

After that, of course, we had to conduct a complete sweep for bugs. We had no idea where they'd been or what they'd done. The Secret Service conducted as thorough a sweep as it could that night. I told the president and Mrs. Reagan about the incident, and the Secret Service did a more thorough sweep the next day. They never found anything, but we were careful what we said upstairs after that just in case some kind of listening device had gone undetected.

At the conclusion of the Geneva summit, the two leaders announced their decision to meet again. They didn't resolve their sharp differences over SDI and the critical issue of nuclear arms control, but the warmth and rapport between the two men left us with high hopes for future summits.

We left Geneva on the morning of November 21, stopped in Brussels, where Reagan briefed NATO officials, and then headed back to Washington.

In a press conference after the summit, Gorbachev said the one-on-one sessions were frank and long. "Sometimes we had sharp discussions, sometimes we had very sharp discussions."

On the ride home on Air Force One, we were jubilant. We were going to arrive at Andrews Air Force Base at 8:30 p.m. East Coast time, and Reagan was scheduled to go right to Capitol Hill to address a joint session of Congress.

Mrs. Reagan's big concern was that the president get some rest. By the time he got to Capitol Hill, it would be, according to his body clock, 3:00 a.m.

"He's not going to want to sleep, but

he's got to rest," she told me. "I'll tell him that, and you have to tell him that, too. He's got to get some sleep."

Like the rest of us, though, the president was too keyed up to sleep. He and Mrs. Reagan had dinner on the plane, and he worked on his speech. He rested, but never really dozed off.

When we got into Andrews, we climbed aboard Marine One and flew up the Mall to the Capitol while being covered live by all networks.

Flying through nighttime Washington, with the Capitol and the Washington landmarks glowing below us — the stately Lincoln and Jefferson monuments, the spire of the Washington monument — I found myself thinking that maybe we really were approaching the end of nuclear weapons and the demise of the cold war. I thought back to the uneasiness of my childhood and the fear of my family and neighbors that nuclear annihilation might be near. And here we were, playing a small part with this man in his attempt to bring the nightmare of nuclear weapons to an end.

Little did I know that, the following year, in the chilly landscape of Reykjavik, the capital of Iceland, that dream almost faced a collapse.

But in 1985, we were returning in triumph. We landed on the east side of the Capitol and were greeted in the House side of the Capitol by the congressional leadership. The president got thunderous applause from Congress, and even the Democrats were grudgingly complimentary. House Speaker Thomas P. "Tip" O'Neill said he was "more than delighted" that Reagan and Gorbachev had agreed to meet again.

In his address to Congress, Reagan was straightforward. "I can't claim that we had a meeting of minds on such fundamentals as ideology or national purpose, but we understand each other better, and that's a key to peace," he said. "I gained a better perspective; I feel he did, too."

In his Saturday radio address two days later, Reagan told Americans that "if there's one conclusion to draw from our fireside summit, it's that American policies are working.

"America is strong again, and American strength has caught the Soviets' attention," he said. "They recognize that the United States is no longer just reacting to world events; we are in the forefront of a powerful, historic tide for freedom, opportunity, for progress and peace."

Going into the Geneva summit, so many people made the mistake of underestimating Ronald Reagan. Reagan's great strength was his extraordinary vision for America and his ability to articulate it to insiders and outsiders. He never wavered from that goal.

15

FALLING BACK TO EARTH

My first hint that it was not going to be a regular day at the White House on January 28, 1986, was when Pat Buchanan, the White House's chief of communications, sprinted by my office, heading for the Oval Office. Reagan was in an Oval Office meeting at the time with Larry Speakes and Don Regan to discuss his State of the Union speech, which he was scheduled to deliver that night.

As Buchanan rushed past my office, I heard him say, "The space shuttle just blew up on takeoff," as he burst into the Oval Office. By that time, I was right behind him.

There was silence in the Oval Office. The president looked stricken. I told the president that we should go into the study to monitor the network news reports.

Hands clasped, the president watched in pain. The news was horrible, and the televised images were indelible. Just over one minute after a flawless liftoff from Kennedy Space Center, the shuttle *Challenger*, carrying seven astronauts, blew apart in jagged lines of white smoke, five miles above the Atlantic Ocean. It was witnessed with stunning clarity by thousands of spectators at the site and millions more Americans watching on television. To make a tragic situation even worse, schoolchildren across the country had been watching the liftoff because of the presence onboard of Christa McAuliffe, a New Hampshire teacher who had been chosen from 11,000 people to be the first ordinary citizen in space. McAuliffe was scheduled to conduct two "space classrooms" from aboard *Challenger*, to be beamed live to 25 million students nationwide.

That day and the day that we learned that the 241 marines had been killed by a truck bomb in Lebanon were two of the most difficult days of Reagan's presidency. Like the marine barracks' bombing, the *Challenger* explosion was a personal tragedy for the president, and he took it very hard.

We canceled the rest of his schedule for that day and postponed the State of the Union address so the president could, instead, address the nation that evening on the shuttle explosion. White House speechwriter Peggy Noonan took the initiative and began working on a speech for him as soon as we heard the news. As we watched the repeated televised images, I could tell that Reagan was thinking about the families of the seven astronauts and trying to figure out what he could say to them, and to the world, about the tragedy.

Once again, Reagan rose to the occasion. He had a unique gift for talking into a camera as if he were in Americans' living rooms. Later that day, from the Oval Office on a snowy Washington evening, his warmth and intimacy provided solace to the grieving nation. He also tried to comfort the children of America who had been watching the live coverage.

"I know it's hard to understand, but sometimes painful things like this happen," he told them. "It's all part of the process of exploration and discovery. It's all part of taking a chance and expanding man's horizons. The future doesn't belong to the fainthearted; it belongs to the brave."

He ended softly, with quotes from a poem, "High Flight," written by a young World War II fighter pilot: "We will never forget them, nor the last time we saw them, this morning, as they prepared for their journey and waved goodbye and 'slipped the surly bonds of earth' to 'touch the face of God.' "

A few days later, we went to the Johnson Space Center in Houston for a memorial service, where he bade farewell to "our seven star voyagers," even as he pledged that the exploration of space would go on.

Reagan compared the astronaut crew with the pioneers of the Old West. On the Oregon Trail, he told the 15,000 people gathered on a lawn at the space center, "you can see the grave markers of those who fell along the way. But grief only steeled them to the journey ahead.

"Sometimes, when we reach for the stars, we fall short," the president said. "But we must pick ourselves up again and press on despite the pain."

Above, a formation of four T-38 jets, the type flown by astronauts, roared in a tight, low pass over the space center. One craft split off and wheeled upward in a steep climb toward the sun and then swept out of view into clouds.

Before the ceremony, the president and Mrs. Reagan met privately with about 25 family members inside. The Reagans greeted each of them with handshakes, hugs and some private words. Then they went out together for the memorial service.

About midnight on the night of the accident, I got a call at home from the White House. The operator said she had Christa McAuliffe's father-in-law on the line. He was trying to reach the president. I took the call and found myself dealing with a man in terrible anguish and very angry about the disaster.

"This is the president's fault," he told me. "What is he going to do about this disaster?" He wanted to speak to Reagan.

For 45 minutes, I listened to him respectfully so he could let out his pain. I wasn't going to put him through to the president, but I tried to figure out how I could help him, and I promised that he would hear back from us.

After we got off the phone, I called the president's operator, who, fortunately, informed me that a crisis communications center had been set up at Cape Canaveral. I was also advised that Shirley Green, a former Bush staffer I had known since 1980 who was in charge of NASA communications, was at Cape Canaveral. The White House operator got Green on the phone, and she assured me that NASA had a team to help the astronauts' families. A member of that team would get in touch with Christa McAuliffe's father-in-law immediately, she said.

It was a tough time for everyone, most of all for those families. One cannot imagine the pain of watching a loved one die in such a public way.

President Reagan was a tower of strength in settings like that. His low-key style was a major reason. Also, he treated everyone equally, whether it was a head of state, a member of Congress, the White House groundskeepers — or a spouse lost in grief because of the untimely death of a loved one. He simply didn't perceive any differences among people.

Reagan was also not vindictive. For example, one of the worst things anyone ever said about Reagan when he was president was a comment by Speaker Tip O'Neill, who said it was "a sin that Ronald Reagan was elected president."

But Reagan even let that comment roll off his back. He liked Tip O'Neill as an old Irishman, and I never heard him refer to Tip's comment.

If Ronald Reagan had a flaw, it was that he could be too trusting of people. For example, Larry Speakes, who served as Reagan's press secretary for six years, made up quotes and fed them to the press, claiming they were President Reagan's words when Speakes thought that Reagan's actual words weren't flashy enough.

I remember he did so on the July Fourth weekend in 1986 when we were attending the one hundredth birthday celebration of the Statue of Liberty in New York City. We were staying at Pocantico Hills, the Rockefeller estate on the Hudson River north of New York City, and shuttling down to the city on Marine One for various events. On the morning of July Fourth, we were to land on the battleship USS *Iowa* for a "Parade of Ships" down the Hudson River. I was on board along with Press Secretary Larry Speakes and the president and Mrs. Reagan, who were reading the morning papers. Something in one of the newspapers caught Mrs. Reagan's attention.

"Honey, I don't remember you talking to the press last night," she said to the president.

"I didn't," the president said, still immersed in his reading. Mrs. Reagan read aloud a fairly lengthy quote to the president.

The president recoiled. "Hell, I never said that!" he said.

I turned to Speakes. "Larry," I warned, "you heard what the president and Mrs. Reagan just said. You've got to knock this off. They're on to you now."

The Reagans were speaking loud enough that they knew Speakes and I could hear their conversation. I took it seriously, and we thought that Speakes had also. However, Speakes did not halt the practice.

Reagan, naturally, assumed Speakes had stopped. Two years later, the fake quotes finally caught up with Speakes when he wrote a book after leaving the White House boasting of the practice. Although Speakes's book didn't mention the Fourth of July episode, he claimed that he made up a comment from Reagan when he was in a Geneva meeting with Gorbachev in 1985.

After Speakes's book came out, there was a huge press furor about the bogus quotes, and Speakes was forced to resign his job as chief spokesman for Merrill Lynch & Co. Reagan was not pleased and as good a job as Speakes did as spokesman for the president, especially after being thrust into the role after his predecessor Jim Brady was shot alongside the president, this was a terrible disservice to the president.

We used to say that you had to be pretty stupid to upset Ronald Reagan. But one day in 1986, I actually saw an outsider do it. In March, we were at a fund-raiser in New Orleans for Representative Henson Moore, a Republican congressman who was running for the Senate seat of retiring Democratic Senator Russell Long. In a state long dominated by Democrats, Moore actually had a shot at winning, and we had hopes of picking up a Senate seat in the midterm elections later that year.

At the time, Libya was in the news a lot. In early January, Reagan had issued an executive order banning trade with Libya and ordering all Americans out of the country because of Libyan leader Muammar Qaddafi's involvement in terrorist actions against Americans and other targets around the globe. There was much speculation that the United States was preparing to attack Libya, which, indeed, we were secretly preparing for.

Well, when we met Moore in a holding room shortly before the fund-raising luncheon in New Orleans, Moore tried to joke about the Libyan situation.

"There were rumors you weren't coming because of Libya," he said to Reagan. "But I told the audience you were on your way. And I also told them, Mr. President, that you wouldn't sleep through anything with Libya this time, like you did in 1981."

Moore was referring to an incident when Ed Meese had mistakenly decided not to awaken the president to tell him that U.S. Air Force fighter jets had shot down two Libyan MIGs. Meese acknowledged that it was an error and that he should have called the president sooner.

After Moore made his little joke, I thought the president was going to take his neck off, he looked that angry. He leaned in, looked Moore in the eyes and, speaking in a precise and firm tone, set him straight.

"Now look," he said to Moore. "I've been living with this for a long time. Yes, I was asleep. But I was in California, and it was *4:30 in the morning. Most* people are asleep at 4:30 a.m. No, I was not awakened. My staff now has orders to wake me up the minute something like that happens again. We made a big mistake, but *it won't happen again.*"

I looked at Moore. Good, I thought, you got what you deserved — a tongue lashing from Ronald Reagan. You managed to do the impossible — make Ronald Reagan angry!

Later that fall, I wasn't as sorry as I should have been when Moore lost his Senate race to Democrat John Breaux.

* * *

In April 1986, the president agreed with us to go to Baltimore to throw out a pitch on opening day at the Baltimore Orioles game against the Cleveland Indians. Normally, the president didn't like to go to sporting events because of the security risk it brought to other spectators at the event and also because of the inconvenience he knew it caused the other fans. But in this case, we assured him that the visit wouldn't be announced in advance, so the security risk would be much lower and the Secret Service would have to take minimal precautions.

We knew the president would enjoy throwing the ceremonial first ball and then sitting in the dugout and watching a few innings of the game. But we had to undergo sticky negotiations with the Secret Service over the president's position on the field. We wanted him to pitch from the pitcher's mound, but the Secret Service wanted him to stay close to the dugout. We compromised and decided that Reagan would throw to Orioles catcher Rick Dempsey down the third-base line.

But before we left the White House, I suggested to Reagan that he get some practice, pointing out to him that he hadn't thrown a baseball in a while. Reagan took great pride in his athletic ability, and I knew he wouldn't want to look awkward on the field.

Reagan liked that idea and suggested that we use some of the commemorative baseballs in my closet. I gathered a couple of them for our workout.

"Let's go outside and throw them around," said the president.

"I don't know where we can go where someone won't see us," I said, a little nervously. We couldn't play catch in the Rose Garden; the press would see us there. Nor could we go to the South Lawn and be seen by the press or the public.

Finally, we decided to go to a small area just behind the Oval Office that was shielded from public and press view. In the suit and tie that he would be wearing to Baltimore, he pitched, and I caught. His windup reminded me of when he played the pitcher Grover Cleveland Alexander in the movie *The Winning Team*. At first, his pitches were a little tentative; he was concerned he was going to hurt me since I didn't have a glove. But I assured him I was fine, and he started throwing harder. Then harder, until he was satisfied with his delivery.

In Baltimore, it was a gorgeous spring day, and the Orioles had a record crowd of 52,200 people. After we reached the Baltimore dugout, the public address announcer told the crowd that the president of the United States was at the game and coming out onto the field from the Baltimore dugout. Spectators gave him a standing ovation. The White House and Baltimore press started to crowd around as the president stepped out of the dugout and proceeded to third base. Dempsey positioned himself down the third-base line.

I could see that the president was looking concerned. I knew why. He was worried that he was going to hit someone with his pitch, what with all the press hovering around so close to Dempsey. Sure enough, the president was a little tentative with his pitch, and it went wild, sailing about 10 feet above Dempsey's mitt. The crowd roared with laughter.

I looked at the president. His lips were drawn into a taut line; I could tell he was angry and upset at himself for the poor pitch. I rushed over and asked him to throw the pitch a second time, which he agreed to do. I told the Orioles press person to have Dempsey quickly get the ball back to the president because he would throw again.

As the president got the ball again, I looked at him and said: "You know what to do this time."

This time Reagan burned one down the third-base line. It landed with a loud smack right in Dempsey's mitt, and the crowd cheered with great delight.

Reagan settled in the dugout with baseball commissioner Peter Ueberroth, Orioles manager Frank Robinson and Orioles owner Edward Bennett Williams (who, ironically, had represented would-be Reagan assassin John Hinckley in his insanity plea). Munching on a jumbo hot dog, the president chatted with the trio and with the players.

It was nice to see Reagan enjoying himself. There was a lot going on at the White House at the time. Just two days earlier, a bomb had exploded in a crowded West Berlin disco that was popular with U.S. soldiers stationed there. It killed an American sergeant and wounded 50 other GIs. To retaliate for the bombing, the president had been reviewing plans for American strikes at targets in Tripoli. The United States was convinced Muammar Qaddafi had been behind the attack.

But the president wasn't the only one

with Libya on his mind. During the game, Dempsey, who was known for being quite a character, came over and sat next to the president. He had a glint in his eye.

"Mr. President," he said. "I have a question. What would you do if Qaddafi was sitting here next to you right now?"

Reagan gritted his teeth. Now there was a glint in *his* eye. Oh boy, I thought.

"If that guy was sitting next to me now, I'd nail his nuts right here to this wooden bench," Reagan said.

Dempsey just howled with laughter.

Exactly one week later, on April 14, U.S. Air Force and Navy bombers attacked targets in and around the Libyan cities of Tripoli and Benghazi. With continuing terrorist attacks by Libya over the years, Reagan believed that after the West Berlin bombing, the outlaw nation had now gone far enough. There was no question in his mind that it was time to take action. He signed off on Caspar Weinberger's plan for an air strike.

On the afternoon of April 14, Weinberger came to the Oval Office for a meeting with the president, Regan and National Security Adviser John Poindexter.

"They're on their way," Weinberger warned Reagan. "There's no turning back."

"We're not turning back," Reagan answered.

That was vintage Reagan. He was incapable of self-doubt and once he made a decision, he moved on, fully confident that he had made the right judgment call. There was no looking back, no anguish.

The timing of the decision to bomb Libya was probably the most closely held secret of Reagan's second term. Only a few in the White House knew of the attacks beforehand. The president was supposed to go to Paul Laxalt's that evening for the annual "Lamb Fry" black-tie dinner, but the president knew that he must address the nation that night to announce the attacks. Since the president went to the Lamb Fry each year, I told Don Regan that we couldn't back out at the last minute or everyone would know something was up. So we let the staff and the Secret Service get dressed in black tie, as if we were actually going, and had the motorcade all lined up. But at the last minute, we canceled. The Oval Office was quickly broken down so that the television equipment could be moved in, and Reagan gave his address.

He told Americans that the United States had solid evidence that Libya was directly involved in the West Berlin bombing. He said the United States, with the help of allies, had aborted numerous Libyan terrorist attacks, including a planned massacre, using grenades and small arms, of citizens waiting in line for visas at an American embassy. He said that he "spoke to the outlaw Libyan regime in the only language that Colonel Qaddafi seems to understand."

As soft-spoken as the president was in private, he was a bold leader. As with Libya, he knew when to take tough action, and he knew when to hold firm to decisions with which others might disagree. Although he wasn't a tough-talking table pounder, he always got what he wanted. On the other hand, he liked to help people, and he always said yes when he was being asked for small favors. In fact, my job was to make sure he didn't say yes too often in those situations!

The president always kept his overall goals for the country firmly fixed in his mind. He knew he wasn't there to manage the government; he was there to make the world safer and grow the U.S. economy. He was always looking ahead to the next task that would further those goals. He never forgot that his time in office was limited and he was focused on accomplishing his agenda within that time frame — whether it was four years or eight years. He would remind cabinet members and White House staff over and over again: "That's why we're here, to make positive changes for the American people." Also, he reiterated many times during his eight-year presidency how important it was to "listen to the people."

Although he didn't like to hurt people's feelings, he didn't hesitate to say no when he believed their positions weren't moving the country toward those goals. Transportation Secretary Elizabeth Dole, for example, was adamantly opposed to a bill that Reagan was about to sign in his second term raising the speed limit outside major population areas to 65 miles per hour. It had been lowered to 55 in the '70s during the energy crisis. She requested a meeting with the president. Shortly before she arrived for the meeting, the president commented to me that he was determined to stick to his decision to raise the speed limit.

Dole tried to talk him out of it, but didn't get far.

The president spoke softly, but firmly. "I've given this a lot of thought, but I think it is in the best interests of the country to raise the speed limit."

Dole didn't give up. She came back at the president, saying that studies had shown that a higher speed limit caused more traffic fatalities. She reeled off other facts and figures and was relentless in her presentation.

The president didn't budge. "I understand, Elizabeth, but I think about the far West. If people want to put their pedal to the metal, I don't have a problem with that."

Dole tried again with more arguments and statistics. She rambled on for a few more minutes. The president heard her out, but refused to be dislodged.

"Elizabeth, I understand," he said again, still speaking softly. "But I think this is what we need to do."

Dole finally got the message, and the higher speed limits went into effect.

In 1986, Reagan had a similar encounter with the formidable Imelda Marcos, former first lady of the Philippines. Her husband, Ferdinand, had been ousted as president of the Philippines in February 1986 in a revolution fueled by "people power" — ordinary Filipinos tired of the Marcos regime. The Marcos family fled to Hawaii, and the United States had formally recognized the government of Corazon Aquino, the widow of Marcos's former rival. Until the revolution, the Reagans had had a good relationship with Ferdinand Marcos and the first lady, and the Marcoses had come to Washington for a state visit in 1981. The United States had considered Marcos an ally until his strong-arm tactics stole the election from the rightful winner, Aquino.

In April 1986, the Reagans stopped in Hawaii en route to the Asian Pacific region for meetings with Indonesian President Suharto, along with Southeast Asian foreign leaders and the annual economic summit meeting in Tokyo. They stayed not far from the new home of Mr. and Mrs. Marcos. We got word that Mrs. Marcos wanted to see the Reagans and ask them to help them return to the Philippines. That request was turned down, but the president called Mrs. Marcos and ended up talking to her for more than 30 minutes. Mrs. Reagan also got on the phone. National Security Adviser John Poindexter was in the room during the phone call, as was Don Regan.

Mrs. Marcos argued passionately that she and her husband should be permitted to return to the Philippines. She told the president and first lady that they just wanted to return to their homeland — that they were finished with running the country. Reagan listened courteously but didn't waver. He said he could not get involved, and there was nothing he could do.

But Mrs. Marcos was a strong-minded woman, and she didn't give up. She pleaded, she argued. Both Reagans listened patiently but said the Philippines had a democratically elected government and that they couldn't intervene. Reagan knew that if the Marcoses returned to the Philippines, even if Marcos didn't attempt to regain power, it would stir up trouble in the country.

Finally, Reagan tactfully ended the call. "I know we've been on the phone a long time," he said. But they would have to go, he told Imelda Marcos.

Again, Reagan held firm.

In another instance, Senator Steve Symms of Idaho was in the Oval Office in 1986 to have some footage made with the president for Symms's campaign commercials. Symms was part of a larger group of senators who came in for the video session that day, but each member came into the Oval Office on a one-on-one basis. Symms was the last senator to meet with Reagan, and before Symms's videotaping began, he asked me to close the door so he could speak with Reagan privately. I remained in the Oval Office and heard Symms tell the president that he had a plan for dealing with the Sandinista government in Nicaragua. The Marxist regime had taken power in 1979. Reagan passionately supported the contras, rebels who opposed the Sandinista government, but congressional Democrats weren't as supportive as Reagan. Congress had twice passed legislation banning aid to them.

In his closed-door meeting with Reagan, Symms suggested a plan to deal with the Sandinistas.

"Just send twenty-five thousand marines down to Nicaragua, Mr. President," said Symms. "You can wipe out the Sandinistas in two weeks. The Communists would be gone, the war would be over and we would win."

The president's reply was swift and unequivocal. "Steve, I realize that would work, but I can't do that," he said. "I appreciate the suggestion, Steve, but I just can't do that."

The most dramatic example of Reagan's capacity to keep his eyes firmly fixed on his goals for the country was his second summit with Mikhail Gorbachev in Reykjavik, Iceland, in October 1986. We had been doing a lot of traveling domestically in September and early October, making campaign appearances for the midterm elections coming up in November, as we were trying to retain Republican control of the Senate.

The Reagan administration and the Soviets had been working for months to put together another summit. A stumbling block that fall had been the Soviets' arrest of Nicholas Daniloff, a Moscow correspondent for *U.S. News & World Report*, whom the Soviets had accused of spying for the United States. Daniloff's arrest had occurred shortly after the United States arrested a Soviet intelligence officer, Gennadi Zakharov, in New York. After Daniloff's detention by the Soviets, Reagan ordered 25 Soviet diplomats expelled from the United States and wrote Gorbachev to assure him that Daniloff wasn't a U.S. spy.

When that didn't work, the president called in Soviet Foreign Minister Eduard Shevardnadze and upbraided him for the arrest of Daniloff on such trumped-up charges. Shevardnadze delivered to Reagan a letter inviting him to another summit as soon as possible.

After a period of negotiations, Daniloff was released, and Zakharov was delivered into Soviet custody. Those actions immediately opened the door to the next summit — in less than two weeks, in Reykjavik in early October. Reagan read voluminous briefing books to get ready, on top of his heavy campaign schedule for the '86 Senate elections.

Flying to Reykjavik on Air Force One on October 9, we had such optimism about this meeting between the two world leaders. So much had been accomplished the last time around. Imagine what we could achieve at the second summit.

We met at the seaside Hofdi House, an Icelandic government guesthouse that, rumor has it, was haunted. Nick Ruwe, Reagan's former director of advance and scheduling in the '80 campaign who had resigned when campaign director John Sears had departed, was now our ambassador to Iceland. Ruwe worked closely with the White House as summits usually take months to plan, and the Reykjavik summit had to be put together in a matter of days. The Icelanders had proposed staging the talks in a hotel, but Ruwe had argued that we needed a site that would be preserved for posterity.

Mrs. Reagan opted not to go to Reykjavik, partly because the Soviets told us that Mrs. Gorbachev would not attend, either. Well, wouldn't you know it, but Raisa Gorbachev showed up in Reykjavik. It appeared that she wanted to upstage Mrs. Reagan.

Before we departed, the president mentioned that he was taking a favorite coat with him — a heavy overcoat from his Hollywood days that he hadn't had a chance to wear since he had gotten to Washington. He was very proud of it and made sure it was packed for the trip.

In Iceland on the first day, we were scheduled to get together in the afternoon with the president of Iceland for a meeting and photos. The weather was fairly mild but Reagan was determined to wear his heavy overcoat.

Eddie Serrano pulled it out. After one look at it, I swallowed hard. It was awful. Big, with wide shoulders and fur-lined lapels, it looked like something out of a 1940s Hollywood movie filmed somewhere in Siberia. Not only that; it didn't even fit the president. Rather, it seemed to engulf him.

The president, on the other hand, was thrilled to wear it, and the photos with the

Icelandic president were shot with Reagan in that coat.

Unfortunately, Mrs. Reagan was monitoring the news coverage of Reykjavik from the White House. And I called Mrs. Reagan at the White House on the secure telephone before dinner on the first day, as I'd promised to do daily. I got an earful.

"Jim, what is going *on* over there?" she asked as soon as I reached her.

"Everything is fine," I reassured her.

"No," she said, "that *awful* coat. Why did you let him take it?" She had no idea that the president had taken it.

I said I hadn't actually known that the president had brought the coat until Serrano pulled it out in the ambassador's residence that morning.

Mrs. Reagan was exasperated. "He shouldn't have worn it. It looked horrible. I don't ever want to see that coat again. *Lose the coat,* you got it?"

I knew better than to argue. "Yes, ma'am," I said.

I lucked out after that. Rather than having to persuade the president to give up his beloved coat, the weather stayed mild so there was no need for coats. Plus, we'd already worked it out with the Soviets beforehand that neither Reagan nor Gorbachev would wear coats for any of their meetings in Iceland. The Soviets weren't going to get rolled on the coat maneuvering again!

As with Reagan and Gorbachev's initial meeting in Geneva, we arrived first and waited in the foyer of Hofdi House for Gorbachev's arrival. The windows in the foyer were set high, so it was difficult for our people to tell when Gorbachev arrived. We looked at our watches, figuring someone would tell us when they arrived. Finally, the naval aide above us shouted down, "They're here!" I grabbed the president and opened the door. Well, Gorbachev had already gotten out of his car and made his way to the door, so he and Reagan were nose to nose when the door opened.

The near collision didn't stop there.

That first day, negotiations between the Americans and the Soviets went very well, and Reagan was very encouraged. Gorbachev had proposed the two agree on the complete elimination of Soviet and U.S. intermediate-range nuclear missiles from Europe. However, Gorbachev proposed that work on the strategic defense initiative (SDI) be confined to the laboratory. And he proposed a moratorium on nuclear weapons testing. The two leaders talked about eliminating all nuclear weapons. Negotiators hammered away at the details all night.

On the second day, the scheduled noon conclusion came and went. Gorbachev, Reagan and their negotiators kept hammering away at what would be the most massive weapon reductions in history. It was looking good for an agreement.

Then a gigantic boulder landed in the middle of the road: SDI. Gorbachev insisted, as he had the previous day, that development of SDI be confined to the laboratory. It could not be deployed. Reagan rejected that stipulation, saying he had made a promise to the American people to deploy SDI. He offered to share results of the SDI research with the Soviets. Gorbachev rejected that offer. Reagan said he refused to discuss anything that involved eliminating SDI.

There was silence in the small room where the two were negotiating in the presence of Secretary Shultz and Foreign Minister Shevardnadze. Then Reagan stood up, closed his briefing book and walked out. After a moment's hesitation, Gorbachev followed.

We had been waiting outside the room

where Gorbachev and Reagan were negotiating with a sense of growing anticipation. The consequences of such an agreement — the elimination of all nuclear weapons — would rewrite history. As the bargaining went on into that Sunday evening, we assumed we could be staying another night in order to finalize the details of such a historic pact. The two leaders had spent almost 10 hours in sessions together, working through their differences.

But then Reagan and Gorbachev emerged. Reagan looked as angry as I have ever seen him. His lips were pulled tight, he moved stiffly, hands at his side.

"There is still time, Mr. President," Gorbachev told him. But Reagan replied that there was not.

As Gorbachev passed Don Regan, he said, "You should speak to the president, Mr. Chief of Staff."

"Mr. General Secretary, the two of you have been speaking to each other for two days," Regan replied. "Whatever the president has decided is what the president will do."

Reagan and Gorbachev walked to their motorcades together. Neither said much. They reached Reagan's motorcade first. Gorbachev told the president that he was sorry that it didn't work out.

"You could have said yes," said Reagan. Those were his final words.

And it was over.

At that point, we still weren't certain what had happened, except that the talks had ended abruptly on a bad note. According to our schedule, the president was supposed to go to a reception at the American embassy in Reykjavik after the conclusion of the talks, then to the naval air station, where he would speak to the 6,000 U.S. Navy and Air Force personnel stationed there before taking off.

But Reagan seemed so distraught, we weren't sure what to do next. His Secret Service detail looked at me, and someone asked me whether we were still going back to the embassy or whether we were going straight to Air Force One at Keflavik Naval Air Station.

"I don't know," I said. Obviously, something had gone very wrong. The talks had clearly fallen apart. Why, we didn't know for sure.

"The president might just want to get on the plane and get out of here," I said. "Although, I think he's going to want to do the right thing and meet with our people."

By this time, the president was in the

limo. He was looking straight ahead, in deep thought. His face displayed a great sense of loss. I got into the car with him.

"Mr. President," I said, "I know you have a lot on your mind, but we've got to figure out what we're doing here. Do you want to go to the airport or do you want to go to the embassy?"

Reagan didn't answer. He was still looking straight ahead, then off to his left. I couldn't tell whether he had heard me.

"Mr. President, you've got to make a decision," I said. He didn't respond.

Finally, I grabbed him by the arm. "Mr. President," I said, "we're scheduled to go to the embassy for you to meet with the staff there. Do you want to go to the embassy or do you want to go right to the airport?"

At last he responded, turning toward me, although I could tell he wasn't really focused on me. I had never seen him this upset before. Normally, Ronald Reagan could roll with just about any punch. Insults, defeats, setbacks — nothing got to him. But he wasn't rolling right now.

"Stay with the schedule," the president said finally.

We drove back to the embassy, where we went into the gardens to await the reception. It was a mild October evening, and the president and I waited quietly. I wanted to ask him what had happened but, out of respect, I left him alone. When it came time to greet the embassy staff, Reagan was gracious but, to me, he had a forlorn look on his face. We had the staff move through quickly, as Reagan was far from his normal self.

I was getting very worried. I was confident he would eventually snap out of it. But when?

En route to the airport, Pat Buchanan, who was on the trip, revised Reagan's remarks to the U.S. troops to reflect the collapse of the talks. At the military base, Buchanan, Poindexter and others huddled in a back room, revising the speech until the last minute. When the president delivered his remarks, you would never have known the extent of his disappointment. That larger-than-life public persona stood him in good stead, and he spoke with composure and grace.

Reagan said that the talks had helped the two sides move toward an agreement on reducing intermediate-range nuclear missiles in both Europe and Asia. But, he said, Gorbachev had rejected his proposal to delay SDI for 10 years in exchange for the complete elimination of all ballistic missiles from the arsenals of both countries. Gorbachev wanted the United States to restrict SDI to laboratory research. That, said Reagan, "would have killed our defensive shield."

"We came to Iceland to advance the cause of peace," said the president, "and though we put on the table the most far-reaching arms control proposal in history, the general secretary rejected it."

On Air Force One, en route back to Washington, we had a quiet dinner.

We all wondered how long the president was going to be this way. None of us had seen him this distraught before.

Halfway across the Atlantic, the president emerged from the stateroom, a smile on his face, and came down to the senior staff section of the aircraft. His eyes sparkled again.

Ronald Reagan was back.

"You guys were probably worried about me back there for a while," he said to us. "I know I was quite upset." He said he wasn't sure, in walking out of the talks, whether he had done what was best for America.

But, he said, he couldn't give up our insurance policy, SDI, not for America's future. "I'm now sure that I made the right decision back there."

The president also said that we would go forward from here and see what happens.

It was very hard for him to come so close to a monumentally historic agreement, after all those decades, all the fear, all the billions of dollars expended on weapons designed to wipe out entire civilizations. To walk away from the opportunity to finally end MAD — it tortured him until he determined he had made the only possible decision for his country.

Later, in a speech from the Oval Office, the president explained to Americans his refusal to compromise. He said he couldn't agree to Gorbachev's demand that the United States confine SDI testing and development to the laboratory for the next 10 years. SDI, he said, was "America's insurance policy" against cheating or the possibility of a madman's getting nuclear weapons. But he emphasized his optimism that the United States and Soviets could overcome their deep differences over SDI.

"Our ideas are out there on the table," he said. "They won't go away. We are ready to pick up where we left off."

The reviews of the Reykjavik talks were, predictably, scathing from some quarters, although looking back on the critics' comments almost two decades later, they were breathtakingly off base.

Senator Edward Kennedy, for example, told the media that the opportunity for a historic arms agreement was lost because the president had insisted on pursuing the SDI defense shield.

Stephen Cohen, an expert on Soviet affairs at Princeton University, was quoted as saying, "I think it was a tragedy. I think a moment has been missed. It's not clear it can be regained."

But Republican Senator Pete Wilson said that Reagan had successfully avoided a trap, and "I commend the president for being smart enough to recognize it and resist it."

In retrospect, Reykjavik was actually a critical turning point in disarmament negotiations. When you're down so low, there's nowhere to go but up, and that's what we did in negotiations leading to the next summit, in Washington in 1987. At the time, though, we had no way of knowing that triumph awaited us around the corner.

Years later, when all the major figures were out of office, George Shultz said he asked Gorbachev what he believed was the turning point that led to the end of the cold war. Gorbachev's reply, Shultz said, was immediate.

"Reykjavik," he told Shultz. The two leaders, Gorbachev said, according to Shultz "for the first time . . . had a deep conversation about everything. We really exchanged views, and not just peripheral things, but some central things. And that's what was important about Reykjavik."

Shortly after Reykjavik, however, we were struck by a crisis that dwarfed the summit: Iran-contra.

16

THE IRAN-CONTRA AFFAIR

On Election Day 1986, three weeks after the Reykjavik summit, we were in Los Angeles finishing up a weeklong campaign swing through the South and West. Reagan had been campaigning hard for Republican candidates to try to hang on to the Republican majority in the Senate, which Reagan had brought in on his coattails in his 1980 victory. But now, in 1986, that majority was endangered, and the midterm elections were crucial.

As we boarded Air Force One on November 4, a member of the press shouted out what sounded at the time like an odd question: "What about Bud McFarlane going to Iran?"

Reagan did not respond. McFarlane was Reagan's former national security adviser who had resigned in December 1985 and was replaced by his deputy, Admiral John Poindexter.

As it turned out, reports from the Mideast had claimed that Bud McFarlane had gone to Iran with several other Americans, arriving aboard a plane carrying military equipment that Iran had purchased from international arms dealers. The men, the reports said, had posed as aircraft crewmen and traveled on Irish passports. They also brought with them revolvers and a cake as gifts for top Iranian officials.

With that shouted question on November 4, 1986, we were launched into the bizarre rabbit hole of the Iran-contra affair.

Stretching from the steep slopes of Nicaragua to the narrow streets of bombed-out Beirut, the Iran-contra matter ultimately would lead to the ouster of Poindexter, the firing of NSC employee Oliver North, the departure of Don Regan, the suicide attempt of McFarlane — and accusations that would threaten Reagan's legacy as a world leader.

I won't attempt to give a blow-by-blow chronology of the twists and turns of the Iran-contra affair in this book, but it had its roots in the president's deep concern about the American hostages who were being held captive in Lebanon: journalist Terry Anderson, the Reverend Lawrence Jenco, CIA Station Chief William Buckley, American University Administrator David Jacobsen, American University Librarian David Kilburn, the Reverend Benjamin

Weir and Thomas Sutherland. Their plight just tore him apart. Almost every day at his 9:30 a.m. security briefing, he asked about them — whether American intelligence knew where they were and what kinds of efforts were being made to find them.

He met several times with families of the hostages, just as he had met with family members of the TWA hijacking hostages. In fact, just five days before revelations about McFarlane's trip to Iran, he had been quite upset with his staff because he missed an opportunity to meet with the family of one of the Beirut hostages. We were in Spokane for a campaign appearance in October 1986. The morning that we arrived, Reagan saw a news report on a local television station on which the family members complained that they had contacted the White House, seeking a meeting with Reagan, but had been turned down.

When I checked in on him that morning, he had just gotten out of the shower and had wrapped a towel around himself. He had just seen the television report and was quite angry that he hadn't been told that a hostage's family wished to see him.

"Why didn't we let this family meet with me?" he insisted.

In the end, we weren't able to arrange a

meeting between the president and the family because of the tight schedule, but Reagan did call them. The president was upset with the National Security Council, which had been earlier contacted by the family but refused the family's request to meet with the president.

That was the genesis of the Iran-contra affair: the president's intense desire to free the captured men. The president held meetings in the White House residence in 1985, exploring the possibility of shipping arms through Israel to moderates in Iran who might be able to influence the release of the hostages. While in the hospital recovering from his colon surgery in July 1985, the president approved McFarlane's request to open contact with a group of moderate Iranians through the Israelis. Those moderates, McFarlane told the president, had offered to persuade the terrorists to release the seven American hostages.

In January 1986, the president signed a secret intelligence finding authorizing arms shipment to Iran. And in May, McFarlane and NSC staff member Colonel Oliver North traveled to Iran with a planeload of weapons. Other planeloads were to follow. In late October, David Jacobsen was released. But we were saddened to learn that Kilburn and Buckley had died in captivity. And, unfortunately, other Americans were taken as hostages.

Shortly after the Iran-contra scandal broke, Reagan tried to quell it with an address to the nation, telling Americans that it was "utterly false" that the United States had paid ransom to Iran for the American hostages in Lebanon. He said the United States had covertly sent arms to Tehran to gain access and influence there in the hopes of ending the six-year-old Iran-Iraq war and stemming international terrorism.

"We did not — repeat, did not — trade weapons or anything else for hostages, nor will we," Reagan said.

In the president's mind, the weapons shipments to Iran weren't part of an "arms-for-hostages" deal. Rather, he believed strongly that the arms could potentially help the group of moderates take over in Iran. And if those moderates helped us get the hostages back, then so be it. But he stubbornly never saw it as a direct quid pro quo. It was a viewpoint akin to the way he viewed his colon cancer — "Hell, I didn't have cancer." He simply willed himself to believe that it hadn't existed.

In a news conference on November 19, Reagan stumbled badly at times in answering questions about the deal. The president had done his usual prepress conference preparation in the small theater in the White House residence. In Larry Speakes's book, published later in Reagan's second term, Speakes had complained that readying the president for a press conference was like "reinventing the wheel." I disagree. As with most presidents, we rehearsed press conferences, generally two hours the day before the press conference and 90 or so minutes on the day of the news conference.

But Poindexter briefed the president poorly on the Iran arms deal, failing to provide him with the full details and, of course, never revealing the most explosive information — that some of the profits from the arms deal had been diverted to help fund the contra rebels in Nicaragua. He really put President Reagan in the middle of a very difficult and unfair situation, and the press conference should never have taken place. But we were following Reagan's maxim — full disclosure — without knowing that Poindexter had been less than forthcoming about his full knowledge of the entire affair.

Americans responded to the president's explanations skeptically. A *Los Angeles Times* poll showed that only 14 percent of Americans believed the president when he said that the Iranian initiative did not involve exchanging arms for hostages.

But that wasn't the end of the revelations. Attorney General Ed Meese looked into the matter over the weekend of November 22–23 and briefed the president Monday in the Oval Office. His findings were staggering: Between $10 million and $30 million collected from the Iranians for the U.S.-shipped weapons were siphoned off, Meese said, and had gone to the Nicaraguan contras, who were fighting the Marxist Sandinista regime in that country. The only people who knew about the transfer, Meese told the president, were National Security Adviser John Poindexter and NSC staffer Colonel Oliver North.

In the Oval Office that morning, the president listened carefully to the information. The color drained from his face when he heard about the contras. Then, after closely questioning Meese, his reaction was unequivocal.

"We have to disclose this information as soon as possible," he said. That was the Reagan doctrine — when in doubt, always full disclosure. Get the facts out as fast as possible. Reagan had a deep faith in the American public and believed Americans expected, and deserved, that.

The next day, the president and Meese went to the White House press room and told them everything they knew. The president announced he was naming a commission to investigate the matter and that the Justice Department would launch a probe of how the money was handled to determine whether federal crimes were committed. He told reporters that Poindexter had resigned to return to the navy and that North had been "relieved of his duties."

It was a tense time in the White House, and we struggled to maintain some sense of normalcy. The day after the Meese press conference, for example, the president was scheduled to have the annual presentation of a live Thanksgiving turkey at the White House. In the morning staff meeting that day, Pat Buchanan urged us to cancel the turkey presentation. If not, he warned, the press would make all kinds of turkey analogies to the president's current mess. It was not the kind of story, Buchanan suggested, that we wanted to have the day after the Meese report.

I called Don Regan, who agreed with

Buchanan. But I felt differently, arguing that it made matters worse if the president canceled an annual event like that. It would appear that the president had something to hide, and this was clearly not Reagan's style.

I finally went to the president about it. That morning, I went up to the White House residence and explained Buchanan's and Regan's objections and told him it was his decision whether to carry on with the traditional turkey presentation. But my recommendation was that he go through with it.

The president agreed, saying it was "nonsense" to consider canceling the event just so there wouldn't be the possibility of turkey analogies made about his situation.

"We're going through with the event, okay?" he told Regan in the morning Oval Office meeting.

And so we did. The president was peppered with questions about the Iran-contra matter and its effect on his presidency, but he remained silent on the issue and continued with his usual ceremony of "pardoning" the turkey from ending up on someone's dinner table the next day. And I didn't see any turkey jokes the next day in the media.

The white-hot heat of the Iran-contra affair continued for months. There were more revelations — that North and his assistant, Fawn Hall, had shredded documents related to the matter in North's White House office after the diversion of funds to the contras was uncovered, for example, and that CIA Director William Casey had been deeply involved in finding sources of funding for the contras. The commission that the president had promised, the Tower Commission, was headed by former Senator John Tower and with members Brent Scowcroft, a retired air force lieutenant general, and former Senator Edmund Muskie. Lawrence Walsh was later appointed as an independent counsel to conduct a criminal inquiry. In 1987, congressional investigations went on for almost a year.

Just when things couldn't have gotten worse, we got news in mid-December that Bill Casey had collapsed in his office. In early February, a depressed Bud McFarlane tried to commit suicide with an overdose of Valium on the day he was supposed to be questioned by the Tower Commission. Reagan was especially concerned about McFarlane's welfare.

In the midst of it all, Reagan was described in some press reports as being deeply depressed about the crisis. One morning when we were walking from the residence to the Oval Office along the Colonnade, the president stopped and looked at me.

"Jim," he said, "how do I look to you?"

I examined him. His face had its usual glow, and his eyes were bright. He had the same smile and the same vigor.

"You look great, as always," I responded. "Why do you ask?"

"I just wanted to know if you thought I looked as depressed as the papers say I am," he said. "Everybody says it's doom and gloom over here, that there is a cloud over my head. They say I'm quite depressed."

He looked at me again. His face was sober, but there was a glint in his eye.

I laughed. "You never look depressed to me. I've rarely seen you even *close* to that state of mind."

He grinned. He seemed a bit relieved. "Thank you."

Naturally, the whole mess bothered him but he certainly wasn't operating in a deep state of depression. Even so, he read the papers every morning, and he must have wondered at times whether he really was as disheartened as the media claimed he was.

But that simply wasn't in Ronald Reagan's character. He wasn't distracted by the crisis. What bothered him the most, actually, was not that his presidential legacy was in danger of being scarred by Iran-contra, but that people lost their jobs because of it. When Poindexter stepped down and North was fired, Reagan worried about the effect on their careers. He was never concerned about himself. He believed that North and Poindexter had acted in what they believed to be the best interests of the country, but that the affair had gone off course. North and Poindexter had gone too far, and that was wrong. Although North and Poindexter had betrayed the president, Reagan never felt personally betrayed. As always, he felt no bitterness toward them. On the day North was fired — November 25 — Reagan called him to thank him for his service. Even after revelations that North had shredded documents, the president called him a "national hero" in a *Time* magazine story.

"My only criticism," Reagan told the magazine, "is that I was not told everything."

While Reagan wasn't angry at North, the

rest of Reagan's staff was mighty perturbed with him, especially when North claimed later that he had met one-on-one with the president. After that claim, we combed through White House records and found that over a 17-month period in the Reagan White House, North was in 18 meetings with the president. But at all of the meetings, there were always several other people present. North was never alone with the president. He was also never in the White House residence or at Camp David with President Reagan.

But if Oliver North's actions and claims didn't upset the president, the Tower Commission report did. In fact, the day the Tower report was released — February 26 — was one of only three days during Ronald Reagan's presidency when he seemed off stride. (The other two instances were the day the Reykjavik talks ended with Gorbachev and the day of Nancy Reagan's breast surgery.)

The day of the report's release, the president seemed preoccupied, uneasy and even nervous. I was surprised. He didn't have anything to hide; he had known nothing about the diversion of funds to the contras and was confident that the Tower Commission would also make that finding. He had told the Tower Commission everything he knew about the matter. But the commission had refused to allow the president to read the report before it was released, so there could be no accusations that the president had influenced it in any way. But it meant Reagan had no idea what the report said, yet he was expected to appear at a news conference with the Tower Commission moments after the report was released. It put the president in the awkward position of appearing at a news conference where Tower Commission members would discuss the results without actually having read the report himself. Quite unfair for anyone, let alone the president.

In fact, while the report criticized the president's handling of the weapons deal, it confirmed the president's assertion that he did not know about the plan to use profits from the sale to support the Nicaraguan rebels. And it said that he did not intend to mislead the American public or conduct a cover-up.

The Tower Commission did fault Reagan for operating in a management style that placed "especially heavy responsibility on key advisers," yet, it said, the president did not insist they be held accountable for their actions.

It wasn't the president's management style to micromanage or to constantly look over the shoulders of subordinates. He was very trusting — probably the most trusting person I've ever worked with or been around. But, clearly, he had trusted Poindexter too much, and he had gone too far. Don Regan was chastised for not having better control of the NSC on behalf of the president.

After the Tower report announcement that day, Reagan bounced back and was his old self again. After the news conference, he had lunch with the Supreme Court justices that day, and we were back on track.

One of Reagan's great strengths was that he could move beyond crises. He simply moved on to the next thing. His reaction was the same with great triumphs as well. After he signed the landmark INF treaty with Gorbachev at the 1987 White House summit, he came back to the Oval Office and went back to work the very next day. He wasn't one to dwell on past triumphs any more than he brooded over mistakes.

Before the Tower report, it had become increasingly clear that Regan had to go. He had served the president loyally for six years. He worked hard, and I enjoyed working with him. But his imperious manner and his tendency to cut off communication between the president and his senior staff hurt the president at times. He seemed to be seeking a larger-than-usual starring role for a White House chief of staff. For example, when he jumped into the historic photo of Reagan and Gorbachev seated on the couch in Geneva. At a campaign stop in Malvern, Pennsylvania, for example, he was announced onto the stage prior to the president — again, not a customary practice for White House chiefs of staff, who are expected to be more low profile. He also had Secret Service protection, which didn't sit too well with many White House staffers and the press corps. It was unprecedented for the White House chief of staff to have his own Secret Service detail.

Even the president had joked about Regan's role as American "prime minister," as Regan was sometimes called. At the annual Alfalfa Club dinner earlier in 1986, the president personally wrote a joke about Regan in his remarks. It was a mock advisory to the audience, much like the one made at public events attended by the president.

"In compliance with our long-standing Alfalfa tradition," President Reagan read, "at the conclusion of the evening, will you all kindly remain at your tables as the most powerful man in the world makes his exit through that door?" He turned to Senator Fritz Hollings, the chairman of the dinner: "Well, Fritz, once Don is gone, is it okay if I go out the same way?"

He got a roar of laughter from the Alfalfa crowd, but it was also a sign that Reagan was very aware of the attention Regan was getting.

Regan hadn't won any friends on Capitol Hill, either. Privately and publicly, members of Congress were calling for Regan's resignation. Members of the cabinet found him difficult to deal with. At one point, Regan was warned not to attend a Republican congressional leadership meeting in the cabinet room because a member was going to make a serious appeal to the president to dump him. With Regan sitting only a few seats away at the leadership meeting, Congressman Sylvio Conte of Massachusetts told the president that it was time for him to go. Things were becoming quite tough for Don Regan.

Regan's worst sin was his strained relationship with the first lady. In Reagan's first term, Mrs. Reagan had been accustomed to calling Mike Deaver frequently to ask questions and make comments about the staff and how things were working for the president. When Deaver left, she naturally began to telephone Don Regan, and I heard from her frequently as well. But her calls drove Regan, a former marine and the former hard-driving chairman of Merrill Lynch, a little crazy. The first lady came to believe that Regan was no longer serving the president well.

One day Regan came to me. "I did something really bad," he said. He appeared rather ashamed of himself.

"What did you do?" I asked, wondering what on earth had happened.

"I hung up on the first lady," he said.

"You *what?*" I said. I couldn't imagine someone doing something like that to the first lady. *Hanging up on the first lady?* "You shouldn't have done that, Don," I said.

"I know," he said.

There were those who were laying the groundwork with the media for Don's demise months before the Tower report was released. In fact, months before the Tower report, President Reagan was asked by the media on the way to Marine One to head for Camp David if he would keep Don

Regan as his chief of staff. Reagan endorsed Regan with the press. That led to a rather volatile discussion between the president and the first lady when they arrived at Camp David.

The senior White House staff had been talking for weeks about the need to bring in a new chief of staff, but Regan — a proud man and, like the president, a stubborn Irishman — resisted the pressure to resign. In the meantime, he became less and less effective as the press commented and speculated on his imminent departure.

The president, even though he knew there had to be a change, was reluctant to fire Regan. He hated to terminate people, and he didn't like confrontations. In the Oval Office, I talked to the president about the situation.

"You know there is going to need to be a change, Mr. President," I said. "And you're going to have to make that decision at some point soon."

"I know Don has worked hard," Reagan said. "He's served me well. He did an outstanding job as secretary of the Treasury."

"Yes, I know," I said. "He deserves an A plus as Treasury secretary. He's also done a very good job as chief of staff. But I know you're at the point where you have to make a change."

"I know Don's made a few mistakes along the way," the president said thoughtfully.

I asked the president what kind of mistakes he thought Regan had made. The president mentioned the photo in Geneva the previous year. So, he had picked up on the comments about that, I thought. Ronald Reagan never ceased to amaze me.

It pointed out to me, once again, that Reagan knew a lot more about the goings-on at the White House, and elsewhere, than he let on. Even though he chose not to get involved in such matters, that didn't mean he was oblivious to them. Over the years that I worked for him, I figured out that he knew about much of the infighting and the office politics of the White House, but he stayed out of it. He understood that it was part of the natural process, but he never really thought he needed to step in, knowing that it would work itself out. Rather, the president concentrated on staying focused on the issue of the day, kept rolling and kept his mind on the big policy picture.

He also seemed to have some sources for information that the senior White House staff didn't know about. For example, after a speech to the American Newspaper Publishers convention in May 1987 on Ellis Island, the press started shouting questions to Reagan, asking him if he would comment on media reports that a young woman — later identified as Donna Rice — had spent the night at the home of Democratic presidential front-runner Gary Hart while Hart's wife was out of town. It was the first we'd heard about it, but Reagan knew all about it.

In 1987, when Don Regan finally bowed to the inevitable and agreed to go, he wanted more distance between the Tower report and his departure. But Mrs. Reagan and the White House staff wanted him gone as soon as possible so the White House could move forward with a clean slate. In meetings with Mrs. Reagan, Paul Laxalt and Mike Deaver in the White House residence, the president decided on former Senate Majority Leader Howard Baker as his next chief of staff — if Baker would take the job. Baker had great rapport with Republicans and Democrats on Capitol Hill, and the president badly needed to repair his relationships with Congress what with the ongoing rancor of the Iran-contra affair. But Baker was now a high-paid Washington lawyer and might be reluctant to return to the relatively low pay of government work.

Reagan's philosophy was to hire the best person for the job and, often, the best person for the job was someone who was willing to take a pay cut. Deaver approached Baker, who responded positively and agreed to meet with the president, who then would ask him formally to become his chief of staff.

On February 27, the day after the release of the Tower Commission report, Baker came into the White House through the southeast White House entrance to evade the ever-watchful press. Paul Laxalt had ridden over with him in a White House car. I was in the diplomatic reception room and went down to greet them and get them up to the White House residence, where the president was waiting, to keep the meeting more private than it would have been in the Oval Office.

Laxalt came charging out of that car like a colt that had just broken out of the barn. Baker emerged much more slowly, almost dragging his feet and looked at me with a half smile.

"Oh, Jim," he said. "What am I doing?"

"You're doing this because the president

needs you, Senator," I told him and led him upstairs. "You're doing a great thing."

But how to get Don Regan to depart gracefully, and quickly? Vice President Bush stepped in and performed some tactful shuttle diplomacy. He went back and forth between the Oval Office and Regan's office until the details were worked out, and Regan agreed to depart the following Monday, four days after the release of the Tower report.

On Friday, the day after the Tower report, the news leaked, and CNN reported that Baker would replace Regan as chief of staff.

Furious, Regan dictated a terse resignation letter. "Dear Mr. President," it said, "I hereby resign as Chief of Staff to the President of the United States. Respectfully, Donald T. Regan."

I received the letter and passed it along to the president, who called Regan after he read it. It was a difficult conversation. The president told Regan he was sorry for what happened, but confirmed that Baker would be his next chief of staff. Regan, understandably, was angry. He'd worked hard for the president for six years.

"I deserved better treatment than this," he told the president. "I'm through."

"I'm sorry," said the president.

The Don Regan era was over.

Howard Baker moved into the White House chief of staff job as if he'd been doing it for years, although I know he did sometimes regret that pay cut. One day in 1987, prior to an Oval Office meeting with the president, Baker asked me: "Jim, do you know how much money I made last year?"

"No, I don't, Howard," I said. "How much?"

He laughed, but a bit sadly. "Over a million dollars."

The president didn't let himself get distracted by the Iran-contra affair, even through the lengthy congressional hearings in 1987. He simply compartmentalized it into one part of his mind and kept moving forward with his agenda for the country.

Nevertheless, Reagan occasionally brought it up. In June 1987, for example, during the congressional hearings, we were in Italy for the economic summit. We were in Reagan's Venice hotel suite that afternoon, and we flipped on the television to CNN. Fawn Hall was testifying before the Senate-House Iran-contra committee. Reagan looked at the blond-haired young woman curiously.

"Who is that?" he said. Until then, neither the president nor I had ever seen her. She worked in the White House, but the White House is a big place, and Reagan certainly couldn't know all the staff.

"That's Fawn Hall," I said.

"Oh, *that's* who she is," the president commented.

And on July 15, 1987, John Poindexter was scheduled to testify before the Congressional committee on what had become the consuming question of the hearings: What did the president know about the diversion of Iranian arms money to Nicaragua?

We were on Air Force One, readying for departure for a trip to the Midwest on July 13. The president sat across the table from me in the presidential stateroom.

"Jim," the president said, crossing his fingers, "this is the week that John Poindexter clears me once and for all."

Clearly, it had weighed on Reagan's mind for some time.

Sure enough, Poindexter did clear President Reagan on July 15 when he said that the buck stopped with him. Poindexter testified that he had not informed the president about the plan to divert money from the Iranian arms deal to the contras.

"The important point here is that on this whole issue, the buck stops with me," Poindexter told the committee. "I made the decision. I felt I had the authority to do it. I thought it was a good idea. I was convinced the president would, in the end, think it was a good idea. But I did not want him associated with the decision."

17

THE FIRST LADY AND HER "ROOMMATE"

I clearly remember my first head-on encounter with Nancy Reagan. It was the presidential primary campaign in May 1980, and we were in the midst of a blitz of Ohio, a key swing state in that year's presidential race. The Reagans were meeting and greeting voters at the West Side Market in Cleveland, a bustling farmers' market crowded with shoppers on that rainy Saturday morning.

I was the lead advance man for the event, and the plan was for governor and Mrs. Reagan to greet people inside the cavernous structure that held various food booths — beef, sausages, bread, produce and the like — and then to step outside into an open-air market where more farmers had set up shop.

It was gushing rain, however. The heavens seemed to have opened up, and it came down in buckets. The open-air market was covered, but copious amounts of water poured through the leaky roof. I opened the door to the open-air area, planning to lead the Reagans outside despite the deluge. But Mrs. Reagan stopped, eyeing the water dripping from the roof.

"We'll work around the water coming through the roof," I reassured Mrs. Reagan. She eyed me skeptically while Governor Reagan observed politely.

"We're going to go out there?" she asked.

"We're going to be fine, Mrs. Reagan," I assured her. "It's not that bad."

She looked me square in the eyes. "Jim," she said, nodding toward the gushing water, "it's not that good."

I got the message. "I guess we're not going out there, are we?" I said.

"No," she said firmly. "We're not going out there."

That was Nancy Reagan. She had a way of stopping you in your tracks if she believed you weren't acting in the best interests of her husband, later as president to be known as her "roommate."

It's easy to misunderstand Nancy Reagan and, over the years, a lot of people have. The one most important thing to understand about Mrs. Reagan is the depth of her devotion to her husband. Throughout their marriage, she always looked out for him, not for herself.

It's also important to understand something else: Ronald Reagan was just as devoted to her as she to him. He was often quoted as saying that coming home to Nancy was like "coming out of the cold into a warm, firelit room." Even after decades of marriage, they were as in love with each other as the day they were married.

I have never seen two people adore each other so much: Their relationship was almost like a fairy tale. Whether it was upstairs in the White House residence, in Aspen Cabin at Camp David, in a hotel suite or even in an elevator — wherever they were, they behaved as if they were newlyweds, linking hands, looking into each other's eyes, each admiring the other.

In contrast, I remember watching a camera catch Bill and Hillary Clinton as they walked from their hotel to Madison Square Garden when I was watching the Democratic National Convention on television in 1992. For an instant, they didn't realize they were on camera. Then, as it dawned on them that the cameras were rolling, I saw them grab for each other's hand.

The Reagans were just the opposite. You couldn't get them to stop holding hands and looking at each other. Sometimes I just wanted to say "Break it up, you two!" as if they were a couple of lovesick teenagers. In elevators, when we were about to reach our floor and I knew people would be out there waiting for them, I would clear my throat to get their attention. "Mr. President, Mrs. Reagan," I would say, "I need to talk to you before the elevator doors open up." I wanted to prepare them for the moment when the doors opened and hordes of outsiders barged into their private world.

On Friday and Saturday movie nights during weekends at Camp David, when the Reagans would gather their support staff to watch first-run films with them, the Reagans cuddled on the couch as if on their first date.

Theirs was like an old-fashioned love affair from the movies. Only it was real. Throughout their marriage, the president frequently sent her lyrical notes professing his love. A few years ago, Mrs. Reagan collected them in a book: *I Love You, Ronnie.* Reading them can bring tears to your eyes. In cards, on hotel letterhead, governor's stationery and White House note cards, Reagan always found a poetic way to express his passion for her. One note on White House stationery simply read: "I love you, I love you, I love you, I love you, I love you, I love you, I love you, I love you, I love you. And besides that — I love you."

In March 1983, when they rendezvoused in California after a separation of a day or so to celebrate their thirty-first wedding anniversary on the royal yacht *Britannia* in San Francisco Bay with the queen and Prince Philip, the president stepped off Air Force One with a note he'd written for her en route, saying that the day marked 31 years of happiness. He told her that their marriage was, to him, like an adolescent's dream of what marriage should be.

"I more than love you," his note continued. He was incomplete without her, he went on to say, and could only "start living again when she returned to him."

In a way, the Reagans completed and complemented each other, and they didn't need a lot of other people around for entertainment. They were content just being together and enjoying what little privacy they had. For example, they never had a lot of guests at the ranch or Camp David while Reagan was president. They enjoyed having that time to themselves.

I saw their deep love for each other demonstrated again and again but nowhere as much as when Mrs. Reagan underwent a radical mastectomy on her left breast in October 1987 after being diagnosed with breast cancer. At first, the president seemed to take the news in stride. Being the optimistic soul that he was, he was confident that she would be fine and have a full recovery, and he remained upbeat, positive and encouraging to Mrs. Reagan.

The night before her operation, the president took her to Bethesda Naval Hospital, where the surgery would be performed. The president planned to return early the next morning. Again, he was upbeat and comforting with her, giving her a kiss and a hug before departing.

The next morning, I came back to the White House and went upstairs to the residence at 6:00 a.m. and found a changed man. His positive outlook had deserted him completely. He looked hollowed out, nervous, even frightened. The realization that this was serious surgery and the prognosis could be very bad had really sunk in. He was jittery — pacing up and down impatiently as he waited for the motorcade to arrive, utterly consumed with concerns about his wife.

As it turned out, we weren't able to helicopter to Bethesda because of the weather, so we scheduled a motorcade, which was to leave at 6:45 for the hospital. Mrs. Reagan's brother, neurosurgeon Dick Davis, had spent the night in the White House residence and was to accompany the president to the hospital. When I arrived, the president and Davis were ready to go. God knows how long the president had been ready! Probably for some time.

I reminded the president of what he needed to take with him: Some paperwork had to be completed, and he needed to see some other documents. As we were about to head down to the motorcade from the residence, I asked him about one particular document on which he needed to make a decision that day.

"I don't have that one," he said. I said I'd get it from his desk in the Oval Office, and asked him to wait for me upstairs.

"I'll be right back," I said. "Then I'll go down with you to the motorcade."

I rushed into the Oval Office, grabbed the papers I was looking for and headed back out. I glanced out the window to the South Lawn. The motorcade was pulling out!

I sprinted out of the Oval Office, running into Mark Weinberg from our press office along the way, with the White House press pool in tow. Weinberg and the press looked stunned.

"Was that the president?" Weinberg asked.

We went back over to the residence. No one was around. No president, no Dr. Davis, no Secret Service.

"He left!" I said to Weinberg. Reagan hadn't heard one word I'd said all morning, and as soon as he saw that motorcade, he'd jumped in and taken off. Weinberg was upset. The president was going to drive all the way to Bethesda Naval Hospital — about 10 miles — without press coverage. The White House reporters were furious. What if something happened to him along the way, they demanded. The president has media coverage whenever he leaves the White House.

I wasn't really upset about it, though. I knew how concerned he was about his beloved Nancy and how eager he was to get back to her. We rounded up other White House vehicles and, with the press, got to the hospital about 30 minutes after the president.

Ten days later, tragedy struck Mrs. Reagan again. We received word that her mother, Edith Luckett Davis, 91, had died of a stroke. Mrs. Reagan had been extraordinarily close to her mother; they spoke on the telephone almost every day. Mrs. Davis had been in ill health for several years. Even so, her death was going to hit the first lady very hard.

The president's secretary, Kathy Osborne, gave Reagan the news, and Reagan immediately headed for the White House residence, where the first lady was recovering from her surgery. I accompanied him upstairs, but stopped outside their bedroom door as he went in to break the news to her.

"Honey," he said gently, "I've just been notified that your mother has passed away."

Mrs. Reagan broke down. "No . . ." she said, sobbing. The president sat down on the bed next to her. Saying nothing, he simply held her and let her cry. I turned away to leave them alone.

I assumed that Mrs. Reagan would fly with her senior staff to Phoenix, where her mother had been living, and that the president would follow a few days later for the funeral. By the time I got back down to the Oval Office shortly thereafter, Reagan had already called downstairs to tell Kathy Osborne that he would take the first lady to Phoenix.

"I'm taking her out," he told Kathy. "We're leaving tomorrow."

Wow, I thought, he knows just what to do.

The next day, the president took Air Force One to Phoenix with the first lady. The president also accompanied the first lady to view her mother for the first time as they made final arrangements. The president returned to Washington that night, and then we traveled back out at the end of the week for Mrs. Davis's memorial service. Reagan gave the eulogy, writing it himself in the Oval Office with no input from the White House speechwriters. In it, he said that Mrs. Davis was a woman of "wit, charm and kindliness" who had made a friend of everyone she encountered. Mrs. Reagan wept during the service, but laughed a little at her husband's humorous recollections of her mother.

The Reagans had very different personalities. Reagan was the easygoing, I-can't-say-no-to-anyone sort, and Mrs. Reagan was the worrier. She's gotten a lot of criticism over the years for her protectiveness when it came to her husband, but her sole focus was what was best for him.

When Mrs. Reagan was with the president, she was very serious, very focused on him. She fretted every minute she was with him that everything was going exactly as it needed to go — his interactions with people, his security, how he was being perceived, his press. When he wasn't around, she was a lot more fun — more relaxed, with a warm sense of humor. Unfortunately, the public never really saw that side of her.

In 1982, I remember, the first lady was flying to Washington from California. The president had already returned, and I flew back with the first lady and her staff on a plane out of the air force executive fleet. We were sitting in the senior staff section. I was at one table, and Mrs. Reagan and Elaine Crispen, her press secretary, sat across the aisle at another table. Mrs. Reagan, who was wearing a skirt, pulled a blanket over her legs and deftly removed her skirt and slid on a pair of trousers. Triumphantly, she held up her skirt to me.

"Jim, look at this," she said. Her eyes were sparkling.

I laughed. "Mrs. Reagan, I knew something was going on, but I didn't know what."

She laughed, too. "You missed it!"

"This shows how observant I am," I said.

* * *

There was one sure way of getting Ronald Reagan very angry — and that was to attack Nancy. Any enemy of Nancy Reagan became an enemy of Ronald Reagan.

Reagan, for example, was deeply upset by the criticism of her during his first term, when she was accused of lavish spending because of her designer dresses, the formal White House dinners, her renovations at the White House and the $250,000 set of White House china she had purchased. The reality is, Mrs. Reagan raised the money from a private, anonymous donor to replace the aging set of china that came with the White House. In addition, any of the renovations she made to the White House were badly needed. But she still took a lot of incoming fire for her work.

Reagan even went after Lyn Nofziger after he wrote an op-ed piece in the *Washington Post* shortly after Reagan had left office accusing Mrs. Reagan of clearing all the conservatives off the board of the Ronald Reagan Library in Simi Valley. Reagan phoned Nofziger, upset, and really took him to the woodshed about it. Even though Nofziger was a longtime friend and huge ideological ally of Ronald Reagan, Reagan wouldn't stand for that kind of attack on Nancy.

That didn't mean that the Reagans didn't have their differences. I remember once when the first lady was out of town, the president hosted a dinner in the East Room. It was a fund-raiser for the Ronald Reagan Library. One guest asked the president if he could see the White House residence. Mrs. Reagan liked to keep the residence private; relatively few people outside family ever went up there. It was her way of protecting what solitude they had. But Reagan, easygoing as he was, said, sure, he'd take him up. In fact, not only did he take that particular guest, but he also took the entire dinner party to the residence and showed them around! Well, Mrs. Reagan was less than pleased when she heard about that later.

They also had their differences over some staffing issues, with Don Regan leading the list. But Nancy Reagan was Ronald Reagan's ultimate protector, and she was very hard on herself, and others, if she felt Reagan wasn't being served well.

During Reagan's presidency, Mrs. Reagan rarely ventured into the West Wing. Unlike Hillary Clinton, she didn't see herself as a presidential partner in policymaking at the White House.

But her presence was felt every day. She was frequently on the telephone, checking in with people she knew in the White House and elsewhere. Often, she knew what was going on faster than some of Reagan's staff. When I took the job of executive assistant to the president, the most significant advice I got from Reagan intimates like Nofziger and Dave Fischer was that I should expect phone calls from the first lady. They warned me to make them a top priority and learn to deal with them. They were part of the job.

In fact, that's where Don Regan stumbled. Instead of seeing her phone calls as part of the package that came with the job as President Reagan's chief of staff, Regan sometimes saw them as annoying and intrusive. But they were a fact of life in the West Wing.

Dave Fischer gave me some more valuable guidance: Always be honest with Mrs. Reagan, he said. No matter what, never lie to her. If she asks a question and you don't know the answer, Fischer said, just tell her that you don't know.

"You can't do this job without the complete trust of the first lady," he said.

"Sometimes, she's going to ask you about things that she'll know you don't know. Don't try to fake it."

When I was at my desk, I could usually tell when I had a call from Mrs. Reagan. The White House line would flash. "Uh-oh," I would think, and pick up the phone. The White House operator would say: "Mr. Kuhn? We have the first lady calling for you."

Sometimes, she had routine queries: What time would Air Force One take off for a scheduled trip the next day? When were we leaving for Camp David? But often it was with comments and critiques. She read the newspapers and watched CNN and was always on the lookout for how the president was being portrayed. She wasn't afraid to criticize if she thought he was being served poorly. If the White House line rang at 4:30 in the afternoon and it was the first lady, she generally wasn't calling to tell me that I was doing a good job that day. She'd seen something on the news and was going to question us closely about it.

If members of Congress were trashing him that day or if a group of conservatives was complaining that the president was cozying up too much to the Soviets, she could be on the telephone soon thereafter making the inquiry. *Why is Ronnie being berated like that? What are you doing about it?*

And virtually every time, she was right. For example, when she called following the release of the Tower Commission report. It hadn't gone well for the president. He fumbled the report and seemed ill at ease — nothing like his usual smooth, confident public persona. The first lady was not happy.

"Ronnie looked terrible," she told me. "What are you guys doing down there?" She was right. The podium at which he stood was too small, which made it awkward for him to leaf through the 282-page volume. And he hadn't been prepared adequately for the press conference afterward.

The first lady was always on the lookout for the president. She made sure good people surrounded him. She looked ahead, watched everything, protected him and pushed things the way they needed to be pushed.

Nancy Reagan had a major role in getting her "roommate" to the negotiating table with the Soviets. She also made sure that Reagan was engaged in her war against illegal drugs.

She did it for smaller things, too. At the

Naval Academy's commencement in Annapolis in May 1985, she called me the night before to ensure that the president would not be exposed to the sun for hours. She didn't like him to be in the sun too much because of his various bouts with basal cell carcinoma, a form of skin cancer.

She was very sensitive about his image, too. On an '86 trip to Dallas, the president was presented with a new ostrich-skin briefcase. (It is legal for the president and first lady to accept domestic personal gifts of any value as long as they declare the value.) The president loved presents and, as soon as he could, he unloaded the contents of his old briefcase, handed it to me and put the papers in his new briefcase. He was very proud of it. But as soon as the first lady found out the briefcase was valued at $1,800, she called me and laid down the law: No more expensive gifts. She routinely turned over the gifts they received to the White House Gift Unit, which worked closely with the National Archives and Records Administration. The president didn't worry about what people thought, as long as the gift was legal, ethical and appropriate. The first lady, though, was very concerned that the general public not get the impression that the president and first lady were busy lapping up pricey presents.

She did occasionally let down her guard for inexpensive gifts. I remember someone presented the Reagans with a case of locally baked brownies when we were in Malvern, Pennsylvania, during Reagan's second term. The Reagans were delighted with the gift. I tried to remind them that the brownies needed to be checked out by the Secret Service.

"Oh, honey, they're fine," Mrs. Reagan said to the president, opening the case, extracting a brownie and taking a big bite out of it. She and the president both enjoyed the treats, to no ill effect, that weekend at Camp David.

Mrs. Reagan also tried to ensure that the people who worked for him had his best interests at heart. Because Reagan was so nice, she knew people would try to take advantage of him, and she saw her role as having to be tougher than he.

Stu Spencer once said that the best way to describe the relationship between Nancy and Ronald Reagan politically was that Reagan was the boss and the CEO, and Nancy Reagan was the personnel director.

"Nancy always had to take a look at you.

She researched you, she'd find out about you," Spencer said. "She spent all of her time looking for people who would serve her man well."

She was very aware of how his staff was serving the president, and how the press was portraying him. Numerous times, no matter what the issue, Mrs. Reagan was able to uniquely connect with the president when others couldn't reach him, over dinner, weekends at Camp David, or travel on Air Force One. Although sometimes, as with the Bitburg controversy, even she did not succeed.

Maybe if Barbara Bush had played that role with her husband, George, when he was president, he wouldn't have run into such trouble after the first Gulf War when the economy headed south. Bush's economic advisers told Bush the economy wasn't so bad, but Bush didn't have someone as uniquely close to him as Nancy Reagan there to cut through the upbeat messages and tell the president what was really going on.

Conservatives were not fond of Mrs. Reagan. I got an occasional comment about it: "Mrs. Reagan hates conservatives." As evidence, they would cite Mrs. Reagan's influence in getting the more moderate James Baker, instead of a conservative like Ed Meese, named as the president's first-term chief of staff.

Mrs. Reagan wasn't ideologically opposed to the right. Indeed, the president never departed from his core conservative beliefs. But Mrs. Reagan worked to ensure that Reagan looked at all sides of an issue. She brought out his pragmatic side and made him a more effective leader. She looked to make sure that Reagan didn't get pulled so far to the right that his major goals for the country were unachievable. More than once, Mrs. Reagan said to me that if we followed conservatives' line of thinking, "it's over the cliff because they didn't get their way. And then we get nothing." Conservatives didn't always understand that with Mrs. Reagan behind him, the president was able to achieve *more* of his conservative agenda, not less.

She deserves so much credit for his success. Plenty of presidents would have been much more successful if they'd had a Nancy Reagan behind them.

She was excellent at asking good, hard questions. She'd stop you and stand you up straight and you'd know: "She's right. This has to be rethought." She never demanded anything for herself; it was always for her "roommate," for Ronnie.

If there was one area where the first lady was especially protective, it was the president's schedule. The president had four schedules that were constantly in flux: his six-month schedule, where we would block in big trips, to economic summits, for example; the 30-day schedule; the two-week schedule and the daily agenda. She was very watchful to make sure the president's staff didn't stretch him too far, knowing that Ronald Reagan worked most effectively when he had some daylight. She made sure it stayed that way.

She also got involved in some decisions about where and when the president traveled. As has been amply reported, including in the first lady's autobiography, Mrs. Reagan consulted an astrologer. She started the practice after the president was shot. It frightened her so much that she wanted some reassurance that she could at least take some steps to prevent another incident. As she said, it was one of the ways she coped with her fear after he almost died. As much as she felt honored by and enjoyed being first lady, her worries about the president's image and safety made aspects of her role living hell for her over the entire eight years. She turned to astrologer

Joan Quigley for help in dealing with that fear.

Unlike Don Regan, who complained in his book about Mrs. Reagan's reliance on astrology, I never found it onerous. She never interfered with events like world economic summits or domestic events where we were locked into certain dates. Sometimes we heard from her that certain days would be better for the president to travel than other days. That could affect when we, say, scheduled a fund-raiser for a Republican candidate. She might tell us, for example, that a Wednesday was better than a Friday. Generally, she consulted the astrologist for the best days for press conferences, which was absolutely fine. These were events where there was some flexibility. She would talk to the chief of staff, me or Bill Henkel about the schedule. I figured if it made Mrs. Reagan feel better and didn't affect the president's policies or popularity, then I didn't see a downside.

I'm not sure the president ever knew the level of her engagement, though. At some point after Howard Baker started as chief of staff, he was running through the month's schedule with Reagan in the Oval Office and then added casually that he would call the first lady and run it by her, too.

Reagan looked a little irritated. "What do you mean?" he asked. "Why take it to her? I've signed off on it."

I grabbed Baker and pulled him out of the Oval Office. "You have to walk a fine line between the president and first lady," I told him. "We need her to be involved, but we don't need to tell him just *how* involved she is."

"I went too far, didn't I?" Baker asked, shamefacedly.

"Yes, Senator," I said. "But, most important, now you've got it."

18

GETTING PERSONAL AND GETTING "BORKED"

One Saturday in the fall of 1987, when we were at Camp David, I got a call from the Camp David operator. "We have Bill Smith calling the president," he said. As Reagan's executive assistant, I screened all his calls and authorized which ones would be put through to the president. Since the Reagans referred to William French Smith — a close friend, a member of Reagan's kitchen cabinet, and Reagan's first attorney general — as Bill, I assumed it was Smith on the line and instructed the operator to put the call through to the president. I thought nothing more of it.

That night, after we'd watched a movie in the Reagans' cabin, the president mentioned a recent phone conversation.

"I want to tell you about an interesting call I got this afternoon," he said, "from a man in North Carolina who wanted to talk to me about education." Reagan said he'd had a discussion with the man about his education policies and what his administration was doing about rewarding excellence in the classroom.

I was puzzled. Where the hell did that call come from? I didn't remember screening a call from anyone in North Carolina.

"He liked my ideas," Reagan told us happily. "He gave me some of his thoughts. We talked for a long time."

I asked him how long, and Reagan said they'd spoken for about 45 minutes.

"Mr. President, do you remember his name?" I asked.

"Ah . . . yes," said the president. "I believe his name was Smith . . . Bill Smith, it was."

I almost slapped my forehead in exasperation. Bill Smith! The call from the Camp David operator earlier that day — I had believed it was from William French Smith.

Minutes later, I phoned the Camp David and White House switchboards and asked them to pull up the call I had cleared earlier in the day from Bill Smith. They confirmed the telephone call, and said the caller had phoned the public number of the White House, and the call had been transferred to Camp David. I had, of course, cleared the call believing it was from William French Smith.

Reagan had been delighted to get the call. Of course, he knew about the call-clearing system, and I'm sure he was aware when he got the call that there had been a mix-up somewhere. But he was always very coy about things like this. Nonetheless, if a call like that got through to him, he was never going to raise hell about it. That just wasn't his style. Instead, he had a nice talk with Mr. Bill Smith, who probably thought it was perfectly normal to pick up the phone, call the White House and have a 45-minute conversation with the president!

At the same time, Mrs. Reagan certainly was aware that there was a screwup, and she knew that I knew that she was aware of this. No problem, though.

To me, that's a story about how extraordinarily humble Ronald Reagan was about occupying the office of the president of the United States. He was totally unaffected by its power.

At times during his second term, he pulled out money in the Oval Office to ensure that he had cash for upcoming long trips.

"What are you doing?" I would ask him.

"Well, I'm making sure I have money for the trip," he'd say.

"No, no, we've got it covered," I would

tell him. "Don't worry. We've got a budget for these things, unless they're personal, of course."

I would also question him about where he got cash, and he would say with a smile, "I have money, too, you know."

Reagan always believed that the praise, the salutes, the perks went to the office of the presidency, not to him personally. He was able to distinguish between himself and the position of president of the United States. That was how he stayed human in an overwhelming job — he took the position seriously but, once again, never himself.

He lived by the mottoes "Never say never" and "Listen to the people." He believed in these wholeheartedly and said them over and over again as president — in cabinet and staff meetings. He trusted the American people.

Presidents get very little praise and a lot of criticism. But complaints about Reagan's performance as president didn't affect him. He just kept moving forward — a warm, personable man with an unsinkable optimism about life.

That said, he could be extraordinarily wounded if his broadcasting, acting or athletic background was ever criticized. He was very proud of that part of his life, and he often told stories about it and how hard he had worked to pull himself up from the Depression and into the movie industry.

One Hollywood story he liked to tell was when he had to pose for publicity shots — still photos with Errol Flynn for *Santa Fe Trail,* a movie they had made in 1940. He hated doing stills, but that was an important part of the movie promotion. Flynn was slightly taller than Reagan, who was six feet and one-half inch tall. Well, Reagan didn't like the idea of appearing shorter than Flynn in the publicity shots, so he came up with a plan to make himself seem taller. They were shooting outside at Warner Bros., so Reagan unobtrusively pushed together a small pile of dirt with his shoes as he waited for the photographer to set up. Then he perched on the pile next to Flynn for the photos. *Voilà!* Ronald Reagan was taller than Flynn in all the posters and other publicity for the movie.

In April 1987, we went to Notre Dame at the invitation of Notre Dame basketball coach Digger Phelps. The U.S. Postal Service was unveiling a Knute Rockne stamp there. In *Knute Rockne, All American,* Reagan had played the part of George Gipp, a Notre Dame football star who died dramatically two weeks before the final game. (By the way, Reagan always insisted on pronouncing the *K* in Rockne's first name, so it came out as "K-noot," not "Noot." He said Rockne's wife was on the set while the movie was being shot and had stated that "K-noot" was the correct pronunciation.)

At the unveiling in Notre Dame, the coliseum was darkened briefly and the famous clip from the movie — Gipp's death scene where he asks Rockne to "win just one for the Gipper" — was shown. Reagan watched the movie scene backstage with Notre Dame football coach Lou Holtz as his younger self gasped out Gipp's last words. When the lights went back up, I saw tears in Reagan's eyes. That movie meant a lot to him. It had been a turning point in Ronald Reagan's acting career, boosting him out of the B-grade movie level and into life as an A-list movie star. I realized how much that role had meant to him as he drove himself emotionally into becoming a very good actor.

President Reagan also loved to show off his athleticism. We had arranged for Reagan to throw a pass at the end of the Notre Dame ceremony to Notre Dame receiver Tim Brown, the Heisman Trophy winner that year, using the football presented to him by Holtz. It worked beautifully. From the stage, Reagan asked for Brown, who was in the crowd and stood up. Reagan fired a bullet at Brown, who snagged it deftly. Reagan loved that kind of fun stuff.

I saw again how emotional Reagan's past was for him when the family of Chicago Bears quarterback Jim Harbaugh came to meet the president in the Oval Office one day in 1988. Harbaugh, a friend of Mark Weinberg's, had asked if his mother and grandmother could meet the president. They had their photos taken, and we gave them some presidential "goodies," as we called them — trinkets with the presidential seal on them. The president was chatting with them when Harbaugh's grandmother said: "You know, Mr. President, I've been following you for years. I think you're the best president this country has ever had. Everything you're doing — well, I can't praise you enough." Then she added: "But, you know, I never cared for you much as an actor."

I froze. That was the worst possible thing she could have said to Ronald Reagan. She could have told him she thought he was a horrible president, and it would have rolled off his back. But she attacked his acting career!

Reagan looked stunned, as if he'd been hit between the eyes.

I thanked Harbaugh's family and hustled them out of the Oval Office. Closing the door, I turned back to the president. He stood by his desk, looking at the floor. He was devastated, his feelings smashed. What could I say?

I walked over to him and put my hand on his arm. "Mr. President," I said, "she didn't mean it that way. People think that, as president, you have the most powerful position in the world, and she was just trying to contrast that job with you as an actor."

He looked at me.

"Jim," he said, "that's the first time I've heard that. No one's ever said that to me before. Nobody's ever told me I was a bad actor."

"She really didn't mean it," I repeated, trying desperately to think of a way to cheer him up. "I think she was just trying to say, 'You were a good actor, but more important, you're a great president.' I think she got carried away. She doesn't really believe you were a bad actor. Nobody believes you were a bad actor." That took the edge off the situation — at least, somewhat.

Throughout 1987, we were still dealing with the vestiges of the Iran-contra affair. Hearings continued on Capitol Hill, and it emerged that CIA Director Bill Casey had played a key role in organizing support for the Nicaraguan contras. Tragically, Casey died a few months after collapsing in his office in 1986 and undergoing surgery for a cancerous brain tumor.

A crusty New York lawyer, Casey had been close to the Reagans since stepping in and taking over Reagan's 1980 election bid after Reagan fired John Sears in February 1980. Casey was appointed CIA director in 1981.

There was much hunger on the part of the press to discover just how much Casey knew about the Iran-contra affair but, obviously, Casey was in no condition to talk about what he knew or didn't know. But that didn't stop the press from trying.

One night in the spring of 1987, White House doctor John Hutton came by my office in the West Wing. He had gone to the hospital to check on Casey. Naturally, we hoped that Casey would recover but, if he didn't, a new CIA director would need to be appointed. Casey's wife refused to consider that idea while Casey was still alive.

Hutton came back from the hospital and asked if he could close my door. He said that Casey was in bad shape. Then he asked an unorthodox question: "Who was that guy who brought down Nixon?"

"You mean Bob Woodward?" I said.

"That's him," said Hutton. "He was there."

"Where?" I asked.

"Outside Casey's hospital room," said Hutton. "He's lurking around the hallways. He looks like he doesn't want to be seen."

Later, when Woodward's book about the Iran-contra affair came out, there was a dramatic scene where Woodward interviews Casey in his hospital room. After the book came out, some claimed that Woodward had made it up — that he had never even been to the hospital. But Hutton's sighting confirms that Woodward was there, although I doubt Woodward was able to interview Casey. The man was in a deep coma and never came out of it. Maybe Woodward really did speak to Casey, but I simply don't believe that he got a response.

Speaking of Woodward, Reagan once told me that he never believed that there actually was a Deep Throat, the inside source who allegedly gave information on the Watergate scandal to Woodward.

"I'll tell you who I think Deep Throat was," said Reagan. "I believe that Deep Throat was Bob Woodward."

In June 1987, we took a 10-day trip to Europe, this time for an economic summit in Venice, a trip to Rome and then a trip to Germany. In Venice, the Reagans stayed in a villa outside the famous lagoon city. One evening at the beginning of the trip when the Reagans were free, the president said that they would watch one of the movies I had brought with us. I had a special, which had been sent to the president by *National Geographic*, where underwater divers explored the wreckage of the *Titanic*. I gave them a quick tutorial on the VCR and then headed into Venice for dinner. The next morning I asked the president if everything had worked out.

The VCR had worked fine, he said, but the tape — although it was labeled as a *National Geographic* special — was actually the movie *Shanghai Surprise*, starring Madonna and Sean Penn. It was so terrible, they said, that they pulled it out after 15 minutes and watched something else. The movie must have really been bad because the Reagans had seen their fair share of mediocre films in their lifetime!

It was in Berlin where Reagan made his famous speech asking Gorbachev to dismantle the Berlin Wall. Gorbachev had made great strides in opening up the Soviet empire with perestroika and glasnost, but the U.S.S.R. itself still appeared to be standing strong.

It was a dramatic moment for Reagan. Before 20,000 cheering West Berliners, the president spoke from a platform built less than 100 yards from the Brandenburg Gate, with protective glass behind him that allowed some East Berliners crowded on the other side of the gate to glimpse him.

In his speech, the president compared the economic prosperity of West Germany with the pinched economic times of the Soviet empire. Yes, he said, Moscow was talking about a new policy of reform and openness. But there was one gesture the Soviets could make that would advance the cause of freedom and peace, he said.

"General Secretary Gorbachev, if you seek peace, if you seek prosperity for the Soviet Union and Eastern Europe, if you seek liberalization: Come here to this gate," Reagan said in firm, hard tones.

"Come here to this gate, Mr. Gorbachev. Open this gate. Mr. Gorbachev, tear down this wall!"

He said it with such vigor and determination, as if he were supremely confident that the wall would come down and the infamous Brandenburg Gate would swing open. But the gate, a towering rectangular arch supported by columns, looked so solid and immovable that it seemed unimaginable that East and West Berliners would ever travel freely through it. In reading through Reagan's speech beforehand, as real as the prospect sounded when Reagan's words echoed through the divided city and as much as I wanted to believe him, I was sure it would never happen in Reagan's lifetime — or possibly in my lifetime, for that matter.

Less than a year after Reagan left office, the wall would fall, and exuberant Berliners would dance on the gate.

Who could have imagined it? Only someone with the willful optimism of Ronald Reagan.

Only a few months after the speech, in September 1987, the United States and the Soviet Union announced a wide-ranging treaty that included an agreement in principle to eliminate medium- and shorter-range nuclear missiles and a commitment to negotiate 50 percent cuts in their strategic offensive arsenals. For the first time, an entire class of nuclear weapons would be eliminated.

They also announced that Gorbachev and President Reagan would hold a summit in Washington. In the White House press room, where the announcement was made, a reporter shouted to Reagan, "What about the evil empire?"

"Oh, I don't think it's lily white," Reagan said with a smile.

But Reagan knew he was going to face a battle in the Senate to affirm any treaty he would sign with the Soviets. His continuing efforts to negotiate with the Soviet Union concerned many conservatives who believed Reagan was selling out the store in his eagerness to do a quick deal with the Soviet Union. Earlier in the year, in March, Reagan had met with a group of conservative leaders, including Conservative Caucus Chairman Howard Phillips, Paul Weyrich, head of the Committee for the Survival of a Free Congress and Phyllis Schlafly of the Eagle Forum, in the Roosevelt Room of the White House. They had expressed concern that Reagan was going too easy on the Soviets.

Reagan had listened carefully to their concerns, although he didn't waver from his position to press ahead with his efforts to reduce nuclear arms. The group had treated him respectfully, but they had clearly disagreed.

At the end of the meeting, Reagan had departed, looking less than pleased. Usually, when an outside group meets with the president in the White House, someone thanks the president at the end of the meeting, and the group applauds as the president exits the meeting room.

But this time, there had been dead silence in the room.

As soon as we had gone back into the Oval Office, I closed the door. The president asked me if I'd noticed what hadn't happened when he left the Roosevelt Room. I knew what he was thinking, but I wanted to hear his response.

"There was no applause," he said. It was so unlike Reagan to notice such things — he didn't much care whether or not people clapped — but he had expected it at least from this group of longtime supporters. Conservatives had been solidly on his side since the 1960s and now, just when he needed them the most, to help him fulfill his life's work to eliminate the Soviet threat, they had seemed to be off on their own.

Later that year, when Reagan signed the INF treaty with Gorbachev in the White House East Room, some conservatives called him a "useful idiot for Kremlin propaganda," and an "apologist" for Mikhail Gorbachev.

Yet with them or without them, the president was determined to carry on and serve America's best interests. While his core belief system was strongly conservative, he was a pragmatist who didn't let his ideology deter him from embracing what he believed was best for the United States and the world as a whole.

But Reagan's conservative backers were solidly behind him that summer and fall of '87, as they fought beside the president to save the Supreme Court nomination of Appellate Court Judge Robert H. Bork.

Reagan nominated Judge Bork on July 1, 1987, to fill the seat left vacant by the retirement of Justice Lewis Powell Jr. Reagan had already filled two other Supreme Court seats, with Sandra Day O'Connor in 1981 and Antonin Scalia in 1986, when Chief Justice Warren Burger retired. Reagan replaced Burger with Justice William Rehnquist. In fact, when Scalia —

normally a bold, confident man — came to see the president shortly before his nomination, he was quite nervous. Reagan had a calming effect on anyone who came before him, even a powerful legal man like Scalia.

In the case of Bork, there was every reason to believe that his nomination would ultimately make it through the Senate, even though Democrats then held the majority. Bork, said Reagan in introducing him in the White House press room, was the "most prominent and intellectually powerful advocate of judicial restraint." After all, Scalia, with a background as conservative as Bork's, had seen his nomination sail through the Senate with unanimous approval.

Almost immediately, liberals declared all-out war on Bork. Senator Edward Kennedy said Bork stood for an "extremist view of the Constitution." The NAACP, People for the American Way and the National Abortion Rights Action League all came out against the nominee, calling him an "ultraconservative" who would roll back civil rights on several fronts.

Howard Baker went before the NAACP at its annual convention shortly after Reagan announced Bork's nomination to plead with them to withhold judgment until the Senate confirmation hearings. Supporters of his nomination pointed to Bork's stellar qualifications and pointed out that Reagan had the right, as president, to choose high court justices who shared his philosophies.

In a weekly radio address after his nomination of Bork, Reagan urged the Senate to "keep politics out of the confirmation process." But no dice.

Liberals would not back down. The war against Bork accelerated, and the rhetoric against him grew almost hysterical.

Senator Howard Metzenbaum of Ohio declared in a Judiciary Committee hearing that he had found Judge Bork's views to be quite frightening.

At the beginning of October, well before the full Senate voted on Bork's nomination, it became clear that Bork's nomination was doomed. But Reagan, who would never turn his back on someone, kept up his steadfast support. The president's attitude was that if Bork was going to go down in defeat, then Reagan would, too. Many on Reagan's staff hoped that Bork would ask to have his nomination withdrawn, but Bork was as stubborn as Reagan. Just weeks before the full Senate vote, John

Tuck from Howard Baker's office gave me a note to take in to Baker, who was attending a luncheon in the White House East Room. It was a phone message to Baker from Bork, asking that he tell the president that he wanted to fight on.

The president put up a gallant fight, but on October 23, the Senate voted 58–42 to reject Bork.

The next day, Reagan nominated federal appeals court Judge Douglas Ginsburg to the bench. Unfortunately, shortly after that, Ginsburg disclosed that he had smoked marijuana on several occasions in the 1960s and 1970s and, to make matters worse, while he was a Harvard law professor.

It was clear to his staff that Reagan was flogging a dead horse, as we used to say in Ohio. Even with the marijuana revelations, Reagan was determined to stick by Ginsburg's side in the fight to gain Senate confirmation. On November 6, Reagan was scheduled to give a speech in support of his troubled nominee. It was starting to become clear to many that Ginsburg was doomed but, again, Reagan was willing to stick with his nominee to the very end, no matter what the outcome. That morning, though, I read through the president's speech, in which Reagan planned to strongly defend him, asking Americans to forgive Ginsburg and let "this brilliant and able young man continue to serve his country."

I was appalled. It was clear that the Ginsburg nomination was doomed, yet we were hanging Reagan out to dry with a statement like that. I went to Howard Baker and Ken Duberstein.

"We can't let the president go out and say this," I said. "We know that Ginsburg's going to go down. What are we doing to the president?"

Both agreed that the statement should be toned down, but they told me I had to convince Reagan. I worked with Tommy Griscom, director of communications, and cut out most of the more laudatory statements, and then I went to Reagan. He had already prepared and marked his cards; he was ready to go. It took me about 15 minutes to convince him to tone down his remarks. He was being very intransigent but, finally, I said: "Look, you have to leave yourself some wiggle room here. You're not abandoning Judge Ginsburg, but he's hanging on by a thread, and you know it. He may be gone in a couple of days."

He eventually said: "Damn it, have it

your way. But you're right, I'm not abandoning him." He reluctantly made the requested deletions. His remarks still praised Ginsburg, but noted that "Judge Ginsburg erred in his youth. He had acknowledged it. He had expressed his regrets."

The next morning, while we were at Camp David, we got word that Ginsburg would announce at midday that he was withdrawing his nomination. Before then, the president received a flurry of calls from Ginsburg and from Utah Senator Orrin Hatch, a senior Republican on the Senate Judiciary Committee. But I didn't put them through to the president. I called down to Ken Duberstein about it. "I'm not putting those calls through to the president," I told him. "I don't know what they want to talk to him about. They may try to change his mind or something, but the guy's got to go." Duberstein agreed. Fortunately, Ginsburg was history by Saturday afternoon.

Four days later, Reagan announced his third nominee — Judge Anthony Kennedy, a more moderate conservative. The president announced Kennedy's nomination in the East Room on Veterans Day, November 11, and his nomination sailed through the Senate. Notwithstanding the

16 inches of snow that hit Washington on Veterans Day, this was, indeed, a relief for Ronald Reagan.

It might be said that Reagan backed down on his principles by choosing a more moderate conservative. As it turns out, over his years on the bench, Kennedy has proven to be a bulwark of conservative support, voting again and again with Justices Scalia and Thomas and Chief Justice Rehnquist. In the end, Reagan made a shrewd choice. When it became clear that more conservative candidates wouldn't fly in the Democratic Senate, Reagan was guided by his pragmatic instincts. He had solid conservative convictions and principles that he drew on in making tough decisions, but in situations where it boiled down to pragmatism versus ideology, pragmatism invariably won out.

19

THE STREETS OF WASHINGTON AND MOSCOW

The president was livid. He paced back and forth in the Oval Office, looking at his watch. Soviet leader Mikhail Gorbachev was unconscionably late for his meeting with Reagan in the Oval Office. It was December 10, 1987, the final day of an extraordinary three-day summit between the two world leaders at the White House.

Gorbachev was scheduled for a 10:30 a.m. one-on-one meeting with the president at the White House, and he still hadn't shown up. The president wanted updates. *Where is he? When was he coming?* We had no idea.

Then someone told us to turn on the television. The president and I went into Reagan's study to watch an astonishing sight unfold.

The Soviets had now rolled us.

Gorbachev had suddenly stopped his motorcade at the corner of Connecticut

Avenue and L Street in downtown Washington, gotten out of his limousine and begun pressing the flesh like an old-time American pol at one of Washington's busiest intersections. It was a chaotic scene. His KGB motorcade escorts didn't realize the limo had stopped until they were farther down the block. When they figured it out, they roared backward up the street to Gorbachev's car. D.C. police accompanying the motorcade made quick U-turns on their motorcycles.

Delighted Americans clustered around the Soviet leader, extending their hands.

"I shook his hand over the *USA Today* box," boasted Patti Terry, an executive of Wang, a computer maker, to journalists later. "He was saying 'world peace.' I should have tried to sell him a computer."

"Gorby," as Americans called him then, was a hit.

By the time Gorbachev made it to the White House, he was well over an hour late. Reagan mostly kept his irritation to himself and me, although he was a little cold toward Gorbachev after he arrived.

The Reagan-Gorbachev summit in Washington had come together fairly quickly, although not as rapidly as Reykjavik. On November 1, Reagan came back to Washington after the memorial service for his mother-in-law, and we began planning for a Washington summit — the third meeting of the two leaders in three years — to start December 8. As difficult as it was to believe, from the ashes of Reykjavik had come a sweeping nuclear arms reduction treaty.

At first, the White House considered holding the meetings at Dumbarton Oaks, a nineteenth-century mansion in Georgetown where international meetings had established the principles later incorporated into the charter of the United Nations in the 1940s. The Dumbarton Oaks suggestion came from Mike Deaver. But the White House senior staff argued that, for a historic moment like this, a more appropriate location would be the White House, and we prevailed.

Reagan looked forward to seeing Mikhail again. The two leaders were by now on a first-name basis, and their constructive dialogue was the kind Reagan had envisioned for years. Even though Reagan had initial doubts about walking away from a deal with the Soviets at Reykjavik, he was sure the Soviets would come around eventually. And they had. In the preceding months, the Americans and Soviets had worked out their final differences on a treaty that would scrap intermediate-range nuclear missiles, clearing the way for the two leaders to sign it when Gorbachev came to Washington.

On the first day of Gorbachev's visit, Secretary of State Shultz greeted Mikhail and Raisa Gorbachev at Andrews Air Force Base, and they were whisked away to the Soviet embassy in downtown Washington, only a few blocks from the White House.

The big day was the following one, December 8, when a beaming President Reagan and Gorbachev signed the historic nuclear arms reduction treaty — the INF treaty — at 1:45 p.m. in the ornate East Room at a walnut table used by President Abraham Lincoln's cabinet.

Their banter was lighthearted, and so many cameras were clicking all at once that the sound melded into a loud buzz as the two leaders signed, eight times each, the pages of thick leather-bound volumes — blue for the United States and burgundy for the Soviets — as the political and military leaders of both nations burst into applause.

Reagan noted that it was the first agreement ever between the United States and the Soviet Union to eliminate an entire class of U.S. and Soviet nuclear weapons.

"We have made history," he said simply.

Then, almost immediately, the two leaders and their negotiators launched into more talks aimed at agreeing to eliminate long-range nuclear weapons as well.

The president was very upbeat and positive about the summit. He had gotten to know, and to like, Gorbachev in their previous meetings. Margaret Thatcher had been right about the fact that Reagan would develop a chemistry with Gorbachev.

Once again, Reagan had stuck to his principles — not to give up on SDI — and he had gotten the treaty he wanted.

Less than six months later, we traveled to Moscow. After a vigorous battle, the Senate finally ratified the INF treaty on May 27, 1988. Conservatives in the Senate were, again, concerned that Reagan was giving away too much to the Soviets. The president took a more pragmatic attitude: *Doveryai no proveryai* ("Trust, but verify") was his watchword. He believed that enough safeguards had been built into the treaty agreement to allow the Americans to confirm whether the Soviets were living up to their side of the bargain. In his mind, there was no question that the agreement was in the best interests of the country — and the world.

Howard Baker had to wait in Washington for the vote and then bring the articles of ratification for the INF treaty to Helsinki on an air force jet. The signing ceremony with Reagan and Gorbachev at the Kremlin was set for June 1.

En route to Moscow, we spent four nights in Helsinki and then stayed in Moscow for four nights.

Several weeks before the summit, Shultz had suggested to the president that he try to do something that would allow him to be seen by the Soviet public while in Moscow — much as Gorbachev had done with his extraordinary walkabout with Americans in Washington the previous December. Shultz suggested Red Square, but we already knew we were going there for a more formal visit.

In Helsinki, Mrs. Reagan and I talked about the idea. The Reagans were eager to do something "off the record" — White House parlance for an unscheduled movement — on the streets of Moscow. Something more unexpected than just going to Red Square, which would be sealed off anyway so the Reagans wouldn't get a chance to meet ordinary Soviet citizens. I told Jim Hooley, who oversaw the White House advance operation, and head Secret Service agent Ray Shaddick that we were looking for somewhere in Moscow that would expose the Reagans to the people of Moscow.

Our advance team and Secret Service each came up with a site. Our advance team suggested a walk through Moscow's Arbat mall, a popular shopping area for Moscow residents near Spaso House, the U.S. ambassador's residence, where we would be staying. The Secret Service, on the other hand, pushed a more remote, but more secure, location.

Even as we left Helsinki, the advance team and the Secret Service were still battling about which location would be better. Advance was arguing for the Arbat because of the large numbers of shoppers the Reagans would encounter. The Secret Service wanted its more picturesque, but secluded, overlook elsewhere in Moscow.

Riding in from Vnukovo Airport in Moscow, I was struck by the uniform grayness of the city — grim buildings lining the dank streets. I was also trying to figure out how to settle the issue of where the president and Mrs. Reagan could go for their walkabout.

After the Reagans arrived at Spaso House, the location of their off-the-record visit was still undecided. Chief of Staff Howard Baker, who could have made the decision but couldn't be located immediately, and Deputy Chief of Staff Ken Duberstein chose to avoid any confrontation between Advance and the Secret Service on this delicate issue.

So I decided to take it to the ultimate level — the president and Mrs. Reagan. In their bedroom at Spaso House, I met with them, explained the situation and expressed a strong preference for the Arbat site.

"It's everything you've been waiting for," I told the Reagans. But I stressed that they would need to make the final decision. I suggested bringing up Hooley, senior advance man Rick Ahearn, Shaddick and his deputy, Dick Griffin, so the Reagans could hear the pros and cons for each site. I asked the president and Mrs. Reagan where they wanted to meet, and they assured me that the bedroom was fine.

Ordinarily, neither a president nor a first lady would decide their participation in such an unusual event. However, this was the Soviet Union, this was Moscow, and it had been on our minds since Gorbachev's visit in December.

The meeting with the Reagans convened, and each side made its case. The Secret Service made its pitch — their site had a great view and there would be good photos of the Reagans. Hooley and Ahearn then made an excellent case for the Arbat, describing the shopping area and pointing out that the Reagans would meet many more Soviets there, which was key.

As they talked, the president paced around the room. He just wanted to go somewhere. Mrs. Reagan, who was lying on her back on the bed, her feet propped up on the pillows, listened intently.

Secret Service agent Griffin said he had security concerns about the Arbat. Ray Shaddick, Griffin's boss, concurred.

"But if we go to the Arbat," I asked Shaddick, "are you saying that you can't protect the president and Mrs. Reagan?"

"No, that's not what we're saying," said Shaddick.

Mrs. Reagan popped up from the bed. "Fine," she said. "Then let's go."

"Yes," said the president, "let's go."

Within five minutes, we had the press loaded in the motorcade and were headed to the Arbat, a renovated pedestrian street crowded with new cafés and boutiques in postperestroika Moscow.

When the Reagans emerged from their limo on the crowded street, Moscow residents proved to be as welcoming to them as Washingtonians had been to Gorbachev. Smiling shoppers surged forward as soon as they saw the Reagans. Hundreds cheered loudly and applauded as the Reagans strolled through the crowd for about 10 minutes, shaking hands.

So many people surrounded the Reagans that the White House press photographers accompanying us complained that they couldn't get any good photos. Hearing their complaints, Mrs. Reagan looked around and spied an old carriage. She grabbed the president, and they stepped up on it, elevating themselves enough above the crowd to acknowledge everyone assembled and also enabling photographers to get some good shots. Then they stepped back down and, joyfully, took their time greeting more people. As amazing as I always found Mrs. Reagan, she truly impressed me in Moscow that day when we were struggling to get the photo of the day.

In my mind, the score with Gorbachev had been evened.

As we left the Arbat, the Secret Service was so comfortable with everything that we decided to walk back to Spaso House, which was only about five minutes away.

The KGB agents with us, however, were not accustomed to this kind of activity and weren't on their best behavior. They pushed people away from the Reagans; journalists later complained that they'd been punched and kicked as well. At one point, we heard Helen Thomas, the long-time White House correspondent for United Press International, screaming. I turned around and saw that KGB agents were carrying her off after she apparently got too close to the Reagans. I grabbed the president. "Mr. President, look what they're doing to Helen! You have to help her."

The president stopped. "Say there," he said to the Soviet security people, "she's with us." The KGB put Helen down, and the president and Mrs. Reagan put Thomas between them, safe and secure, and continued their walk back to Spaso House.

The rapturous reception the Reagans received at the Arbat was repeated everywhere else we went in Moscow. People lined the streets to watch our motorcade, applauding and cheering.

Nonetheless, we couldn't forget that we

were still in a Communist country. We had been warned that Spaso House might be bugged with audio and video surveillance equipment. So whenever we discussed anything sensitive there, or even if we wanted to examine briefing books, we had to go into the "bubble," a small, secure room set up by the State Department in the grand foyer of the ambassador's residence.

The president wasn't happy with this setup. Damn it, he said, he didn't want to crowd into an uncomfortable secure room every time he wanted to study the briefing books or have a conversation with his staff about the negotiations. On the other hand, Mrs. Reagan firmly believed in following all our security guidelines.

After trying to talk the president into the arrangement, I realized that he had put his foot down, so I gave up and called the National Security Council. National Security Adviser Colin Powell called me back, and I explained the problem and also asked why it was such an issue because much of the information the president was reviewing, he was going to convey to the Soviets anyway in less than 24 hours.

"You're absolutely right," said Powell. "Make sure the president is comfortable.

He's got to get through a lot of material. Because if he doesn't, we're going to lose the whole darn thing."

Later, on Air Force One en route to London, we discovered that the Soviets knew about the secure room and had been sending in microwave signals to try to penetrate it. White House doctor John Hutton asked me on the flight how much time the president, and the rest of us, had spent in and around the bubble because Hutton was concerned about exposure to the microwaves. I was taken aback by his question.

"What difference does it make now?" I asked Hutton. "We've already been exposed to it!" Hutton never said another word about it.

On Reagan's second day in Moscow, in the warm spring sunshine, Gorbachev and Reagan took a tour of Red Square, accompanied by reporters. They met Soviet citizens — although we knew they had been carefully screened by the KGB.

Sam Donaldson called out a question: "Do you still think you're in an evil empire, Mr. President?"

"No," the president replied promptly.

"Why not?" Donaldson asked.

The president smiled, Gorbachev at his

side. "I was talking about another time and another era," he said softly.

That afternoon, the president spoke to students at Moscow State University. In a vast vaulted room on campus, with a marble bust of Soviet Union founder Vladimir Lenin looking down on President Reagan, the students listened quietly through headphones as he talked about faith and freedom, the technology revolution, the free-market economy, democracy — and, quoting Boris Pasternak in the novel *Doctor Zhivago*, the "irresistible power of unarmed truth."

He did a question-and-answer session with the students, telling them that he looked forward to a day when there would be no more nuclear weapons in the world. One student asked him if youth had changed since he was a student. Reagan smiled, recalling the days when he was California governor when "I could start a riot just by going to a campus."

But all that has changed, he told the Moscow State students, "and I could be looking out at any American student body as well as I'm looking out here and would not be able to tell the difference between you."

That was, in my mind, one of the most

symbolic events of President Reagan's extraordinary eight years in office. The aging cold war warrior, entering the twilight of his presidency, sharing his thoughts and wisdom with young people in a country he had once considered the font of all evil in the world.

How far Ronald Reagan had brought us.

The Moscow visit proceeded at a breathless pace. Reagan met with Soviet dissidents at Spaso House and had lunch with cultural and arts leaders. He and Gorbachev met privately several times. And there were the Soviet state dinner and the reciprocal U.S. state dinner.

The Reagans went to the Bolshoi Theatre with the Gorbachevs and then had a private dinner with them at the Gorbachevs' dacha outside Moscow. On their last night, they posed for photos outside the brilliant swirling domes of St. Basil's Cathedral in Red Square.

At the departure ceremony at the Kremlin on June 2, Reagan told the Gorbachevs: "I think you understand we're not just grateful to both you and Mrs. Gorbachev, but want you to know we think of you as friends."

We flew out of Vnukovo Airport and headed to London so Reagan could meet with Margaret Thatcher. It was a quiet flight; the Reagans were drained physically from their visit to Moscow. In London, we had a triumphant ride through the streets, with Londoners waving from along the River Thames, from the tops of double-decker buses and from boats in the lake at Hyde Park. The bright colors and lights of the city were a marked contrast from the muted grayness of Moscow.

We went directly to Buckingham Palace, where the Reagans had tea with Queen Elizabeth and Prince Philip (whose behavior was much better this time). After leaving Buckingham Palace, Mrs. Reagan split off to another event, and the president was supposed to motorcade to No. 10 Downing Street to meet with Thatcher. As he got into the limo, it occurred to me that it wouldn't look right if the president was riding alone in the presidential limo, what with the large crowds of Brits who would be seeing the president along the way. I brought White House press secretary Marlin Fitzwater over to the president's limo before it departed and asked the Secret Service to open up the president's limo.

"What are you doing?" Fitzwater asked.

"Come on," I said. "Mrs. Reagan is off

on another visit, and I don't want the president riding alone from here to Ten Downing Street, so you're going to ride with him."

"I can't *ride* with the *president*," Fitzwater protested.

"Just get in the car," I pleaded. "You're riding with the president." I pushed him in, the Secret Service closed the door and off they went.

When they arrived at 10 Downing Street, Fitzwater got out of the car, beaming.

"Wow, that was unbelievable," he said. "All those people, saluting Reagan." He looked at me. "I always thought that if I was fortunate enough to ride with the president in his limo that it might be from downtown Cleveland to the airport. Not from Buckingham Palace to Ten Downing Street."

Reagan met with Thatcher and briefed her on the events at Moscow. It was amazing to see how things had come full circle since that day at Camp David almost four years ago when Thatcher had brought Reagan the encouraging news about a new leader for the Soviet Union. There had been the highs of the Geneva summit, the lows of Reykjavik, the joy of the Washington summit with its INF treaty signing, and now Reagan was visiting Thatcher to talk of his progress with Gorbachev.

The next day, bewigged, scarlet-robed London officials greeted us at Guildhall, where Reagan gave an emotional speech to several hundred guests.

"Imagine, the president of the United States and the [president] of the Soviet Union walking together in Red Square," said Reagan, "talking about a growing personal friendship and meeting, together, average citizens, realizing how much our people have in common."

And then it was back to Washington, where we arrived to a full-dress reception at Andrews Air Force Base. Air Force One pulled into a hangar, and the Reagans stepped off the plane to a 21-gun salute, a trumpet fanfare and the cheers of more than 4,000 flag-waving White House staff and supporters. Most of the cabinet was there to greet them as well.

"There's no place like home," said Reagan.

As difficult as it was to believe at the time, the Soviet Union was on the verge of crumbling. A mere 18 months after our visit to Moscow, the Berlin Wall came tumbling down. And less than four years later,

Gorbachev resigned, and the U.S.S.R. was no more.

What Reagan predicted before the London Parliament in 1982 had come true — the Communist Soviet Union had been consigned to "the ash heap of history."

20

THE FINAL STRETCH

The muffled echo of loudspeakers drifted across the Ellipse to the White House as the president and I walked along the Colonnade to the Oval Office on the morning of January 22, 1988. Workers were setting up for a demonstration later that day — nothing unusual in Washington — but this was one in which the president took a particular interest. Fifty thousand pro-life demonstrators would rally on the muddy Ellipse that morning to protest the fifteenth anniversary of the Supreme Court decision — *Roe* v. *Wade* — that legalized abortion. As in the past, the president was scheduled to speak to the group via a telephone linked to their public address system shortly after noon.

For a moment, the president listened to the noise from the Ellipse. He suddenly stopped walking. I halted, too.

That's for the pro-life demonstration, he said. Then, he added abruptly: "I'm concerned about making that call to them today."

I was puzzled. "Mr. President, you know what you want to say. You've got your talking points, but I know you don't even need them." Each year of his presidency, the president had telephoned the group and affirmed his support for their cause.

"No, it's not that," he said. He looked thoughtful.

I sensed that he might be concerned about the mechanics of making the call.

"WHCA is all set to do it over the phone," I assured him, "the way you've done it many times. And the phone call will be plugged into the PA system that we're hearing down there. Technically, everything is set to go."

The president shook his head and looked off in the direction of the Ellipse. "No, it's not that," he said.

"What is it?" I asked. The president turned and looked at me. He was concerned about something else.

"Well, I've been thinking about it," he said. He noted that he had been talking to the large pro-life group at its annual Washington rallies each year of his presidency but that, in actuality, a large percentage — 70 percent or so — of American women were pro-choice.

"I'm sensitive to that," he told me, "and to the fact that for all these years, I've been imposing my will on all of them."

I was amazed. This was the first time the president had expressed a sentiment like that.

"That's noble for you to acknowledge," I said. "I assume you still want to do the call?"

"I'm still going to do the call," he said without hesitation. "But I'm just sensitive about it."

We started walking again.

Later that morning, he did speak to the 50,000 demonstrators on the Ellipse. He promised that his administration soon would publish regulations it had promised that would bar family planning clinics from using federal funds to offer abortion counseling or make referrals to abortion services. But Nellie Gray, organizer of the "March for Life," scolded Reagan for signing a budget bill that included abortion funds for the District of Columbia.

Reagan handled it with his usual aplomb. "Well, Nellie," he said, "sometimes these things happen because, as you know, there are people that are in great disagreement with us. But we are continuing to work and to do our best to end any federal funding."

In my mind, aside from being forthcoming, Ronald Reagan displayed deep sensitivity and open-mindedness. Despite his conservatism, he believed in seeing other points of view, even on issues about which he felt strongly. And while he was still very much pro-life, he was also keenly aware of the other side of the debate — that many women in America disagreed deeply with his position on this issue. That concerned him enough that he stopped and reflected about it. "Here's what I'm going to do," he seemed to be saying, "yet I want you to know that it's not easy for me."

In many ways, 1988, the last full year of Reagan's presidency, was also the calmest. The country's economy was humming along, the Iran-contra affair was fading, Reagan's rapport with Congress had rebounded and the cold war was clearly deescalating, although we had no idea at the time that the Soviet Union would crumble so quickly.

In my experience, Reagan never really slowed down in 1988. He kept the same schedule and the same pace as in the previous years of his presidency. His energy level remained strong. After we had been out late in the evenings at various events and had returned to the White House, the president always seemed just as fresh as when he had come down in the elevator that morning from the White House residence. "Take the rest of the night off," he liked to joke to us.

The only difference I saw was a diminished enthusiasm for extensive travel. To be sure, Reagan never much relished domestic travel that required him to spend overnights on the road away from Mrs. Reagan. It was a little different on international trips because Mrs. Reagan was almost always with us but, even so, in Ronald Reagan's mind, there needed to be a real purpose in making the trip as opposed to just going to another country that he hadn't been to.

At the end of 1987, he had been looking forward to his Moscow trip in May 1988 for the fourth summit with Gorbachev. But he stated that the highest altitude he preferred to reach was horseback. He had begun to say that he didn't want to travel unless it was for something really meaningful.

Nonetheless, as we looked ahead to the president's last year in office, Howard Baker decided that the president needed to make a few more international trips.

"I want to talk to you about your last year in office and where you might want to travel overseas," Baker said enthusiastically in a meeting with the president in late 1987 in the Oval Office.

The president looked considerably less enthusiastic. Noting that the Moscow trip and the economic summit in Toronto were already on his schedule, he asked warily: "What else do you have in mind, Howard?"

"I want to talk about places that you haven't been overseas," he said.

"Oh, really?" said the president, his eyebrows starting to climb, "like where?"

This is going to be interesting, I thought. Baker's wading into dangerous waters here. But Baker kept going.

"For instance, Mr. President, you haven't been to Israel," Baker said. "We should think about having you go to Israel."

The president sighed. "Howard, we've talked about that for years. I can't go there, because if I go to Israel, then I'll have to make sensitive decisions regarding which Arab nations to go to. Then where don't I go? We decided it would be better for me not to go to the Middle East but to have the Arab leaders come here. And besides, Israel has been here many times. So, no, I'm not going to Israel."

"Okay," Baker said, undeterred. "What about India?"

"I've been to India," the president said promptly.

Baker glanced at me and back at the president. "I don't remember you going to India as president. When did you go?"

Reagan looked more exasperated. "Well, I didn't go as president. President Nixon sent me to China as a special envoy when I was governor. On the way back from China, we stopped in Bombay to refuel. And, actually, it was in the middle of the night and I was asleep the entire time. But I was there, so I don't need to go to India."

Baker was looking a bit wild-eyed. I was chuckling inwardly. Sometimes it was impossible to argue with the logic of Ronald Reagan.

Baker tried again. "I've got one more, Mr. President," he said.

"*Now* where?" Reagan asked.

"I know you haven't been there, but you need to go," Baker said, determined not to get talked out of this one. "Australia."

"Australia?" the president said. "Howard, they've invited me to go there so many times, and they've been here many times, too. In fact, the prime minister is coming again. I really don't think we need

to make that trip, Howard."

Baker looked defeated. I decided to pitch in.

"You know, Mr. President, I think Howard is right," I said.

"About what?" asked Reagan.

"About Australia," I said, grinning. "You really do need to go to Australia."

"Oh, really," the president said. "Why in the hell do you think I need to go to Australia?"

"You need to go, Mr. President," I said, "because every one of your staff who travels with you wants to go to Australia."

"Well, you guys are all free to go to Australia," the president said, a grin tugging at his mouth, too. "But you *ain't taking me*."

I grabbed Howard, and we got out of the Oval Office.

"That didn't go so well," said Baker gloomily.

"So much for overseas travel in '88," I said.

Reagan certainly had his quirks! One day in 1988, we were doing a fund-raiser in Washington for Senate candidate Pete Dawkins, who was gearing up to run against Senator Frank Lautenberg. The president, me, Mark Weinberg and a few other people were waiting in a holding room before Reagan went out to make his speech. We got into a discussion about state politics, and I mentioned a former Ohio governor, Jack Gilligan, who went down to defeat after one term in the 1970s. It was believed, I told the group, that one of the reasons he was defeated was that he said publicly that he saw a UFO. Well, everyone cracked up — except Reagan, who shot me a scowl.

What had I done? I wondered. Reagan had always told me that when someone tells you a joke, be polite and laugh no matter how many times you've heard it. Okay, so this wasn't a joke, but it was still a humorous story. But Reagan had seemed truly offended by my remark about Gilligan.

I pulled Weinberg aside. "I think I just upset the president," I said, still mystified.

"You did," said Weinberg.

"I did?" I said.

"Don't you get it?" he asked.

"No!" I said.

"You *know* how superstitious he is," Weinberg said.

"Oh, my God," I said. "That's right. He *believes* in that stuff."

The next day, Weinberg showed me a newspaper clipping quoting Reagan as saying he'd seen a UFO while on a plane in California when he was governor.

That was Reagan. If you don't know that it doesn't exist, then maybe it does.

In fact, Reagan displayed his idiosyncrasies mostly on smaller things like that. I recall a flight to Dallas this year as we headed to a rodeo in Mesquite, Texas, a campaign stop for the Bush-Quayle ticket. En route, on Air Force One, Reagan went over his remarks for the event.

"When I say the word 'rodeo,' " he asked, "should I say '*ro*-de-o' or 'ro-*day*-o'?"

"Why would you want to say 'ro-*day*-o'?" I asked.

"That's the Spanish pronunciation," explained Reagan.

"I wouldn't do that," I warned. "This is Texas."

"Well," Reagan said slowly, mulling it over, "I don't know."

"Mr. President, I don't even know if we need to check that with anybody," I said. "Just say 'rodeo' and Texans will be happy."

I thought that had settled it, but not for Reagan.

As we waited in the holding room at the rodeo arena with Texas Governor Bill Clements, the president pulled out his remarks.

"Say, Bill," he said, "I want to ask you a question."

I'll be damned, I thought, he's bringing it up!

"Jim and I were talking on the plane," Reagan said to Governor Clements. "Here, in my remarks, I was thinking that maybe I should pronounce 'rodeo' as 'ro-*day*-o,' the Spanish pronunciation." He started sounding to me like he was ready to go shopping in Beverly Hills.

Clements couldn't restrain himself. He burst out laughing. "Mr. President, whatever you do when you go in there, please don't say 'ro-*day*-o.' "

"Well, all right," responded Reagan.

The president looked at me and I looked at him. I rolled my eyes.

In fact, that was part of the greatness of Ronald Reagan — that with all the success and adversity and the incredible highs and difficult lows of the presidency, it didn't change his essential character. He walked out of office the same man who had walked into the White House. He gained a tremendous amount of knowledge, but he stuck to his basic principles, remained engaged on several overarching goals and was remarkably effective at implementing them.

Part of his success, of course, was his electability — his immense personal appeal and his ability to communicate his vision to millions of Americans. Although he didn't talk much about it publicly, he believed his Hollywood background played a big role in that success. Late in his second term, I heard him say that if it hadn't been for his Hollywood experience, "I don't know how I'd be able to do this job."

Someone once asked him whether he ever got nervous before big speeches. No, he said, because of his movie and broadcasting background.

"You just have to tell yourself when you're in front of that microphone that there isn't anybody else out there listening," he said. "Because if you ever stopped to think about it, you would likely convince yourself that you can't do it."

He was also gifted at governing and, among politicians, those skills often don't come in tandem. Reagan had both — electability and governing skills. His adroitness at governing grew out of his unparalleled ability to stay focused on his ultimate goals and avoid getting sidetracked from his agenda. His was leadership at its best. He worked well with everyone. He was simply incapable of rancor. Privately, he never complained about the White House press corps. If anything, he was always too kind to the press because he couldn't say no to answering their constant questions! Ronald Reagan was also incapable of arrogance.

Like other presidencies, the Reagan presidency had its share of controversy around appointees — some of it deserved and some of it not. Reagan's first Labor secretary, Raymond Donovan, endured years of persecution from congressional Democrats, headed by Senator Edward Kennedy, that eventually led to his indictment and to his resignation as Labor secretary in 1987. Donovan was ultimately acquitted in 1987 and vindicated after spending millions of dollars in legal fees. Attorney General Ed Meese stepped down in August 1988 to distance himself from the president after being accused of influence peddling. He, too, was ultimately vindicated.

Sadly, my former mentor, Peter Voss, the chairman of Reagan's Ohio campaign in 1976, who had been named by Reagan to the U.S. Postal Service Board of Governors, was sentenced to four years in prison in 1986 for embezzlement in connection with a postal contract. He ultimately served two years in prison.

Reagan invariably got questions from the press when a federal appointee got in trouble with the law. He once responded that the federal government was so big that "you go to bed at night as president knowing that there is somebody out there doing something that they're not supposed to be doing."

It wasn't that he took wrongdoing lightly. He just knew that, as president, he couldn't control the behavior of everyone who worked for the immense federal government.

Some of the most moving moments at the White House occurred when Reagan met with seriously ill children. The visits were requested by the Make-a-Wish Foundation, an organization dedicated to fulfilling the wishes of children with terminal or life-threatening illnesses. When the children wanted to meet the president of the United States, Fred Ryan, the president's director of scheduling, always tried to arrange it, and the president was always happy to do it.

It was always such a touching sight to see the president meet with the children in the White House. Many of them were frail, some of them bald from chemotherapy, others in wheelchairs. But he picked up their spirits, offering them jelly beans and asking them about themselves. For the little ones, he got down to talk to them. While the rest of us were fighting back tears, the president always managed to stay strong. He talked to the parents, too. I often wondered if he realized how much he helped those families.

Reagan always maintained that kind of accessibility in the White House. Whenever Ryan called asking if he could squeeze in one more group or individual who wanted to meet the president, Reagan never complained. Without question, there was always an open-door policy in the Reagan White House — even for Reagan's political adversaries.

For example, Senator Robert Byrd, the Democratic Senate majority leader during Reagan's last two years in office, was a vocal opponent throughout all eight years of his presidency. But the president never shut Byrd out of his office. He had numerous Oval Office meetings with Byrd during his presidency, took his phone calls, along with the usual bipartisan congressional leadership meetings in the cabinet room.

I remember one such meeting with the bipartisan congressional leadership in Reagan's second term where members raised various issues. Senator Strom Thurmond, for instance, lectured Reagan on one of his pet issues: the loss of textile jobs in South Carolina. Thurmond always used the same example — military parachutes could someday be made overseas, he said, and what would happen if they didn't open when our troops needed them?

Then Byrd, a perennial passionate advocate for his home state of West Virginia, brought up the plight of coal miners in his state. Coal mines were shutting down, Byrd said; there was massive unemployment. What was the Reagan administration doing to help those people?

"Well, Bob," the president responded, "these workers need jobs, and I want them to have jobs." But, he said, unfortunately, the coal industry was in decline for a number of reasons, including stricter pollution-control rules that were reducing the demand for coal. The answer, the president said, was to retrain coal workers for other jobs.

Byrd's reply was sharp. "Mr. President," he said, "these are coal miners. That's all they've ever done. They don't know anything else. They're not going to be retrained because they're not going to leave their homes in the mountains of West Virginia. They've never lived anywhere else but West Virginia. You can't retrain these people and expect them to go somewhere else. It will not work."

At the end of Byrd's discourse, Reagan was silent. He didn't try to lecture Byrd or even defend his administration's policies. He just listened to Byrd and treated him with respect. If I had been in Reagan's position, I don't think I could have resisted getting in the last word, but Reagan knew that was not always the best course of action. To me, Byrd got through to Reagan on this issue.

Even after the incident, Byrd was still welcome at the Oval Office. At one point, Byrd brought his family by to meet the president and Mrs. Reagan, and they had lunch together in the private connecting study off the Oval Office.

Bear no grudges and seek no revenge was the president's philosophy. Also, Reagan believed that in winning, you do so with dignity without crowing or slaying your opponent.

In 1988, the president campaigned hard for George Bush, despite the opposition of some Reagan supporters. Reagan wanted to get Bush elected not only to see a furtherance of his ideals, but also because of Bush's long-term loyalty to him. Bush was an excellent vice president for President Reagan. He was completely loyal to the president and not once in eight years did he upstage Reagan. Bush also watched the president's back when it came to the political impact of various decisions and issues. Reagan was never interested in how his decisions would affect him politically, only on what would form the best policy, but Bush would speak up at meetings: "How will this affect the president?" he would ask. Or he would say, "We've got to look out for this man" and point to Reagan.

Near the end of Reagan's term, he always got Vice President Bush's input in making cabinet appointments so that Bush could carry those members over to his administration if (and, after November 8, 1988, when) he was elected president. When Ed Meese resigned as attorney general in July 1988, for example, Bush recommended former Pennsylvania Governor Richard Thornburgh as his successor. I well remember when Thornburgh came into the Oval Office for President Reagan to officially ask him to serve as his attorney general. During the meeting, the Secret Service came to me and said that the radiological alarm had been triggered from the Oval Office. I asked the Secret Service if we needed to clear out of the Oval Office and they advised me that they didn't think that would be necessary, but they were checking into it. Shortly after Reagan's meeting with Thornburgh concluded, the Secret Service determined that the alarm was triggered simply because Thornburgh had recently had a chest X-ray.

Thornburgh served as Reagan's attorney general for the remainder of his term and then stayed on as attorney general in the Bush administration. Similarly, Bush brought Nicholas Brady, a close friend, to Reagan as Treasury secretary in the final months of Reagan's term when Jim Baker left the post to serve on Bush's campaign, and Texas Tech University President Lauro Cavazos as Education secretary when Bill Bennett stepped down in September 1988. Cavazos and Brady also remained when Bush took over the presidency in 1989.

There wasn't much uncertainty in the Republican primaries; Bush clearly would become the nominee. But there was plenty of suspense over Bush's choice of a vice-presidential running mate. The press was ripe with speculation. Would it be Senator Bob Dole? Congressman Jack Kemp? Senator Alan Simpson? Senator Pete Domenici? Attorney General Thornburgh? A governor from a key state? Not even the president knew. But Bush gave no hint, not even to his top staffers. Bush could be very secretive. Maybe it was his CIA background or perhaps, because of his many years in Washington, he just didn't trust a lot of people.

The week before the Republican National Convention in New Orleans in August 1988, I happened to walk into the Oval Office study as the president and vice president were finishing up their Thursday lunch together. I started to walk back out, but Bush stopped me.

"No, Jimmy, stay," he said. "I'm just about finished, and I know that you guys have to go."

He continued his conversation with the president.

"No, not Kemp," he said. I realized they were discussing various vice-presidential running mate prospects.

"Really?" said Reagan. "Not Kemp?"

"No," said Bush. "He's just not presidential."

I was in accord. The first time I'd met

Kemp was on the campaign trail in 1980, when Reagan spoke at the Southern Leadership Conference in New Orleans. I was checking out of the Fairmont Hotel and overheard Kemp screaming at the front-desk clerk about his room. I thought of that incident.

At the Republican National Convention in 1988, Reagan was scheduled to come into New Orleans first, make his farewell speech on Monday night and depart the next morning, leaving the spotlight on George Bush. We decided that the two would rendezvous at the airport as Reagan departed and Bush arrived and arranged a short ceremony where Bush and Reagan would each speak briefly.

On Monday evening, Reagan gave a gracious speech at the convention, strongly endorsing Bush.

"I care that we give custody of this office to someone who will build on our changes, not retreat to the past — someone who will continue the change all of us fought for," the president told the tearful delegates. "To preserve what we have and not risk losing it all — America needs George Bush."

The next morning at the airport, it was time to pass the torch. After short remarks on the tarmac, George and Barbara Bush walked the president and first lady to Air Force One. As they did, members of the press shouted out questions about Bush's running mate. Bush was scheduled to make the announcement at midday.

"Who is your running mate, Mr. Vice President?" they yelled. "Does the president know?"

Again and again, the White House press pool shouted from under the wing of Air Force One, asking who was on the ticket with Bush and if he had told the president. Barbara Bush looked at her husband and said, "For God's sake, George, tell the president who it is."

Bush grabbed Reagan and started walking him over in my direction near the nose of the plane. I started backing up to stay out of their press photo. But they kept coming and stopped within a matter of feet from me, facing me, with their backs to the media. Bush looked at Reagan and said two words: "Dan Quayle."

Dan Quayle? The 41-year-old junior senator from Indiana? I had only ever seen Quayle's name mentioned once as a possible running mate in all of the articles and op-ed pieces that I had read.

If Reagan was surprised, he showed no

sign, staying straight-faced and simply nodding. Reagan then boarded Air Force One to head for the ranch, and Mrs. Reagan boarded a second aircraft and proceeded on a separate schedule. But the media had seen Bush say something to Reagan, and they went crazy. I knew a media onslaught was coming and upon boarding went into the stateroom in Air Force One to speak to Reagan.

Reagan was in the bathroom, changing his clothes, and I also knew it would be a matter of seconds before Marlin Fitzwater and B. Oglesby, deputy chief of staff, came to the front of the plane, eager to quiz the president on the burning question of the day — the name of George Bush's running mate.

Sure enough, I opened the stateroom door, and there they were while Reagan was changing. Fitzwater and Oglesby said that the Air Force One press pool, which sits in the rear of the plane, was sending notes to them asking what the vice president had told the president. I knew they wanted to ask the president for the name so they could pass it along to the press, with the president's permission, of course. I told Fitzwater and Oglesby that I would tell the president that they wanted to see him, and that I would come back to get them in the senior staff section of the plane in a matter of minutes.

The president came out of the bathroom and plopped down at the stateroom table and grabbed a handful of grapes. I explained that Marlin and B. wanted to speak to him.

"What's on their mind?" he asked casually. I could tell he knew exactly what they wanted.

"There is a media onslaught from the traveling press pool, and they want you to tell them the name of the vice president's running mate," I said. "But I know you're not inclined to tell anybody because George needs to announce this himself in New Orleans."

He grinned. "No, I'm not going to tell anyone anything," he said.

I went back and got Fitzwater and Oglesby, who came in and sat down on the couch in the stateroom. They were both anxious.

Fitzwater did the talking.

"Mr. President," he said, "the press is all up in arms about the fact that the vice president might have told you who his running mate is."

The president kept popping grapes into

his mouth. "Uh-huh" was his only comment.

"Mr. President, can I ask, did the vice president tell you back there who his running mate is?" Fitzwater asked.

"Yes, he did," said the president, still munching grapes. He said nothing more and sat back in his seat as if to say, "Anything else?"

There was silence. Fitzwater started to say something, then stopped. He and Oglelsby looked at each other, stood up simultaneously, thanked the president and left in frustration.

I wasn't surprised. I knew that Reagan would never upstage Bush, or anyone, for that matter. Everyone wanted to know Bush's choice, but they had to wait. Bush stunned the political world when he announced the energetic young conservative, a "man of the future," at a rally shortly thereafter.

A week later, we went to Long Beach to sign the Trade and Competitiveness Act. On the long ride from the ranch on Marine One, I confessed to Fitzwater that I'd overheard Bush tell Reagan his choice was Quayle. Fitzwater was furious with me! "You should have told me," he snapped. "Don't ever withhold information like that again." But I wasn't going to spoil Bush's surprise, any more than Reagan would have. In Fitzwater's defense, if he had known then, the press would have expected him to convey this information to them.

After a grinding campaign against Michael Dukakis and Lloyd Bentsen, election night proved triumphant for Bush-Quayle. Reagan had worked hard to get Bush elected.

With that, Reagan was able to start looking forward, beyond his presidency, to his legacy and his future. On November 21, 1988, we went to a quiet mountaintop in Simi Valley, about 70 miles south of Rancho del Cielo, for the groundbreaking for his future presidential library.

The site was so new that construction workers had to bulldoze a path partway up the small mountain for us, and we had to walk the rest of the way. It was an extraordinary location — quiet, with breathtaking views and soft breezes that caressed us. Just days earlier, the bulldozers had rousted nests of rattlesnakes.

Former cabinet members William Clark, Ed Meese and William French Smith, industrialist Armand Hammer, MCA chief Lew Wasserman and actor Charlton

Heston shared the moment with a beaming president and first lady.

Characteristically, the president tried to deflect attention away from himself. "This is a most humbling moment for me," he said in his remarks. "The story that will be told inside the walls that are yet to be built here is the story not only of a presidency, but of a movement."

On the way down the mountain, the Reagans decided they wanted to make the site their final resting place, set in the midst of rolling mountains covered with brush, beavertail cactus and wildflowers.

21

AN OFFICIAL FAREWELL, BUT NOT GOOD-BYE

We were in New York City about three weeks after the library groundbreaking for President Reagan's fifth, and final, meeting with Mikhail Gorbachev. We helicoptered to Governors Island in New York Harbor for a low-key lunch designed primarily as a get-to-know-you opportunity for Vice President Bush and the Soviet leader, presided over by the president. Gorbachev and Reagan got the chance to say their final farewells to each other, though, and to celebrate the remarkable friendship that had blossomed between the anti-Communist leader of the free world and the head of the former "evil empire." As a gift, the president presented Gorbachev with a photograph of their first summit meeting, when they had taken that celebrated walk down to the boathouse on the shore of Lake Geneva. The two had accomplished so much, and the president hoped that Gorbachev would have a similarly warm relationship with Bush.

As we left the lunch, Reagan took Gorbachev and Bush for a brief ride to the edge of Governors Island for a spectacular view of the Statue of Liberty across New York Harbor, where Reagan, Bush and Gorbachev posed for photos. Reagan bade farewell to Gorbachev and, as we got ready to depart from Governors Island, there was a plethora of rotor-thumping helicopters waiting to ferry Bush and Reagan in various directions.

"Which one is ours?" I asked someone as we walked with President Reagan. Overhearing me, Reagan turned to me with a wicked grin.

"Jim," he said, "they're all my helicopters."

We all burst out laughing, including the president. We knew he didn't mean it — in fact, that was the joke. He was playing off a similar remark once made by President Johnson when approached by a sailor on an aircraft carrier, who pointed down the deck and told LBJ, "Sir, your helicopter is there."

"Son," Johnson replied, "they're all my helicopters."

That was Reagan. Don't take the perks of power too seriously — they are ephemeral and fleeting. As his remarkable eight-year tenure wound down, he didn't regret losing those benefits — or the job itself. He did say that after leaving office, he would lobby for the repeal of the Twenty-second Amendment to the Constitution that limits a president to two consecutive terms. Reagan stressed that he wasn't interested in repealing the two-term limit for himself, but that he believed that voters should not be restricted in voting for the nation's only at-large elected office.

The Reagans purchased a five-bedroom home in Bel Air and planned a busy postpresidential life of giving speeches, supporting conservative causes, setting up the Ronald Reagan Presidential Library and writing their memoirs.

As a 77-year-old senior citizen in the waning weeks of his presidency, Reagan could have been forgiven for coddling himself a little. But that was never the case. We returned to Washington after the lunch at Governors Island and immediately began preparing for the final press conference of his presidency the next evening. However, that evening, he became ill after giving a speech at an American Enterprise Institute dinner and spent most of the night throwing up. Mrs. Reagan called in White House doctor John Hutton, who filled me in when I arrived at the White House early that morning. The president was resting upstairs in the White House residence, he told me, and he was unsure about the president's physical condition for the day ahead. I alerted Chief of Staff Ken Duberstein, Press Secretary Marlin Fitzwater and other members of the senior White House staff to the situation.

Their reaction was immediate — cancel the press conference. But I strongly urged everyone to hold off until we had talked to the president. The president, I assured them, would be determined to carry on.

"If you want to incur the wrath of Ronald Reagan," I argued, "cancel the press conference. Because I firmly believe he's going to come down in the elevator at some point today feeling okay, and he's going to want to do the press conference. You're all making a huge mistake if you cancel it without talking to the president first."

Sure enough, within a couple of hours, Reagan was on his feet and ready to go. Duberstein and I went up to the residence as President Reagan was also scheduled to call Gorbachev to bid him farewell as he departed New York. On that call, Reagan invited the Gorbachevs to the ranch, and Gorbachev invited the Reagans back to Moscow. Then Reagan strode down to the Oval Office, looking as healthy as ever. After the call to Gorbachev, he acknowledged that he hadn't felt well but said, "I'm fine now."

By 10:30 a.m., the president was in his usual press conference briefing session in the White House family theater, then had lunch with the vice president and conducted two afternoon meetings. It was as if nothing had happened.

That night at his final press conference, the president showed no hint that he had been violently ill as the day of December 8 began. He deftly fielded a broad range of questions about his presidency. The best part of his eight years in the White House, he said, had been helping to improve the state of the economy, while the worst was sending American servicepeople into harm's way.

It was difficult to forget what a dramatically different world it was from the one eight years ago. In 1981, at his first news conference as president, Reagan had blasted Soviet leaders as willing to "commit any crime, to lie, to cheat" if they believed it would advance world communism. At this — his final news conference — he said that those days appeared to be gone.

But he quickly added his own favorite Russian proverb: *Doveryai no proveryai* — "Trust but verify."

"We must remain resolute and without illusion," he said, "and we must speak candidly about fundamental points of differences. We must especially maintain our military strength."

The final weeks sped by. Business continued as usual at the White House but, as the last days of the Reagan presidency crept closer, more and more people called, asking for one last chance to see the president, to shake his hand and say good-bye. I was fielding so many requests that I had to enlist presidential secretary Kathy Osborne and my wife, Carole, to return calls. The president, as always, was happy to oblige everyone who called.

Finally, on January 19, the last night of Reagan's presidency, I realized that I still had a thick stack of photographs on my desk that needed to be signed by the Reagans. They were photos of the Reagans with various people — White House staff, Secret Service agents, friends, political leaders — who had asked me to request that the Reagans sign them.

I stuck the photos in a folder and took them up to the White House residence. Reagan met me in the center hall of the family quarters, and I showed him the pile.

"I know you're busy," I said, "but I've got these photos that need to be signed, and several of them include Mrs. Reagan.

Is there any way I can leave them with you for you to sign?"

"I'll do them right now," the president said promptly.

Mrs. Reagan came into the center hall and looked at the folder. "What's that?" she said.

I explained what the photos were and apologized for bringing them upstairs during their last night at the White House.

"That's fine," she said with a warm smile.

"Honey, I'm going to sign them right now," Reagan said.

"Am I supposed to sign some, too?" Mrs. Reagan asked.

"Yes," I said, "if you would, please." Of course, said Mrs. Reagan. So right there, they both sat down on the floor — the president of the United States and the first lady, and laid out the photographs around them and began signing.

"This is wonderful," I said gratefully. They couldn't have been nicer about it as they signed away for about 45 minutes.

The following morning was Inauguration Day. We had finished clearing out the Oval Office the previous day, and the president had not planned to return. But Duberstein suggested that Reagan go to the Oval Office one final time on his last day in office. That was fine with Reagan, so we went back shortly before the preinaugural reception.

It was odd to see the room so vacant and quiet after eight years of watching so much history take place there. Sunlight streamed across the presidential desk, which was bare except for the white multiline telephone that the president had used so many times over eight years. Gone were the family photos on the credenza, the western sculptures and the barrel desk chair that Reagan had brought from California. The room seemed almost to be breathing peacefully — empty, expectant, awaiting its next occupant, as it had for almost 100 years.

For a moment, alone, Reagan stood quietly and gazed around the room, fingers folded lightly in front of him, almost as if in prayer.

I couldn't help but drift back over eight years ago, when Reagan was ambivalent about leaving his beloved California and moving to Washington. And now, here he was, returning to put roots back down in Los Angeles and at the ranch after an extraordinary two terms in the highest office in the land.

On that morning, the president made one last phone call from the Oval Office —

fittingly to Lyn Nofziger, who had played such a big part in propelling Reagan to the White House. And, also fittingly, it was a quintessential call for Ronald Reagan to make — he wanted to ask about the health of Nofziger's daughter, who was hospitalized.

Some members of Reagan's senior staff began to trickle into the room — Kathy Osborne, who was weeping quietly into a handkerchief, Duberstein, Fitzwater and Colin Powell, who put his arm around Osborne to comfort her. White House photographer Pete Souza had mounted a remote camera on the wall behind Reagan's desk and got some shots of the president in his final moments in the Oval Office. Reagan opened the drawer of the desk to make sure the note that a departing president traditionally leaves for his successor was still there. It was.

"You'll be in my prayers," part of it said. "God bless you and Barbara. I'll miss our Thursday lunches." He signed it "Ron."

As staff members filled the room, the president brightened up and moved on to other business. He pulled out the white laminated card with the nuclear code on it and turned to Powell.

"Say, Colin," he said, "what am I supposed to do with this card?"

I quickly stepped forward. I had already worked out with the military aide who was in charge of the football that day that the president would turn over the card to the aide later that morning after the reception with congressional leaders, the first lady, president-elect and Mrs. Bush, but I hadn't had a chance to brief the president on the arrangement yet.

"You're still president, sir," I said. I told the president that he would be giving the card to the military aide just prior to departing for the Capitol. I also told Powell that we had everything covered.

The president put the card back in his pocket for two more hours.

Powell gave Reagan his last security briefing, saying simply: "The world is quiet today, Mr. President."

Weinberg brought two groups of press photographers into the Oval Office for one last photo op — and that was it. At the congressional reception, the president was back to himself, laughing and upbeat. Whatever emotions he had been feeling in the Oval Office that morning were gone, and he was looking ahead again.

I, too, was getting impatient to move on. I had been in the White House for eight years, and all eight had been at a full sprint. I had chosen to remain on the job seven days a week during my four-year stint as executive assistant. I don't do anything in moderation, and I figured that there would be plenty of time for downtime later in my life.

The inaugural ceremony seemed to race by for me and, before I knew it, President Bush and the new first lady were walking the Reagans down the steps of the east side of the Capitol to the marine helicopter that would fly us to Andrews Air Force Base, where we would pick up our flight to California. As we lifted off from the Capitol, the Bushes waved good-bye. And then they were gone.

For the last time, we skimmed over the Washington monuments, and the pilot took us over the White House. The president peered out the window. He was quiet again.

"There's our little bungalow down there," he said to Mrs. Reagan.

At Andrews, the Reagans were greeted by more than 2,000 cheering people waving signs and American flags. SO LONG, GIPPER, said one placard. They received a 21-gun salute, and then we boarded Special Air Mission 27000 — the same big old

707 that had brought us to Washington in 1981 and, as Air Force One, had ferried the Reagans around the country and the world for eight years. It was piloted by Colonel Bob Ruddick, who had flown us for the entire Reagan presidency.

Every seat was filled with White House staff — well, now they were former White House staff — as well as their families and other friends and supporters of the Reagans. My wife, Carole, and I were on board, as were Kathy Osborne with her daughter, Duberstein and his wife, White House doctor John Hutton, first lady Press Secretary Elaine Crispen, B. Oglesby, Stu Spencer, and Mark Weinberg, who would be the Reagans' press secretary in California. Also on the trip was longtime correspondent Jerry O'Leary.

One person was missing: the military aide carrying the football. After eight years by Reagan's side, he was now with President Bush. Of course, the Secret Service was on board, because the Reagans would have security for the rest of their lives.

It was such a strange feeling to be untethered from the White House after all those years. For eight years, my life had belonged to the presidency. It had been an unbelievable experience for me and my family, but now it was time to return to a "normal" life and a "real" job again.

Weinberg had brought a bottle of Cristal Champagne on board, and the two of us sat on a bench about halfway down the plane. We said little and just drank deep, as the Reagans and the others walked up and down the aircraft. For the first time in eight years, we were able to let down a little bit.

We had a lunch of chicken, rice and broccoli; we all had slices from a cake inscribed THE REGAN YEARS 1981–89.

As we neared Los Angeles International Airport, Reagan slipped into the seat behind Ruddick to watch him bring the jet in for him one last time. I went into the cockpit to give the president his customary prearrival briefing.

"Mr. President," I said, "I want to tell you about what's going to happen at LAX."

"Jim," he growled playfully, "I'm trying to fly this plane."

I grinned. Fine, I thought, for once I'll stay out of your way and come back later.

The weather was warm and overcast when we emerged from the aircraft to hundreds of well-wishers. The University of Southern California Trojan band played

"California, Here I Come" and presented Reagan with a Trojan hat, which he donned at the end of the ceremony. The Reagans were greeted by comedian Rich Little, William French Smith and actor Robert Stack.

"You are an example of the true American success story," Stack told his old friend. "You changed the course of history."

Wearing an air force jacket, his arm around Mrs. Reagan, Reagan told the crowd that there weren't enough words to express what was in his heart now that he was back in California. Staying in Washington for eight years left him in a "perpetual state of homesickness," he said.

From there, a few of us — the Dubersteins, John Hutton and Carole and me — accompanied the Reagans to their new home while the rest remained at the plane. We drove in a small motorcade — Secret Service but no press — to their rambling stucco home on St. Cloud Road. Carole and I had already decided how to handle ourselves. We knew the Reagans wouldn't want a weepy, emotional scene, so we took our cue from Stu Spencer, who treated the farewells lightly back on the plane — a sort of "we'll see you soon" approach. And, really, it wasn't good-bye. The Reagan presidency was over, but we knew we would stay in touch and see them regularly.

Carole and I were the only ones returning to LAX for the flight back to Washington, so we stayed at the Reagans' for only about 20 minutes. The president wasn't a hugger when it came to men, so he and I had a long good-bye handshake. We had shared so much over the years that we didn't really need to say much to each other. Mrs. Reagan gave me a big hug and a kiss, and also embraced Carole. Then we left.

As dusk settled over Los Angeles, we were driven back to the airport for our flight home. The car took us right to the steps of Special Air Mission 27000 — one of the final perks of the presidency. As I leaned back to look up at the gleaming, powder-blue jet with the presidential seal painted on the side, I suddenly felt breathless. I realized my life was about to change drastically again, but this time in the direction of normalcy.

This time, our aircraft was just another plane on the congested runways at LAX. I counted 15 planes lined up ahead of us for takeoff.